MW00449699

Mother!
The Frank Zappa Story

Mother!

The Frank Zappa Story

Michael Gray

Plexus, London

All rights reserved including the right
of reproduction in whole or in part in any form
Copyright © 1993, 1994 by Michael Gray
Published by Plexus Publishing Limited
26 Dafforne Road
London SW17 8TZ
First printing 1993
Revised and updated 1994

British Library Cataloguing in Publication Data

Gray, Michael
  Mother! The Frank Zappa Story. – 2 Rev ed.
  I. Title
  781.66092

ISBN 0 85965 217 3

The right of Michael Gray to be identified as author of
this work has been asserted by him in accordance with
the Copyright, Designs and Patents Act, 1988

Printed in Great Britain by J. W. Arrowsmith Ltd, Bristol
Cover Design by Phil Smee

This book is sold subject to the condition that it shall not,
by way of trade or otherwise, be lent, re-sold, hired out,
or otherwise circulated without the publisher's prior consent
in any form of binding or cover other than that in which it is
published and without a similar condition including this
condition being imposed on the subsequent purchaser.

10 9 8 7 6 5 4 3 2 1

Contentz

Thankz

for help with the new version of this book go warmly to Sarah Beattie, the children, Wolfram Altenhövel, Andrew Darke, Andy Greenaway, Lee and Pam from Birkenhead, Bob Linney, the staff of Mount Pleasant in Reigate, Kent Nagano, Ned Smism, Pravoslav Tomek, Fred Tomsett, editor of the Zappa fanzine *T'Mershi Duween*, and Danny Tyrrell. For help with the 1985 version of the book, on which the early part of this new edition is founded, I thank again Karl Dallas, Paul Eggett, Gabriel Gray, Urban Gwerder, Pamela Harvey, Mick Watts and Pamela Zarubica. None of these people are responsible for the bits you don't like the sound of.

Acknowledgmentz

are due for recent assistance by David Bailey and his office; Martin Cassini; Susan Dewey of the Chicago Symphony Orchestra staff; Nick in the Folk Department of Decoy Records, Manchester; Endcape Ltd. for faxing facilities; Katrina Erskine; the information service of the National Sound Archive (available free on 071-589-6603); Peter Doggett of *Record Collector* magazine; the Royal Northern College of Music in Manchester; G&S Music; and especially Liz Wells of Music for Nations, Zappa's record-company press-officer in the UK, for official and unofficial help. Likewise I acknowledge previous-edition assistance by: CBS Records' London press office; David Hughes; Tim Read; Moira Bellas and the people who gave permission to republish extracts from the work of others in the course of this book.

Introduction

When Bob Dylan went on a world tour in 1981, he made his musicians rehearse for five days. When Zappa went on a world tour in 1988 he made his musicians rehearse ten hours a day, five days a week for four and a half months.

He was always a Stalinist; he fired his musicians if they drank or took drugs, he maintained his decades-long marriage apparently through his wife's complete acquiescence in all things, including Zappa's unilateral decision to name his children Moon Unit, Dweezil, Ahmet Rodan and, in mellow old age, Diva.

He used to tour a lot, with many different successive line-ups, but his last two tours were back in 1984 and 1988. Right up to the end of his life, he was still mixing tapes of some of these concerts, and released a phenomenal amount of 'product' after giving up trying to work with big-company labels or get his work played on the radio. In the late 1960s he 'invented' advertising rock albums on Sunset Boulevard billboards – which has become a big-money fixture of the scenery there over the last two decades; at the beginning of the eighties his hit single 'Valley Girl', with daughter Moon Unit monologuing, led to merchandising that included a Valley Girl doll that said 'Bag your face!', clearly prefiguring Bart Simpson and capturing the mood of the decade. But by the mid-1980s, having been signed to most of the major labels and having ended up in legal dispute with each of them, Zappa switched away from the mega-approach to disseminating his music.

With his own label and small-scale distribution deals, including much stress on mail-order sales, he issued all this in the last nine years of his life: 1985 – one LP and a seven-LP box; 1986 – two LPs and a nine-LP box; 1987 – a three-LP box, a cassette-only sampler, an LP and another 9-LP box; 1988 – two double-LPs and three single-LPs; 1989 – one CD; nothing in 1990; in 1991 two live CDs, a double-CD and a ten-LP box set; in 1992 three double-CDs and an eleven-LP box-set; and in 1993 two further CDs! This was *alongside* the CD-release of many, many back-catalogue vinyl items, most of which have been altered in the process, requiring dedicated fans and completists to (re-) buy all these as well. He also issued commercially four videos in 1985, one in 1987, two more videos and his 'autobiography' in 1989, another video in 1990 and yet another in 1993.

His rock music was always one-part sub-cultural satire, one-part fond parody of doo-wop-cum-pre-Tamla-r&b and one-part complicated-as-jazz instrumental music offering odd chords and several different awkward time-signatures played simultaneously – which Zappa wrote, arranged and produced, and to which he contributed as an electric-guitarist of much talent.

Zappa was also a long-term composer of 'modern classical music', writing and scoring experimental film-soundtracks as early as 1963, spending vast amounts of money getting symphony orchestras to perform and record some of this work. He worked with Pierre Boulez and the new Music Director of Manchester's Hallé Orchestra, Kent Nagano, and pioneering a computer-keyboard instrument, the Synclavier, on which he also composed and played 'classical' music.

The Synclavier is a modern equivalent of the pianola which plays automatically by means of a piano roll with holes punched out for the notes. The connection goes beyond the similar mechanical and electronic programming of the notes, in that while Zappa's orchestral music was influenced not just by the famous moderns like Stravinsky, Webern and Stockhausen but also very specifically by the French American composer Edgard Varèse, so with his Synclavier work he was very influenced by a naturalized-Mexican born in Arkansas in 1912 called Conlon Nancarrow, who, after initially composing for modernist string-quartets, came back from fighting for the Republicans in Spain, moved to Mexico and switched, in the 1940s, to composing for the Player-Piano, as Americans call it. He used it because he realized that it was possible to programme it to play music far more complicated than human hand/brain co-ordinations could manage. Nancarrow punched the holes in the rolls himself, one by one: an extremely laborious process whereby a five-minute composition could take many months to programme, on top of whatever time it took to compose in the first place. It's my belief that this perverse workaholism is part of what appealed to Frank Zappa about Nancarrow. Recently, at 80, Nancarrow started writing for orchestra and human pianos again, for the first time in almost 50 years.

Zappa's own workaholic talent was also for splicing and editing different tracks together in a way that I don't think anyone else has ever had the ambition to achieve. For instance, it's fairly common to come across, on a Zappa LP sleevenote, a bit of tiny print that says something along the lines of: 'Side 1, track 3: the first half of the guitar-solo was recorded live in Detroit 11/3/78, the second half of the guitar-solo and the brass-section were recorded live in Chicago 9/11/77 and the bass, drums and rhythm-section were recorded at Power Plant Studios New York 6/6/77.' There are plenty of people who will overdub a bit of *subsequently* studio-recorded guitar solo on top of a slice of live performance with a few dodgy notes they want to unplay (though their sleevenotes don't generally admit it), but no-one but Zappa required or managed the audacity and technical wizardry of overdubbing live work on top of basic tracks recorded on a previous occasion in the studio or on top of other live work recorded later.

Any compilation-tape of 'The Essential Zappa' should straddle these different aspects of the Zappoid Universe, from early delights like 'Call Any Vegetable' and 'What's The Ugliest Part Of Your Body?' right through some of the best instrumental rock-music of the 1970s and '80s to much more recent material, including a 1988 live performance of Ravel's 'Bolero' (issued 1991) that, if you didn't hear the applause at the end, you would certainly assume to be a carefully-crafted studio-job, so immaculately is it played and so vividly recorded.

Zappa was also a great promoter of other talent, producing albums by Captain Beefheart, Jean-Luc Ponty and others, recruiting to his band many musicians who subsequently got their own record deals, including Don 'Sugarcane' Harris, George Duke, Jean-Luc Ponty again, and heavy-metal guitarist Steve Vai, and commissioning videos that introduced the plasticine-animation artist Bruce Bickford.

Zappa also gave good sound bite (as we media people like to call it), including, in the context of one of his favourite late-sixties pastimes, hippie-baiting: 'If we cannot be free, at least we can be cheap!', and a definition of the music press as 'people who can't talk interviewed by people who can't write for people who can't read'. I like, too, Zappa's response to a journalist who asked him how he could have burdened his son with the name Dweezil: 'It could have been worse. I might have called him *Ralph*.' (Dweezil has grown up to be an electric-guitarist just like Dad.)

Then there were Zappa's intrusions into the political scene down the years. These ranged from telling the agit-prop students of the LSE in the late 1960s that 'Revolution is this year's flower-power' through fighting a lengthy, informed and skilful campaign against the censorship proposals of the so-called Washington Wives in the mid-1980s to 'doing a feasibility study' into the prospect of standing as a US Presidential candidate in 1992.

So there he was, living in Los Angeles, working in his basement studio, composing, mixing and re-mixing, right up till the last possible moment before cancer killed him. 'I don't like Los Angeles but it's the only place I know I can get my equipment fixed.' He never stopped.

1. Let's Make The Water Turn Black:

Zappa's Childhood & Adolescence In Brown-Shoes-Don't-Make-It America

Frank Zappa was a child of the American forties, and an adolescent of her fifties. Those decades clarify much of what is notable and important about Zappa's later pre-occupations as a composer/writer and as a personality, both public and private.

The 1940s in America remains a very under-documented time and place: eccentric, bulbous and charming. It surrounded its citizens with the naive beginnings of mass-production objects, which were delightful just because they were naive beginnings. Corporate America had yet to learn how to in-build the inhuman element. So there they were: ludicrous pop-up toasters; grotesque bedside lights; giant refrigerators so intimidating that the Americans never had the nerve (as did the British in the face of far punier equivalents) to shorten their name to 'fridges'. From chairs to wall-clocks to coffee-grinders – all things bright and bulbous, the forties brought them all – particularly cars. The huge bullfrog automobiles that rolled out of Ford and General Motors at the start of the decade – and then again, after stoppage of production during wartime, from 1946 onwards – represented a kind of conveyor-belt surrealism that was to disappear, along with every other anti-orthodoxy, during the fifties.

In calamitous contrast to the forties, the fifties was the new, cold (and Cold), boring era. An age of unparalleled orthodoxy in American life. Mass-production grew up, and learnt to remove most of the eccentricity from its output. 'Bulbousness

11

must go,' said the company presidents, 'and utility-tackiness must replace it.' It did, so that the only bulbous things left were the company presidents themselves, grown obese in their new-found boom-time affluence.

Frank Zappa reacted against this fifties aesthetic. It's obvious from his work that he's never forgiven it. One of the notable features of the artwork Cal Shenkel has done for Zappa album covers is its unswerving resurrection of forties bulbousness in, for example, the cars on the covers of *Uncle Meat* and *Just Another Band From L.A.* It isn't Shenkel's preoccupation so much as Zappa's – and it extends beyond automobiles. Zappa was so pleased with the forties 'fulsomeness' of a vacuum cleaning device used at the small recording studio he bought in 1964 – of which more later – that he made Captain Beefheart pose with a similar one on the inside cover of the *Hot Rats* album. The *Chunga's Revenge* album also has a grotesque vacuum cleaner featured inside its cover, no doubt again in memory of the same hallowed original. Indeed, ten years after signing his first major record deal, Zappa still held this original artefact in sufficient affection to describe it lovingly to me as 'this funny little bullet-shaped vacuum cleaner with a big hose'!

Lastly, take a look at the sofa on the cover of the *One Size Fits All* album – released a quarter of a century after the end of the 1940s. 'It's one hell of a sofa,' Zappa told me proudly, 'if you appreciate fulsomeness.'

There was one area, though, in which this forties-good, fifties-bad syndrome did not apply: popular music – and unpopular music too. Music tended to be awful in the 1940s, and improved all round in the decade that followed – particularly the kinds of music that had real impact on Frank Zappa. The popular music of the forties was dominated by the crooners we all know and loathe; unpopular music, such as the pioneering 'serious' composing of Zappa's early hero Edgard Varèse, suffered too. Varèse produced major work in the twenties, thirties, and fifties – but none in the forties. (And it was in the forties that Charlie Parker felt so desperate that he implored Varèse to take him on in any capacity – even as a cook – in exchange for composition lessons.)

In the fifties, though, the demand for wartime escapist slush slackened off and other things happened in music. The crooners took a dive; Varèse came up with his *Deserts* and *Poème Electronique*; rhythm 'n' blues grew into what Zappa considered (and still considers) a truly wonderful thing; and black music began to break down the walls of white radio. Rock'n'roll emerged. And in the face of all developments to the contrary in other areas of American life, even the music *objects* of the fifties improved. You can't beat a 1957 juke-box.

Not unnaturally then, since in music it was forties-bad, fifties-good and in all other respects vice-versa, Frank Zappa's sense of all-American social solemnity diminished and his interest in music burgeoned as he left Edgewood, Maryland, the forties and childhood behind and coped instead with the environment of the Mojave Desert, the fifties and adolescence.

His brief autobiography on the cover of the first Mothers Of Invention album, *Freak Out*, ran like this:

'I was born in Baltimore, Maryland, December 21, 1940 and grew up in California. I am a self-taught musician, composer, blah, blah, blah. When I was eleven years old I was 5ft 7in with hairy legs, pimples and a mustache . . . for some strange reason they'd never let me be the captain of the softball team. Got married when I was twenty . . . a lovely girl: almost ruined her life, filed for divorce, moved into my recording studio, joined forces with Ray, Jim and Roy, schemed and plotted for a year, working in beer joints, blah, blah, starved a lot, etc., played a lot of freaky music and stayed vastly unpopular (though notorious).'

This may not tell us a great deal of Zappa's personal history, but it makes clear an attitude: it is more of a hit-back than an exposition.

It may of course be true that whatever the era or its aesthetics, all kids rebel and Zappa was just one of them; but he was very definitely a child of his particular times. Born in 1940 and uprooted from Edgewood, Maryland to the vast no-man's land of the Mojave Desert in California in 1950; child in one decade and adolescent in the other. So it's illuminating to look a bit closer at both.

America had climbed back to self-confidence after the Wall Street Crash of 1929 and subsequent Depression of the thirties. When Zappa was born in December 1940 things were looking up, even though Europe was at war. Europe could seem a long way away, if you wanted it to. But then came Pearl Harbor – one of those phrases that children hear repeated for years, as no doubt the young Frank Zappa did, without ever having its significance explained.

What it meant was that without any declaration of war, the Japanese attacked America's main naval base (in Hawaii) early on Sunday morning, 7 December 1941. Two hours later, 2,400 people were dead, 120 aeroplanes destroyed and 19 ships, including five battleships, were sunk or out of action. The next day, the American Congress ('The people in their righteous might . . .' as Roosevelt put it) declared war on Japan; three days later, Japan's allies, Germany and Italy, inevitably declared war on the USA. America was in the war.

The war meant hardship, but it also meant a massive build-up in activity so far as the US military and its associate industries – defence, weaponry, research – were concerned, and Zappa's father, a graduate of the University of North Carolina, spent most of his adult working life in these associated industries. It was for this reason that Zappa's family rarely spent more than one or two years in any one place.

'See even though it seems like there was this thing that the forties was an era of fulsomeness,' Zappa told me, 'and the fifties had this tremendous conformity aspect to it, the contrast wasn't that great for my family because we moved so many times. I was never in one place for more than a few years because my father was employed by the government, either directly or indirectly, for most of his life. So he would be transferred from one place to another all the time – and *never* to any place where it was any fun to be. Because it was always in conjunction with some sort of military installation and they are always in boring places.'

Russia, of course, was an ally of the Americans and British in the Second World War, but at the end of the war, American foreign policy became sharply anti-Russian, and a corresponding anti-communism built up at home. Roosevelt died on 12 April 1945 – urging just an hour before his death that the USA should 'minimize the general Soviet problem as much as possible'; yet less than a fortnight later Truman contrived his famous first confrontation with Soviet Foreign Minister Molotov at the White House. That November it was Truman, not Joseph Stalin, who terminated the meetings of the so-called Big Three and so initiated a ten-year period in which there was no meeting between American and Russian heads of state. (Indeed, in 1950 Dean Acheson, then US Secretary of State, vetoed a proposal by Churchill that a Stalin-Truman conference take place.)

In the United Nations General Assembly, America called the tune. In this immediate post-war period, 1946-1953, only two resolutions supported by the US failed to become adopted, and out of 800 resolutions that were adopted, the US was defeated on less than 3 per cent. While a country like India, free from American pressure, voted with the US only about one-third of the time, the following American-supported dictatorships voted with the US more then 90 per cent of the time: Greece, Peru, Turkey, Venezuela, the Dominican Republic, Nicaragua, Taiwan, Thailand, Honduras, Paraguay and Haiti.

Even though the very notion of Russia contemplating military aggression immediately after the war was ludicrous – Britain had spent the war contending with six German divisions, Russia coping against *185* – everything America did under Harry S. Truman's presidency (and later under Eisenhower's) was founded on the suspicion that Russia would be an aggressor that 'needed to be stopped'.

Thus on top of the UN machinations and Truman's deliberate reversal of Roosevelt's attempts at US-USSR friendship, there came in 1947 the Truman Doctrine speech, which, as it were, formally opened the critical Cold War period. March to August 1949 saw the formation of NATO – before, that is, the creation of the Warsaw Pact (which so many school history books still suggest NATO was designed to combat). In the kind of political atmosphere that this inexorable sequence of events indicated, some of the events of 1948 were of crucial significance. In the US it was election year; Truman was re-elected but his administration was hamstrung by a Republican majority in Congress and the growing tide of McCarthyism; abroad there came the Czech coup in February and the Berlin blockade in June. Panic all round – if mostly self-induced. Thus it was that the same year Congress voted for peacetime conscription for the first time in

American history. In 1952 the Republicans came to power, with John Foster Dulles ('a man with a notorious aversion to negotiated settlements') as Secretary of State.

The openness and brave confidence with which the American people had started the 1940s had been squeezed out by all these events. Coincidental with this anti-Russian foreign policy was the McCarthy era of anti-communist witch-hunting at home. No-one in America escaped its repressive, narrowing, orthodoxy-imposing effects, and families like the Zappas suffered more than most. For two reasons: Frank Zappa's parents were not all-white all-American Americans, and Zappa's father made his living from work in defence-contract industries where 'security' was all-important.

It was in October 1946 (when Frank Zappa was five) that J. Edgar Hoover announced that communists were at work at every level and in every organization in America. Five months later came the Truman Doctrine speech, in which (in effect) Truman declared war on international communism, and less than two weeks later he ordered two and a half million government employees to undergo a security check.

This order was soon extended to include three million members of the armed forces and three million defence-contract employees. Thus (as D. F. Fleming notes in his book *The Cold War And Its Origins 1917-1960*): '. . . at least 8,000,000 Americans [were] always under the shadow of having to prove their loyalty. . . . Including the families of 8,000,000, about 20,000,000 American citizens [were] subject to investigative procedures at any time'.

These procedures got more and more vicious and ominous as the forties slid into the fifties. In 1947 the Loyalty Boards had to have 'reasonable grounds' for dismissing people. In 1950 this was changed so that they only had to have 'reasonable doubts' about people. In 1953 Eisenhower made it even vaguer and consequently more difficult for anyone to protect themselves against any kind of rumour-mongering, however ill founded. Tragedy did, as ever, eventually end up as farce, at least insofar as Truman found himself, on 6 November 1953, being accused of having knowingly harboured a communist spy; but neither that, nor his subsequent declaration that McCarthyism was 'the shame of our time' could do much to lessen its all-pervasive, repressive effect upon millions of ordinary American citizens.

When Frank Zappa talked to me about it, he remained restrained, but quite obviously, this whole gamut of accelerating orthodoxy the Zappa family hit hard: 'We had two problems. One was the Security Clearance; the other was the fact that my father was born in Sicily and my mother was first-generation, from Italian and French parents. And most of the places we lived, anybody that was not one hundred per cent all-white American was a threat to the community, y'know? And being associated with somebody of foreign parentage made it tough for me in school, and made it tough on them. There was that whole aspect of American life. And I never did understand it.'

Enlarging on the Security Clearance aspect of all this, Zappa told me: 'And once you had your Security Clearance you had to guard it very carefully because if you lost it you couldn't get a job. So my father was concerned about his Security Clearance all through his life. During the time that I was in high school he was always telling me, every time I would get in trouble at school he would flip out because he worried that it would effect, in some roundabout way, his Security Clearance. And since he was cleared for Top Secret, every time the school would call up, there would be a panic.'

By the end of the forties, then, the 'era of fulsomeness' was well and truly over; American politics – and thus American social life – had come a long way from the kind of dumb and vulgar, yet disarmingly naive, attitudes embodied by this gem of a remark by one Senator Wherry, discussing contemporary US friendship toward China: 'With God's help we will lift Shanghai up and up, ever up, until it is just like Kansas City.' A 1940 crowd cheered that remark, and as late as 1946 American exports to China were booming and posters were promoting US-Chinese friendship along with exports of Coca Cola. In 1949 this Randy-Newmanesque fantasy was destroyed by Mao Tse-Tung, and American reaction to the 'loss' of China came close to echoing the 'Let's drop the big one and pulverize 'em' sentiment expressed in Newman's song 'Political Science'.

In the realm of sexual politics too, the atmosphere of openness and potential for change which was in the air at the start of the 1940s had been squeezed out by the end of it, so that among the numbing orthodoxies under which American families of the 1950s were expected to live out their lives was the renewal of a stringent oppression of women. (And so, indirectly, of children too.) The change in attitude is well documented in the pages of American women's magazines of the forties and fifties as traced by Betty Freidan in her book, *The Feminine Mystique*.

In Hitler's Germany in the 1930s, women were forced back into their narrow 'biological role' under the slogan 'Kinder, Kuche, Kirche' (Children, Cooking and The Church). But in America, the so-called New Woman emerged, and by 1939 the idea was being promoted and encouraged even by the traditionally conservative women's magazines. The heroines of their stories were American women who demanded more out of life than a husband and babies – women who effectively carved out their own lives and who, when they did get romantically involved, were loved by men who actually valued these women's strengths and sense of independence.

A counter-attack soon came. As early as 1942 a book called *Modern Woman: The Lost Sex*, by Farnham and Lundberg, argued that careers and higher education led to 'the masculination of women with enormously dangerous consequences for the home . . .' Gradually, as America moved toward the 1950s, this pernicious theme began to win out over the New Woman. By 1949 only a third of women's magazine heroines had careers, and most of these were shown in the stories to be giving them up for the 'happier' life of the housewife.

(The magazines were eventually forced to admit that all this repressive re-narrowing of women's horizons was not accepted gladly by women themselves. In 1956 *McCall's* published an article called 'The Mother Who Ran Away'; it got them the highest readership of anything they'd ever run, and Betty Freidan reports an editor of the time as saying: 'We suddenly realised that all those women at home with their three and a half children were miserably unhappy.' Nevertheless, the anti-careers, anti-education drive as regards American women kept on thriving into the 1960s.)

I asked Zappa whether in addition to the pressures of

Security Clearance and foreign origins, this destruction of the New Woman era had been another significant factor in the air for the Zappa family when he was growing up.

There was certainly nothing New Womanish, he agreed, about his mother; nor did her life afford her any of the kinds of choices available to the New Woman of the early 1940s.

'I think,' he told me, 'that if there was any impressed conservatism of that nature attached to my mother, it was probably there anyway from her family. My mother is Italian-French, and she's from a very strict religious family, and pretty much a poor family too.'

The Zappas, despite Mr Zappa Snr's qualifications and defence-contract work, were hardly well-to-do either.

'Right,' Zappa explained. 'That's another thing, you see. I don't think my mother ever read *McCalls* or the *Ladies Home Journal*: I don't think she could afford them. She'd probably have read 'em if she could have afforded them, but we were desperately poor.

'Even when my father was working for the government we were really poor. At one time he was teaching at the Naval Post-Graduate School at Monterey, California, and we were so poor then that on weekends – Monterey is a sea-coast town and right near it is a town called Salinas, which is in a valley a little way from the coast; and the main industry in Salinas is the raising of lettuce. And there were always these trucks, with open tops, full of lettuce, going down the highway to Monterey. And inevitably some of the lettuce would blow off onto the road. And my father used to put us in the car and we would drive toward Salinas and try to find a lettuce truck and wait for something to fall off it. And then we would stop the car – which was a Henry J., an obsolete, extinct, crummy little car – and he would get out and gather up armfuls of lettuce and take it back to the house and boil it. And that's what we'd be eating.

'And in the forties too, when we lived in Edgewood, Maryland, I used to go with him fishing, down to this place where you could catch catfish or you could catch crabs – and so besides working however many hours a day he did at his job down there, he was also out there hustling to get food to feed the family.'

Zappa's father, with his Sicilian background, was hardly the type to encourage Mrs Zappa's hankerings after a less constrictive life either. Mr Zappa is quoted by Walley* as saying, while discussing his autocratic policy-making on bringing up their children (Frank, two younger brothers, Bob and Carl, and their younger sister Candy): 'She didn't understand my motives and I wasn't about to explain'. They may all have been poor, but at least Mr Zappa had his jobs – his contacts with the outside world – and these were a lot more varied and interesting than Mrs Zappa's endless round of ekeing out and doing chores.

As well as working for the U.S. Naval Post-Graduate School in Monterey for three years, Zappa senior also worked: at the Army installation at Edgewood, Maryland; as a metallurgist for Corvair in Pomona, California; for the government in Florida; on the Atlas Missile in San Diego; and different work again in the town of Lancaster, California. They did indeed move around a lot.

The two most important places, so far as Zappa's childhood and adolescence were concerned, were Edgewood, Maryland – where the family lived for several years up to the time when Zappa was ten – and Lancaster, California – where Frank went to high school and found his own teenage life.

I said to him in a conversation in 1975 that although I'd read several accounts of what Lancaster was like, I'd never read anything about him in Edgewood, Maryland.

'Well,' he said, sensing another opportunity for hitting back, 'I'll be delighted to tell ya!' What followed, though, was both hitback and exposition, and in astonishing detail. (Zappa sometimes appears to suffer from total recall.)

'Edgewood, Maryland is a place where I lived on an Army housing project. The houses had walls that were approximately an inch thick, and they were heated by coal furnaces which heated actually just one room – the kitchen. There was coal and there was a small gas water-heater – very small – with a coil of copper tubing in it and a little gas burner at the bottom. It heated about three ounces of water at a time.

---

* *No Commercial Potential*, David Walley, Outerbridge and Lazard, New York, 1972; 2nd edition E. P. Dutton, New York, 1980.

'It was 15 Dexter Street we lived at. Down the street were some woods, with a little polluted crick running through them, which had creatures called crawdads in it. A crawdad is a little shrimp-like object that will bite your toe. And it had a few snakes.

'I used to go down and play in the woods, climb trees, ride a bicycle, and chew tar from the paving – because all they had done was spew tar onto the dirt. It was a cheap housing project.

'Everybody who lived on the project had a gas mask because the Army installation nearby was engaged in chemical and biological warfare experiments. They had tanks of mustard gas within close range of the housing project so that if any of the tanks ever leaked it would kill everybody who lived on the project. So you had to have a gas-mask in your house.

'So I had a gas mask and a can opener. Do you know how a gas mask is constructed? There's a mask, there's a hose and there's a tin can with a diaphragm on one end of it; and inside the can is an assortment of salts and charcoal that's supposed to filter out the bad aspects of whatever it is that goes into it.

'I was curious as to what was in that can, see? So at six years old I popped open a gas mask. Thereby disabling it; but it made it much more fun to play with, because once you got the can off, the hose was much more, er, mobile. The can weighed about a pound, so without it it was much better for a kid to play with.

'So that was my space helmet. I used to play with it in the coal bin that was in back of the house. It was like a large wooden bin with a lid on it, which served as a spaceship.

'It snowed there once every couple of years and when it snowed I'd get a piece of cardboard and slide down the hill. The snow was always about 1½ inches deep and it melted in one day, and it was always too cold to have any fun out there, but when it snowed you can believe that I was out there with the cardboard.'

Friends? Or was Zappa, even at six, truly a loner?

'I had three friends. One was Paddy McGrath, a boy who was crippled and lived up on the hill. I used to go to his house and have contests eating peanut butter sandwiches with him.

'I had another friend named Leonard Allen. He was interested in chemistry. I used to go over to his house and we would work on experiments. And it's difficult when you're six years

21

old to find the right things to make gunpowder, but we managed to do it.

'I had one other friend, named Paul – I can't remember his last name – who was from Panama. I used to go over to his house and his grandmother would make omelettes with spinach in them. I thought this was a very peculiar thing to eat, but I recognised the fact that he was from another country and so I thought maybe that's what they eat down there.'

Gruesome pleasure flits across the Zappa face, as he recalls something else, which illustrates the awfulness of children:

'Paul used to tell me stories about how you take a bat and tie firecrackers on its wings – this is what you do if you live in Panama and you wanna have a good time – tie firecrackers on the bat's wings and light 'em and let the bat go.

'Also Edgewood is a place where my younger brother Bobby caught fire. We used to wear these flannel pyjamas with a trap door in the back for taking a shit, and the only warmth in the house in the winter time if you were the first person to get up was, you had to go stand by the water heater in the kitchen. And that heater was so small that there was no heat coming out of it unless you opened the door in it and exposed the coils and the flames that were heating the coils.

'And one time right around Christmas my brother Bobby went into the kitchen one morning and opened the door of the water heater and stood there – and his pyjama trap door fell down and his pyjamas caught on fire. And my father, through an elaborate series of mirrors, was laying in bed and could see through these mirror images bouncing all over the house that my brother was on fire. So he ran out and beat the flames out with his bare hands – and burned his hands all up; and my brother's back was all messed up. And that was the first time I ever heard about sulphur. It was a new chemical thing at that time and they treated the burns with sulphur – which is why they don't have any scars today.

'And that,' says Zappa, 'is the complete Edgewood, Maryland report!'

The Zappa family moved away from Edgewood, Maryland, in November 1950 – the month before Frank's tenth birthday and less than a year into the shabby new decade. They lived briefly in Florida, and then – partly following Mr Zappa's job opportunities and partly on account of Frank's asthmatic problems – they moved to sunny California. And within that state, despite changes of location every couple of years, they stayed.

If Frank could claim only three friends, as he told me, in Edgewood, he was no luckier in his teenage days. Nowhere that his family went did he find himself more than one or two replacements for Paddy McGrath, Leonard Allen and Panamanian Paul.

'I didn't,' Zappa has often remarked, 'have too many friends.'

Out in California, he grew less keen on chemistry – partly just from the enforced estrangement from his gunpowder-plotting cohort from Edgewood, but also in part because as Zappa grew into his teens he grew predictably less keen to emulate his father – less keen 'to be a scientist like my Dad' – and more inclined to be defiant.

This relationship between the two Zappas was for a long time misunderstood by the interested sections of the music press. The misunderstanding arose from Zappa saying in an interview that he used to listen to his father rather than talk to him. People assumed that indicated an almost reverent respect for Zappa Snr. But when P. and B. Salvo put a question based on that interpretation to Frank in 1974 (*Melody Maker*) he disabused them sharply:

'It's not so much,' he said, 'that my father was providing me with these pearls of wisdom for me to cherish. My favourite expression that he said was: "The road to hell is paved with good intentions." The only other thing he said was: "You're going to lose all your teeth by the time you're 25." That was for eating too many candy bars . . . I said a few things to him of course, but they never did any good.' Elsewhere, he's described his relationship with his father as – in an evocatively formal wording – 'cordial'.

So, Zappa began to turn his mind more and more towards the arts. Music first and above all else. Reportedly he joined a school band as early as 1951, although it must have been one of those teacher-supervised sessions where you get handed out toy drums and triangles and tambourines, because Frank didn't acquire any instrument of his own until he was 12 – that is, 1953. 'I wanted to play drums,' he told Jerry Hopkins (*Rolling Stone*, 1968), 'so I got some sticks and started beating the hell out of the furniture to the extent that my parents gave up and got me a snare drum.'

Around the same time, Frank began to find he could write music of his own. It was nothing to do with rock'n'roll or pop or rhythm'n'blues, though: it was orchestral music. Later Zappa, stimulated partly by his stumbling across the pioneering 'serious' composer Edgard Varèse's work, was to develop this talent for orchestration via various college courses on harmony and so on – and he was to keep on writing pieces for large orchestras for years and years, before ever being in a position to actually hear such work performed.

Sometimes, Zappa claims that during his teen years he *only* wrote this rather esoteric kind of stuff: 'I started writing when I was 14 – pieces for orchestra which had nothing to do with rock'n'roll. I didn't write anything resembling rock'n'roll till I was 20. All that time, I had absolutely no success at getting a piece of music performed. That was the beginning of my biggest problem, which has always been getting my music played so I can hear it . . . I get my kicks through my ears. So when I couldn't hear it any other way, I decided my only hope was to put together my own group.'

That implies that Zappa didn't front a group till he was 20 or so – that is, until around 1961 – and that when he did it was in order to play some kind of orchestral music. Neither implication is anywhere near true. In fact, Zappa practised his drumming sufficiently to join a band – The Ramblers, in San Diego – when he was 14. And it was, in a way, an r'n'b band. 'Our repertoire,' he told Keith Altham, 'consisted of early Little Richard stuff.'

Even that is doubtful: true early Little Richard stuff was both obscure and religious in content. It isn't likely that the Ramblers played that. Zappa was listening to r'n'b and in the Ramblers was for the first time getting something in the way of an opportunity to play it. 'I used to listen to r'n'b a lot –

Johnny Watson when he used to play guitar; Clarence 'Gatemouth' Brown; the Orchids and the Nutmegs . . . I heard some r'n'b and I wanted to be in an r'n'b band.' So there was Frank Zappa at 14, terrifying his father because of his indifference to the high school ethic, playing drums in The Ramblers and listening to strange old rhythm'n'blues records, while at the same time composing ambitious and unconventional orchestral pieces he had no real hope of hearing – and living in the intensely claustrophobic environment of a fifties lower-middle class Californian home.

There is a photograph of the Zappa family in this habitat in 1953: and it shows a living room with not a single interesting object in it beyond the almost surreal ugliness of young Frank's teenage face. The curtains are like an ad for rufflette tape; there's a G-Plan type coffee table – mass-produced and plain and yet somehow fussy-looking and apologetic; a prim sofa with an anonymous floral cover; tiny prissy little picture frames. It was there that Frank had to operate, driven towards all sorts of artistic endeavour not by the poor American's hunger but by an increasing sense, as he grew through adolescence, of aesthetic revulsion.

It produced the fascination with r'n'b – culturally strange black music – and the desire to write unorthodox orchestral work, and other things too. 'About 1955-56,' Zappa told *Melody Maker*, 'I started writing stories which were either science fiction or pachucco-type humour. And then I started doing 8mm films and experimental stuff like exposing the roll five times, doing opticals inside the camera.'

Although both press fiction writing and film experiments were to re-emerge as part of Zappa's arsenal of weapons after he got famous in the 1960s, in the mid-fifties too it was the music-making and composing that prevailed.

The interest in orchestral music got its most potent stimulus from Zappa's discovery of Varèse's work. Reportedly, Zappa read an article in *Look* magazine about Sam Goody's New York record store, in the course of which an album of Varèse's work *Ionisation* was singled out as an example of something notably 'obscure'. This was enough of a challenge to Zappa – a hint of something which, if he could get hold of it, would guarantee him a possession and an experience none of his acquaintances or teachers would be familiar with: something to emphasize that he was set apart from those around him.

According to legend, it took him a full year to track down a copy of this album – which would probably have been the one on Candide Records, catalogue number CE31028, containing the 1931 work *Ionisation* along with the earlier Varèse works *Octandre* and *Offrandres*. (However, again there's some doubt – and again it's created by Zappa himself, because in listing his all-time favourite Top Ten records for *Let It Rock* magazine, June 1975, he says that '*The Complete Works of Edgard Varèse, Vol. 1* . . . was the first album I'd ever heard of any of Varèse's music.')

The legend, however, continues with Zappa's eventual acquisition of whichever album it was and his playing it once in that aesthetically hostile living room, on the family record player that Zappa described as 'genuine lo-fi', with the result that – probably just as he had hoped – his mother forbade any repetition of the performance. Thus encouraged, Frank, of course, fell immediately in love with Varèse and over the years, he has got a lot of mileage out of his early knowledge of, and respect for, Varèse's work.

At the age of 14 or so he simply liked the sheer weirdness of it, and the alienating effect that weirdness had on others. A piece on Zappa by [Barry] Miles, written in 1970, sheds some light on Zappa's attitude in this respect. Miles talks about Zappa's interest in competition, and says: 'When Frank was young and studying music, he began to read *Counterpoint, Strict and Free* by H.A. Clarke, Philadelphia, 1929. On the second page it said: "Never write any of the following successions. . . ." so Frank played them and said "Great!" and never read any further.' A neat little story – and even if it does show more of a dilettante attitude on Zappa's part than Zappa likes to suggest he held in those days, it shows too that he took the trouble to pick up a book like *Counterpoint, Strict And Free* in the first place.

Zappa's devotion to Varèse bloomed. On his fifteenth birthday, the money he got from his mother was spent in trying – eventually successfully – to get through to the maestro by telephone to

Greenwich village. According to the David Walley book, Zappa was thrilled to be told by Varèse that he was engaged in writing a new work called *Deserts*: a good omen of their compatico, Frank thought, since he, right over on the other side of America, was living in the middle of the Mojave Desert.

That too, though, seems a little fanciful – Zappa was telephoning on 21 December, 1955, and Varèse's *Deserts* was written between 1950 and 1954. But no doubt Zappa did telephone him, and no doubt he did eventually get hold of the album of *Deserts* on Columbia Records MS-6362.

About 18 months after the phone call, Zappa followed it up with a letter to Varèse, asking if he could visit him. He got a handwritten, if noncommital, reply: one of many documents Zappa has kept and treasured.

By this time, the Zappa family had moved to Lancaster, in Antelope Valley. Antelope Valley was politely described in fifties guidebook publicity as the 'New Empire of Urban and Industrial Progress in the Southland.' In other words, it was horrible. As for Lancaster itself, a town near the Edwards Air Force base and Palmdale – right in the middle of the Valley (the Valley in turn being in the middle of the Mojave Desert) – Zappa has often described it graphically: 'It was about 100,000 population but it was spread out over 200 square miles. Okies dying in their yards. You know how you always have to pull up a Chevrolet and let it croak on your lawn.'

Talking to Jerry Hopkins in the 1968 *Rolling Stone* interview, Zappa touched on the relationship between his feelings for the town and for r'n'b music: 'It was a funny small town, Lancaster. They had a bad experience about 1954, prior to the time I moved into the Valley. Joe Houston and Marvin & Johnny and some others came and did an r'n'b show. This was the first time any people in that part of the world had ever seen r'n'b. And *of course* with the groups came the dope-peddlers, and the town was really scared.

'In those days the police were afraid of teenagers. It was a bad scene. Gang fights and all that. Then I came to town . . . I got a band together and we stayed together long enough to learn ten songs. There was a negro settlement outside of town called Sun Village and it was those people who supported the group.

'We had these huge negro dances and this upset the people in the town. The police arrested me for vagrancy the night before the show and I was in jail overnight. My parents bailed me out.

'The band stayed together until everybody got to hate each other's guts. After that I left the group and it turned into the Omens . . .

'Don Vliet [Captain Beefheart] was in the band. Don and I used to get together after school and would listen to records for three or four hours. We'd start off at my house, and then we'd get something to eat and ride around in his old Oldsmobile looking for pussy – in Lancaster! Then we'd go to his house and raid his old man's bread truck and we would sit and eat these pineapple buns and listen to these records until five in the morning and maybe not go to school next day.

'It was the only thing that seemed to matter at the time. We listened to those records so often we could sing the guitar leads. We'd quiz each other about how many records does this guy have out, what was his last record, who wrote it, what is the record number.'

By this point, Frank had more or less given up drumming and while with the group referred to above – which was called The Blackouts – he took up the guitar.

On 4 December 1957, just before his seventeenth birthday, he sold part of his drumming equipment, and hired out another part to another local band called The Bluenotes; the contract for that deal is another of the biographical artefacts Zappa has kept to this day.

The beginning of Zappa the entrepreneur.

The switch from drumming to playing guitar was inevitable. When Zappa had joined The Ramblers back in San Diego, the guitar – as he told Jerry Hopkins – 'wasn't the solo instrument: the sax was. Then I started hearing a few guitars . . . I stopped playing the drums and I got a guitar when I was 18.'

He saw it, bid for it, and bought it, at an auction.

'It cost $1.50 . . . It was one of those old arch top F-hole jobs. The strings were so high I couldn't play chords on it, so I started playing lines right away. I didn't learn to play chords until after about a year but in four weeks I was playing shitty teenage leads.'

Shitty or not, Zappa became lead guitarist for The Blackouts. *Acoustic* lead guitar, that is.

'When I was 21 or 22,' Zappa told Hopkins, 'I got an electric guitar, but I found I couldn't play it and I had to start all over again.' It must have been at 22, because there's a photograph of the 21-year-old Zappa still strumming his acoustic, in the *Progress-Bulletin*, Pomona, California, Friday Evening, 9 March, 1962.

But back to The Blackouts. It was, by all accounts, a strange and multi-racial band. God knows what its standard of performance was. But the year was 1958, and one gets a background fill-in just from considering the sort of music Zappa himself was assiduously listening to at this time.

Years later he told Mick Watts (*Melody Maker*) that there was a distinction to be made between black group music on the East and West coasts: 'The West Coast music had a sense of humour, but the stuff from the East Coast was kinda desperate. Group music was brought to California by black people from Texas, and the ghetto situation in LA wasn't as nasty as it was in Harlem, so it developed a different aura. Do you know The Coasters' 'Shoppin' For Clothes'? That's the sort of thing I mean.'

But Zappa loved all of it, whichever side of America it came from. He told me: 'Well, you know, you sit around and you intellectualize about these records, but during the fifties I was in school and it was *real*. When those records came out I listened to 'em and I said, "Yeah – they're really tellin' me somethin"'.

'I *still* listen to those records. I still got the 45s and I still take 'em out and I got 'em all catalogued in boxes. It's not like a fetishist collection. I mean, that is music that I *like* and is alive for me. All the records that I have, it's because I enjoy them and not because I wanted to have every copy of something that so-and-so did. I'm not crazy like that. I've got records that I enjoy listening to. And there's two or three people who'll come over to the house even now and we'll sit around for hours and play those things – and just go nuts because they're *so good*, and they're so real. Those were made in a time when people actually believed in what they were singin' . . . I'm not into love songs. Unless of course they're being sung by The Spaniels, or, y'know,

29

someone I can trust! Somebody who is *really* in *love*, see? Those people believed in it back then.'

I asked him why, granted that he still loved that kind of music, and granted that he has the facilities for acting as a producer for a group like The Spaniels, why doesn't he do that? Couldn't he produce that kind of music?

'I could produce the shit out of it!', he said. 'And love every minute of it. But I really don't believe there is a market for it; I think that outside of the personal satisfaction it would give me to work on something like that, I'm not sure that the time and effort spent on doing it would be rewarded in record sales, which would pay for the project.

'People who are really hard-core r'n'b fanatics know that it's already happened – that it's what's on those old records that exists. And there is no immediate audience for a rebirth of that kind of music done in exactly the right style.'

But he gave another avowal of his love for the music to Keith Altham in a 1970s interview: 'I love r'n'b. It sounds good to me. It has definite musical merit. Just because it could be considered musically illiterate in some instances by academic standards, that has no relationship to what the real value of that music is.

'The emotional quality of the music of the fifties, and the feel of those performances – everything they have is cheap. But the sound that comes out is just great, it inspires you. When they have the cheapest stuff they come out with a piece of art at the end.' (Years later – in 1966 – when Zappa was enjoying his early peak of notoriety as a fresh and outrageously freaky recording artist and performer, he was to declare, self-mockingly: 'We sing songs with feeling like they were done in the late fifties in El Monte Legion Stadium!')

What, then, more specifically, was the high school Zappa listening to within this r'n'b milieu? He told *Melody Maker*: 'I used to listen to Buddy Holly and the Crickets too, but I *was* more interested in black music . . . I went to high school with the Drifters' "Ruby Baby". I really like that. But it is very slick compared to the funky r'n'b sound they used to play: "Steamboat" and "Your Cash Ain't Nothin' But Trash" . . .'

And he told *Let It Rock* (June 1975):

'"Three Hours Past Midnight." Johnny Guitar Watson. One

of the best guitar solos on an old r'n'b record. "Story Of My Life": Guitar Slim. Another of the best guitar solos on an old r'n'b record. "Who Will Be Next?" Howlin' Wolf – because it is *very* serious. . . . "Newly Wed" by The Orchids – one of my very favourite group vocal r'n'b tunes . . . "Can I Come Over Tonight?": The Velours. Any musicologist that can find that record should listen to the bass singer. He's singing quintuplets and septuplets. And considering where it came from and when it was made – it was on the East Coast Onyx label – it was amazing.

'"Let's Start All Over Again": The Paragons. That's also prototypical and it has the unmitigated audacity to have the most moronic piano section I ever heard on any record – and it repeats it often enough to convince me it's deliberate.

'Anything that Richard Berry did. Without getting the credit for it he made so much of what happened in r'n'b possible and so many people wouldn't have been there at all without him. He was one of the most important secret sources behind West Coast r'n'b in the fifties – and now [1975] he's walking around trying to get a contract.

'I interviewed him when I did a piece for *Life* magazine, and he told me he sold the rights for "Louie Louie" for 5,000 dollars. He was working with a Latin band at a place called the Harmony Park Ballroom and the band had an instrumental that went so, and Berry scribbled the lyrics out on a paper napkin in the dressing room.

'It's always been one of my favourite fantasies that songs like "Wooly Bully" get written on a lunch bag in blue crayon . . .'

Imagining Zappa cruising around downtown Lancaster in Beefheart's old Oldsmobile with all these musical cheesecakes and fantasies in his head, I asked him whether he'd seen the first big movie that made some attempt to recapture that era, *American Graffiti*.

'No,' he said, with more than a hint of reproach.

Was that, I asked him, part of a policy of not getting distracted from his own work by paying attention to other people's?

'No,' he said, 'it's just that the idea of *American Graffiti* never appealed to me. I just knew that it couldn't possibly be real.'

I said I was asking because all American musical milieux come to British people vicariously, and *American Graffiti* struck me as evocative – and renewed a feeling in me that, like most English people who grew up on rock'n'roll, I wished I'd been in America in the 1950s, even though other than for musical reasons it's an insane sort of wish.

'No,' said Zappa, 'you're right. You should have been there, it was great. But there is no movie and no description that's ever been made that comes anywhere near to what it was like. It's all *so* jive.

'See, the thing about the fifties in the USA was – the fifties you're talking about, the good stuff, and the source of the good music, was only happening in a few places. It's just like when long hair and flower-power and all that happened. It was really only happening in one or two places. The rest of the country might as well have been Venus, y'know: it just wasn't there.

'And for me, living in places like Lancaster – it was good but it was *very* frustrating. Because things were really happening in Los Angeles, which was 80 miles away. Can you imagine how that felt? – knowing that there it all was, but 80 miles away! I mean, so near and yet so far.'

I asked Zappa if he'd ever liked Elvis – because though Elvis was white, he was, as it were, a hell of a lot blacker than any of the other white singers thrown up by rock'n'roll. Zappa the purist would have none of it – even though he himself was, of course, in his fifties bands (The Ramblers, for instance) engaged in exactly the same white covering of black r'n'b material he so resented and despised in others.

'No, the only record of Elvis I ever liked was "Baby Let's Play House" I was fantastically offended when he did "Hound Dog" in '56, because I had the original record by Willie Mae Thornton and I said "*How* could anybody *do* that?" Anybody who bought that Elvis record was missing out because they'd obviously never even heard Willie Mae Thornton's.

'See, they didn't play black records on the major radio stations. The only way you could hear the sort of music that I fell in love with was to pick up some scratchy station from a million miles away, or else go down to a juke-box record dump, something like that, where you could find these unusual labels –

Peacock, or Excello, or things like that.

'So most of the kids I went to school with had no idea and no knowledge of that kind of music. The only thing they knew about rock'n'roll was when some white person decided they were going to, ah, memorialize on one of them r'n'b records. I mean, it's been said before but it's true – Pat Boone singing Little Richard numbers was an absolutely disgusting phenomenon.

'How about his "Tutti Frutti"?! Ah! that's the one! "Too-ty Froo-ty, oh, Ru-dy"! Can't you just hear his white buck shoes stomping in the distance?!'

But The Ramblers doing Little Richard numbers was OK? And *wasn't* Elvis a lot blacker than most? Zappa will have none of it:

'There was just no appeal there. And the people that I was hanging out with, the mere mention of Elvis' name would bring about peels of laughter – because he wasn't *doing* anything: it just wasn't real.'

Neither, compared to the delights of all this music, was Antelope Valley High School, and Frank Zappa graduated – or rather, didn't quite graduate – on Friday 13 June 1958.

He took a course in harmony, under a Mr Russell, at the Antelope Valley Junior College, and in the spring of 1959, when the Zappa family moved again – this time to Claremont (still in California) Frank took the opportunity to go his own way, and moved to Echo Park, Los Angeles. He'd made it across that 80 mile gulf. He didn't cut all ties, though, either with his family or his old school. (Indeed his continued preoccupation with high school – including a continued animus towards it – is a marked feature of Zappa's adult work.)

The very first thing Zappa worked on, after leaving home and school and making the move to L.A., was the musical score for a cheapo-cheapo cowboy film scripted by Frank's old English teacher, Don Cerveris. The film was called *Run Home Slow*. The score was completed, but to Zappa's desperate chagrin – he had been counting on it to make him a little money to survive on – the film disappeared without trace until much later.

Meanwhile, Zappa was busy elsewhere in a musical outfit called Joe Perrino and The Mellotones, which operated out of San Bernadino, and, hate it as Zappa might, what they played was cocktail music. Muzak for half-drunk tone-deaf cocktail bar patrons in places like Tommy Sandi's Club Sahara on East Street, San Bernadino.

It was from a ten month stint in that band that Zappa's inspiration came for the parody masterpiece 'America Drinks And Goes Home' on the early album *Absolutely Free* which The Mothers Of Invention were to release in the mid-sixties.

Zappa made just about enough money from playing guitar in Joe Perrino *et al.* to enrol for another college course that same year (1959) – this time Chaffey College, in Alta Loma. It was, again, a harmony course.

At Chaffey, Zappa met and married Kay. Kay had a secretarial job at the First National Bank of Ontario, California, and she kept it on after her marriage. It was a good thing she did, too, because life with Frank didn't last long. Their divorce didn't happen for years, but their separation was more or less complete by the end of 1963. 'We shacked up for a little while,' Frank was to say of their relationship years later.

Things were dragging for Zappa as the 1960s began. He'd quit Joe Perrino and The Mellotones; he'd got less out of his harmony courses than he'd hoped for, and less also from the composition course into which he'd unofficially crept at Pomona College. Money was difficult stuff to come by, and his marriage was no honeymoon.

For a while, he was apparently drawn towards Zen and yoga, but his acerbic personality was never really suited to it; Zappa's myopia quotient used to be much lower than that of most rock musicians. As he explained it to an interviewer: 'I was interested in Zen for a long time. That's what got me away from being a Catholic, fortunately. But it's my observation that Eastern religions are wonderful if you are living anywhere but the U.S. The best they can do for you here is, uh, give you a certain feeling of calm . . . The real goal(s) of Eastern religion . . . are difficult if not impossible to achieve in an industrial society.'

In 1961, Zappa returned to film soundtrack scoring, this time for a film called *The World's Greatest Sinner**. According to Walley's book on Zappa, the orchestral recording involved was

---

* This score, says *Zappalog*, includes a prototype (slow) version of 'Holiday In Berlin' which recurs (twice) on the 1969 album *Burnt Weeny Sandwich*, partly live from a 1968 gig! (*Zappalog*, by Norbert Obermanns, was published in Germany in 1981.)

done with just two microphones and was mixed down to monaural in a truck parked outside the auditorium the musicians were using.

What isn't clear is which 'small rock'n'roll group – eight musicians' was used for recording parts of Frank's score. It can't have been the group which Zappa himself had involved himself with before the Joe Perrino outfit, in '61. Each of these groups had four members, not eight. The Boogie Men didn't even have the money for a bass player. Their line-up was: Frank Zappa, lead guitar; Kenny Burgan, saxophone; Doug Rost, rhythm guitar; and Al Surratt on drums.

The Boogie Men played two-chord soul music – stuff like 'Night Owl', a song that still pops up frequently in Zappa's conversations about music, as we shall see – and their audiences came from high-school weekend dances. The experience heightened Zappa's scorn for clean-cut high school kids, but being a Boogie Man had probably been one step better than being a Joe Perrino Mellotone. All the same, things seemed not to be moving forward.

Then *The World's Greatest Sinner* went through its preview/première and got a local run in Hollywood. It had already given Frank one extremely important thing – the opportunity, at last, to actually hear an orchestra playing one of his scores; with its Hollywood run, it now gave him a little money as well.

Zappa, at 21, was somewhere near to being on his way. 'It was rancid,' said Frank later.

2. We Got This Car, When It Hits The Wall:

Early Attempts At Self-Promotion, Selling Jingles & Earning Money From Music

Despite the comparative success of *The World's Greatest Sinner*, Zappa still needed day jobs. There were a number of very ordinary, mundane ones, like those most post-adolescents drift in and out of; but among them was the invaluable experience of working for an advertising agency.

With hindsight it seemed an incongruous alliance between one of the more amorally slick of capitalist endeavours and one of the counter-culture's figureheads. Yet it was an alliance that made perfect sense, granted Zappa's flair for manipulating publicity and notoriety – and later for presenting himself as both the goods and the packaging around them. It was Zappa, when his first big record deal was signed, who was personally responsible for MGM/Verve's successful and imaginative use of an almost unintelligible pop-art advertising campaign for The Mothers Of Invention. Zappa told Jerry Hopkins: 'We wouldn't have sold any records if we had left it up to the company. They figured we were odd-ball. One-shot novelty-a-go-go. But we weren't. We had to show them ways that they could make money on the product. From the beginning it was hard to convince them of what we were talking about. We had to make them understand. First of all, I wanted to take the advertising account. Later they gave me most of it to do.

'. . . MGM had no idea of merchandising in the under-ground press, and in certain periodicals that might tend to be left-wing, hippie oriented, anything that didn't look like establishment media. We went after a peculiar audience – appealing to the curiosity of people who had some curiosity about things.'

Zappa's resourcefulness, and sense of the importance of advertising, was still being somewhat grudgingly admired by his record company as late as 1967 – as this grumpy inter-office memo from MGM's Jack Maher to MGM's Mort Nasatir makes clear:

August 28, 1967

One of the better ideas Herb Cohen and Frank Zappa have come up with since they invented advertising is the use of the billboard on the Sunset Strip.

I have contracted with Grant Advertising to use this billboard for the months of October and November. The price is $3,200 for both months. The billboard will feature all of the Mothers Of Invention albums from *Freak Out* to *We're Only In It For The Money*.

Jack Maher

So it was of benefit to the would-be star back in 1962 that he landed a day job with an ad agency. And by a small coincidence perhaps, the company which Zappa's ad work was designed to promote was the same company for which his first wife Kay worked as a secretary: 'Yes, around 1962,' he told me, 'I was writing copy for the First National Bank of Ontario. Mostly for them, anyway. It was a small agency.'

Another not too dissimilar day job Zappa got was working for a manufacturer of greetings-cards. He told me: 'That was in Claremont. I was doing advertising work for trade magazines relating to those greetings cards. And I was designing greetings cards. And I was making silk-screens for them. That sort of thing. I could have run the place single-handed. My training in school, aside from the music things that I was doing my own, was mainly in art. I supported myself part time from working in commercial art. That's why my album covers were so good later on – not because I did 'em: Cal Shenkel has always done them – but I was very aware of the potency of that side of things.

'I really liked it too. I still have a scrap book collection of some of those greetings cards and stuff.'

So there was Frank Zappa, back in the early sixties, learning the tricks of the self promotion trade – and at the same time trying to crash his way into some of the media beyond the local papers.

One of the first of these excursions – and one which of course he made very sure the local press reported – was Zappa getting on television with Mr Steve Allen by playing 'a bicycle concerto for two'.

By the autumn of 1963, Zappa had also started forming his own music publishing companies, operated from his home address at 314 West G Street, Ontario, Cal., and was submitting material to record companies, agencies and television stations. The first music publishing company was, typically, called Aleatory Music, and was simply Zappa making his submissions of material seem slightly more professional and impressive.

In a sense, this material *was* impressive – Aleatory Music sent material in to the A&R department of the massive Dot Records Inc. which, Zappa claims, 'included the original of "Any Way The Wind Blows," the original instrumental version of "Take Your Clothes Off When You Dance" and a recording of Don Vliet [Captain Beefheart] singing "Slippin' & Slidin"*.' All the same, it is hardly surprising, in the light of how the music industry thought and worked in 1963, that Dot Records Inc. declined to take on titles like 'Take Your Clothes Off When You Dance' and voices like Captain Beefheart's torturing 1950s material.

Accordingly, Milt Rogers of Dot's A&R Dept sat his secretary down on 19 September 1963 and had her write the following rejection note to Frank Zappa – or rather Vincent Zappa, as he was calling himself at the time:

September 19, 1963

Mr V. Zappa
Aleatory Music
314 W. 'G' St.
Ontario, California

* This 'Any Way The Wind Blows' and 'Take Your Clothes Off When You Dance' plus another track from the same period, 'Fountain of Love', have been issued on the bootleg *Necessity is . . ..*

Dear Mr Zappa:

Let me thank you for submitting your material to Dot Records for recording consideration. This material has been carefully reviewed and while it does have merit, we do not feel strongly enough about its commercial potential to give you any assurance of a recording. It is, therefore, being returned to you.

Please accept our sincere thanks for thinking of Dot Records and let me wish you every success.

Milt Rogers

Artists and Repertoire

When Zappa got the letter, he responded in two ways – both equally characteristic. First, he put his copy of what was clearly just a standard rejection letter in his scrapbook. Second, he phoned up Milt Rogers and argued about the rejection of his material.

He was more than a little peeved that, cornered on the telephone, Milt Rogers could finally only explain his failure to sign up Captain Beefheart on the grounds that 'the guitar was distorted' on the submitted recording of 'Slippin' & Slidin''. This was progress indeed.

By no means discouraged, Zappa spent the early part of 1964 juggling about further with his music publishing empire, eventually formalizing it all into Frank Zappa Music, and getting that properly affiliated to BMI. He also spent a lot of time hanging around, and working, with Paul Buff, an electronics wizard cum cronie, who had actually built himself a five-track recording studio in Cucamonga, California at 8040 North Archibald Avenue.

A five-track studio was unique at the time – no-one had got beyond making the transition from two-track to four-track. Not even Dot Records Inc. But Paul Buff had a five-track. He was that sort of person. He and Zappa, who had known each other since the start of the sixties, had a considerable rapport.

Not unlike Zappa's father, Buff had been working with a missile company until he quit to build the Cucamonga studio. 'He's a real unsung hero,' says Zappa. 'He taught himself sax, piano, bass and drums, and learned the basic rock 'n' roll licks, so that he could make all the records by overdubbing himself. He wrote songs too – and they sounded like every other song you ever heard, because he wrote them to a formula.'

Zappa and Buff started working together closely in the Cucamonga studio. Frank told Mick Watts of *Melody Maker*:

'We made records that we knew we couldn't sell to anybody, but we'd spend days on them. Things were so absurd.'

But their basic project *was* to sell their records. They dreamt up catchy little rock'n'roll recordings – 'little symphonies for the kids,' as Phil Spector called the dreams *he* was externalizing at around the same time. And having put them on tape, Zappa and Buff took them round the Hollywood record companies trying to sell them.

They came up with a weird and wonderful collection, and a limited success.

Part of that success was due to Paul Buff's Rec-O-Cut Lathe. That is, a cheap but ingenious machine that turned tape-recordings into acetate records – demo records. When they went round the Hollywood record majors, they found it a lot easier to get noticed and listened to with a demo record than with just another ordinary tape in a whole pile of tapes which cascaded into the majors' offices daily.

Zappa recalled the whole process fondly, telling me: 'Before we would go into Hollywood to try and sell our demos, we wouldn't take in a tape, we'd take in an acetate dub, made on the Rec-O-Cut, which was like a cheap grade dub-cutting unit. In fact it was quite humorous. You know when you cut an acetate there's quite a bit of spewage of the stuff that the needle digs out of the acetate? And it's highly inflammable, and if not collected it just gathers on the disc and you blow it away, or else you have to scrape it off after you cut the disc.

'Well Paul Buff arranged this device which uses a vacuum cleaner similar to the one held by Captain Beefheart on the *Hot Rats* album cover. This funny little bullet-shaped vacuum cleaner with a big hose. And he would accumulate all of these acetate grindings in this vacuum cleaner, and when it was jam-packed he would take this bundle – which looked like a bale of purple hair – and he would take it out into the street and throw a match into it and it would make a quick bonfire in the middle of the night.

'We'd get to have a little celebration like that once every couple of weeks.'

As that implies, they were busy and prolific. Paul Buff played every instrument on a single called 'Tijuana Surf' – 'by the Hollywood Persuaders' and Zappa wrote the B-side. It was put out by DJ Art Laboe's Original Sound label and, Zappa says, 'was Number One in Mexico for 17 straight weeks!'

It was also for the Original Sound label that Zappa, with Ray Collins – later a Mother of Invention – had written and produced the reputedly beautiful 'Memories Of El Monte' by The Penguins. It features lead singer Cleve Duncan of the original Penguins (their big hit was the original of 'Earth Angel') but for 'Memories Of El Monte', Zappa told Mick Watts, 'the rest of those Penguins were just a bunch of guys from the car wash'.

It has the virtue now of being a sought-after oldie – Zappa told me that in fact 'you can order it from Village Oldies or you can order it direct from Original Sound Records in Hollywood: they still press it' – but at the time it didn't sell at all. Not even in Mexico.

In fact Zappa managed, as part of this busy and variegated programme of trying to crash into the music business, to write and make around ten non-sellers for Art Laboe's Original Sound label. He also worked, he told Mick Watts, with 'a label that's so obscure that if you found any of their records (even today) they probably wouldn't be worth anything'.

This was Vigah Records, and it nearly gave Zappa a hit. In fact it actually was a local hit, though only in San Bernadino. The record was called 'The Big Surfer' by Brian Lord and The Midnighters (Vigah 001) and featured a San Bernadino disc jockey impersonating President Kennedy judging a dance contest. Zappa wrote it.

Capitol Records bought the master – paying the then quite large sum of $7,000 – but just as they were launching the record, confident of its humorous punch-line mention of Medgar Evers, Evers was inconsiderate enough to get himself killed. That killed the record – except of course in San Bernadino, where the DJ featured on the single wasn't going to

give up playing his own record just because of a little unde-
served bad luck.

At this time Zappa also took what opportunities he could to
hang around the bigger studios; on one such occasion he was
impressed yet dismayed to find himself watching the Beach Boys
in action. It was just after Capitol had bought the 'The Big
Surfer' master, and Zappa muscled in on seeing producer Jim
Economides mixing a couple of early Beach Boys tracks, 'Surfer
Girl' and 'Little Deuce Coupe' – as well, according to Mick
Watts, as 'Dick Dale's Secret Surfer Spot'. Zappa's dismay
centred around his observation first of Brian Wilson's absence
from the whole proceedings – which didn't at all fit with his subsequent image as the indispensible 'genius' behind that excellent
band – and secondly of the fact that Economides 'spent most
of his time trying on new Italian sports coats sent up from a
nearby men's outfitters'. It wasn't at all the way things were
done at Cucamonga.

There, Zappa and his friends also put together a single called
'Break Time' by The Masters – i.e. Frank, Paul Buff and Ronnie
Williams* – on Buff's own label Emmy; 'Every Time I See You'
by The Heartbreakers and 'How's Your Bird?' by Baby Ray and
The Ferns, both for the Del-fi/Donna company owned by Bob
Keene; and 'Hey Nelda' by Ned and Nelda, inspired by 'Hey
Paula' by Paul and Paula (Vigah 002).

'Baby Ray', Zappa told Mick Watts, 'was Ray Collins, and
that was the first record to feature a snork, which we have since
featured more strongly!' And the B-side of the Baby Ray record
was . . . 'The World's Greatest Sinner'.

Somewhere in amongst all this enthusiastically executed output was yet another characteristically-titled Zappa opus, 'Mr
Clean' by Mr Clean.

As time went by, however, Zappa got more and more interested in the Cucamonga studio, and Paul Buff less and less so.
Eventually – through a contract dated 1 August 1964 – Buff
sold the studio and all its equipment to Zappa for a thousand
dollars.

---

* Williams was the snot-hoarding Ronnie who inspired the song 'Let's Make The Water
Turn Black'. Later he disappeared and then, to Zappa's amazement, turned up at one of
his concerts in the early part of 1974.

The reason why Zappa had that much money to spend was that the movie he had scored for, *Run Home Slow*, had finally, slow but sure, come home. It re-surfaced to a limited success, but enough to earn Frank the money for a decent electric guitar, the studio and some auctioned-off Hollywood movie sets that he dragged home with him in a hired truck.

Paul Buff moved out of the studio and Frank-as-owner moved in. Buff went on to invent a whole range of recording equipment, not least among them the Kepex noise-reduction unit, and run his own successful manufacturing companies.

Zappa told me in 1975: 'I talk to him once in a while still. In fact in a sense today we still work together – that is in the sense that Paul invented the computer mix-down system that's being used at the Record Plant in Los Angeles, and the Record Plant is a studio I use quite a lot.

'In fact right now you know what is sitting there at the Record Plant? All those masters from the Cucamonga days – I've been working toward an album of that material – all those Ned & Nelda things. Well as you know those original masters were recorded on a five-track machine, and in order to re-mix those masters the original heads from that machine had to be remounted on another chassis; and this has been done, and that machinery is sitting in the Record Plant. So at the end of this 1975 European tour I'll go back in there and provided no damage has occurred to the machine – because it's in a very fragile condition – it's just mounted very lightly onto this Ampex chassis – I'll be able to have stereo mix-downs of pieces that pre-date the first album or the earliest things that were done with Captain Beefheart.

'So anyway, that's what happened to Paul Buff!'

Back then, when Buff moved out of the Cucamonga studio and Zappa moved more firmly in, he re-named it Studio Z and held a party . . . and he *taped* the party. He told me: 'At the party was Beefheart, a guy named Bob Narcisso, Ray Collins, Motorhead, Beefheart's little girlfriend Laurie, another guy who used to play drums in our band, Al Ceraeff; I think that was about it. It was the night I took possession of Studio Z, and we just went into the studio and turned on the tape recorder and so

I've got tapes of Captain Beefheart singing "Night Owl" and Ray Collins singing "Louie Louie" and then we'd get a background going and be fucking around and making up lyrics on top of that.'

Frank's work pace was increasing. He was still making tapes; still writing his unplayable orchestral music; still playing in stranger r'n'b bands; and also doing a radio show – at least through the earlier part of 1964. 'It was on the college station at Pomona College. I not only played r'n'b records – I sang, talked, gave lectures, demonstrated ways in which a person could have fun at a party, ahem, by playing r'n'b records.

'I remember one show was dedicated to explaining to the college audience the two chords that you needed to know in order to play the background for "Night Owl" and 50,000 other r'n'b songs that had the same chord changes.

'Things like that. I still have (of course!) a tape of that show – and that piece of tape is to be included in the ten-album set that I've been trying to put on the market ever since 1968!'

But despite the radio show for educating college kids into the mysteries and joys of r'n'b – an educational drive Zappa was to pursue again and again after he became a recording artist in his own right – his main activities back in 1964 were playing live and using his newly-acquired studio.

'Once I learned how to use the studio equipment,' he told the Salvos (*Melody Maker*, January 1974), 'I would sit there twelve hours at a time and play all the instruments myself onto the tape' – just as Paul Buff had done before him – 'and I'd practise what I was going to do later when I got into a bigger studio. It was a lab for me.'

The Salvos asked Zappa whether the studio also helped create the forerunner of The Mothers Of Invention, The Muthers.

'Yes,' said Frank, 'it was a three-piece group with Paul Woods on bass, Les Papp on drums and me on guitar, and we worked at a club called the Saints and Sinners in Ontario, Cal. and it was close to an Eric Clapton-Cream-type format.'

But aside from The Muthers, there was also Zappa's involvement with Captain Beefheart's tentative excursions into recording and performing, mostly through the near legendary *I Was A Teenage Maltshop* project and the short-lived Soots.

I Was A Teenage Maltshop, possibly the world's first rock opera, was, says Zappa, 'strictly fantasy stuff. It was the idea of an old man who has a daughter Nelda who was a cheerleader. The old man has a recording studio that hasn't hit and there's an evil landlord who's going to foreclose on him. So there's this group that comes in with a teenage hero that goes to the high school called Med the Mungler, a teenage Lone Ranger. It was just a fantasy-type thing with rock'n'roll music on it.'

A synopsis and sample extract was submitted to Joseph Landis, the producer of the Repertoire Workshop at KNXT, a CBS TV station, and rejected by him thus on 2 December:

December 2, 1964

Dear Frank,

I received your outline last week, and have read and reread it at least six times.

As you know, both Leon Drew and myself are enchanted with the thought of programming a rock and roll opera.

Unfortunately, we remain unconvinced that the outline submitted can insure a quality show.

Therefore, I must advise you that we will only be interested if we receive a complete script with all narration, dialogue and music.

I have enjoyed our talks in the past and feel you have a great deal of imagination and talent. I wish you all success for the future.

Joseph Landis.

I Was A Teenage Malt Shop later became *Captain Beefheart vs. The Grunt People*. This, too, was rejected.

After the prototype *Malt Shop* had been rejected by the CBS Repertoire Workshop, Zappa and Beefheart formed The Soots, though it didn't survive very long. Still, things were pretty hectic and confused, the bands Zappa played with at this time shifting and re-shifting rapidly, but nothing was wasted and they all served Frank's over-riding ambition: to get into the music industry, to impose his own taste in music on others, to become a financially and artistically successful composer/musician/ entertainer/producer.

One of the most interesting bands out of all these shortly-before-the-Mothers permutations was a line-up from earlier in 1964, with which Zappa had regular work at the Village Inn in Sun Village.

Zappa told me: 'I've got a tape – you know the *Roxy* album [1975]? You know the song about Sun Village? – I've got a tape from the Village Inn where I worked in 1964 and it's got this *character*, I don't know what his name was, some black gentleman there who got drunk and thought he was the MC of the show and grabbed the microphone and started saying "D'y'all like the band? D'y'all like the band?" and the people in the audience were saying "Yeah, we like the band but we don't like you, now *get off!*" and he says "Well little Mary we like you an' we just wanna say that we're gonna have many coming attractions here to the Village Inn and er now we want you all to have a good time and er, er the bar is gonna close soon" – and going through all those raps and then he says "Now, Toby on drums and Johnny Franklin on bass and er Frankie Zappo on guitar!"

'But from the tape you can really get back to how the whole thing was. You can just feel the atmosphere in that place. And it just happens to be a stereo tape so you can hear some room tone and the *old air* that was hanging there. And right after this guy, on the tape, is a selection that we played that night, with this woman called Cora, who was one of the customers.

'She was this huge lady, who wore white socks rolled down over her shoes and sang like a man. She's got a baritone voice and she's singing an old blues song called "Steal Away" with the group – and, incidentally, with *Motorhead* on *sax!* He didn't have the first idea of how to play a sax. And sitting in the audience was, again, Captain Beefheart. And it's actually quite a nice performance of "Steal Away".*'

By the end of 1964, then, Zappa had done quite a bit and expended massive amounts of energy trying to crash his way into the mainstream of the music business. Yet like so many other would-be comers, he could never bring himself fully to

* 'Steal Away' was subsequently made available on the 'Mystery Disc' in the first box of *Old Masters*.

knuckle down and record/play/produce exactly the formula things that the music industry would have taken and rewarded him for. His surfing records were typical of this – 1963 had seen him making surfing records because surfing records were commercially creamy: that year's sound of success. Yet Zappa, perhaps to his credit, could never quite channel his talents into bringing off a conventional, formularized surfing record: his had to laugh at the whole thing at the same time as imitating it; his had to contain Frank's barbed intimations of disapproval at the whole mindless-body-worship-white-Americana element that surf music glorified. Ned and Nelda weren't really *likely* to have the same sort of appeal back then as gooey Paul and Paula. And Zappa knew it.

Luckily, something else was happening by the end of 1964. Los Angeles was breeding a freak scene out of the subterranean remnants of the beat scene, while on the East Coast of America, Bob Dylan was about to put surrealism and rock'n'roll music together into something not only more barbed and, as it were, anti-surfer, than anything the post-adolescent Frank Zappa had come up with, but also something which was to prove commercially viable.

Dylan hastened a shift in taste and a widening of what it was possible to do in the music industry. In the process, the industry moved closer to Zappa. He didn't have to go straight in order to succeed in it; it readied itself to embrace a new range of interests and modes of expressing them, that could accommodate Zappa's already established musical weirdness. At the same time, Zappa's obsessional interests and targets were becoming less directly post-adolescent and more informed by the L.A. freak culture as 1965 boomed.

But before 1965 came, and a major record deal for Zappa came with it, there was the Studio Z Porn Bust Incident.

Plenty of rock stars manage to get busted on sordid-sounding charges after they are famous, and to the extent that their famousness is interesting, so too is their bust. Frank Zappa managed to get himself busted in a creditably interesting way *before* he was famous.

Under the headline VICE SQUAD RAIDS LOCAL FILM STUDIO and the sub-head 2 A-GO-GO TO JAIL, reporter

Ted Harp of local paper the *Daily Report* wrote:

> 'Vice squad investigators stilled the tape recorders of a free-swinging a-go-go film and recording studio here Friday and arrested a self-styled movie producer and his buxom, red-haired companion.
> 'Booked on suspicion of conspiracy to manufacture pornographic materials and suspicion of sex perversion, both felonies, at county jail were:
> Frank Vincent Zappa, 24, and Lorraine Belcher, 19, both of the studio address, 8040 N. Archibald Ave.
>
> RENT MOVIE
> The surprise raid came after an undercover officer, following a tip from the Ontario Police Department, entered the rambling, three-room studio on the pretext of wanting to rent a stag movie.
> 'Sgt. Jim Willis, vice investigator of the San Bernadino County Sheriff's Office, said the suspect, Zappa, offered to do even better – he would film the movie for $300, according to Willis.
> 'When Zappa became convinced the detective was "allright" *sic* he played a tape recording for him. The recording was for sale and it featured, according to police, Zappa and Miss Belcher in a somewhat "blue" dialogue.
>
> MORE ENTER
> 'Shortly after the sneak sound preview, the suspect's hopes for a sale were shattered when two more sheriff's detectives and one from the Ontario Police Department entered and placed the couple under arrest.
> 'Zappa, who recently was the subject of a news story on his hopes to produce a low-budget fantasy film and thus bring a share of Hollywood's glamor to Cucamonga, blamed financial woes for his latest venture.
> 'Inside his studio when the raid came was recording and sound equipment valued at more than $22,000, according to Zappa.

MUSICAL INSTRUMENTS

'Also a piano, trap drums, vibraphone and several electric guitars were stored among the Dalian litter of the main studio. On the walls, Zappa had hung such varied memorabilia as divorce papers, a picture of himself on the Steve Allen television show, a threat from the Department of Motor Vehicles to revoke his driver's licence, several song publishers' rejection letters and works of "pop" art.

'Among Zappa's completed musical scores were such titles as "Memories Of El Monte" and "Streets Of Fontana".

'The latter, written before several utility companies had forsaken the budding composer, opens:

> "Sweeping Streets"
> "As I was out sweeping the streets of Fontana
> As I was out sweeping Fontana one day
> I spied in the gutter a moldy banana
> And with the peeling I started to play . . ."

'Assisting Sgt Willis in the raid were sheriff's vice investigators Jim Mayfield and Phillip Ponders, and Ontario detective Stan McCloskey.

'Arraignment for Zappa and Miss Belcher next week will bring them close to home.

'Cucamonga Justice Court is right across the street from the studio.'

Frank Zappa's version of the same events differs from reporter Ted Harp's more than just in prose style. The passage of almost a decade and his own licence with historical fact no doubt contributed their own twists to the account of the porn bust which Zappa gave the Salvos (*Melody Maker*, January 1974); but for better or worse, it went like this: 'I was set up by the Vice Squad . . . they sent a guy into my studio disguised as a used-car salesman requesting material to present to other used-car salesmen at an alleged party that was supposed to take place the following Wednesday.

'Because I got a lot of publicity in the Cucamonga area through the studio, I was attempting to raise money to produce a science fiction film called *Captain Beefheart vs. The Grunt*

People. They had this whole big spread on the studio in the Sunday papers.

'It was directly across the street from a holyroller church and a block away from a grammar school in a town of 7000 population – so they came to me.

'I was the only guy in town that had long hair even though it was shorter than a crew-cut. It was weird.

'So there was a bunch of animosity in the community about what I was doing.

'They came to investigate me and performed what is known in the trade as an "illegal entrapment". They requested that pornographic material be manufactured.

'He specified what he wanted and I didn't make him a film, I made him a sound tape 'cause I had no idea that the manufacture of such a tape would be doing anything illegal. And I thought I was doing a public service to a bunch of used-car salesmen who wanted to get their rocks off.

'So I made this tape for a price of $100. It sounded really fine to me at the time because I wasn't eating, and he came back next day and offered me $50 and I said "Wait a minute, there's something strange here." And he whipped out a badge and all these guys came in with cameras and this whole big thing.

'I didn't have any money to take it to court and I couldn't have fought the case. So I pleaded, which means: I give up, I don't have any money, I can't afford a lawyer but I did not say I'm guilty. The judge said, "We'll give him six months with all but ten days suspended and three years probation." So I went to San Bernadino jail for ten days. Tank C.

'No film was ever shot. Anyway the sound tape was no worse than side four of *Freak Out!*'

The use of 'conspiracy to' in the charge on which Zappa and Miss Belcher were arrested is important, as Zappa was later to explain to David Walley: 'The California penal code works it out this way: a crime is a crime. If it's a misdemeanor, it's a misdemeanor – unless you talk about doing a misdemeanor with somebody else. If you discuss it with somebody else, it's a conspiracy, which means it's not a misdemeanor, it's a felony.'

(The fact that as a result of the case Zappa became a convicted felon had one good result, as well as the theoretical inconvenience of not being able to associate with unmarried women of under 21: it meant that he couldn't be drafted.)

There is an interesting discrepancy between Zappa's account of the whole affair as told to the Salvos and as told to David Walley. He told the Salvos that he couldn't afford any lawyer; yet he apparently told Walley that he hired an extremely good one, who cost him a thousand dollars, but that this lawyer 'sort of sold me down the river to a 27-year-old DA who was really a prick. He just didn't like me, no matter what.'

It is a pity that I have not been able to trace Ms Belcher for her side of the story. It's odds on that she suffered worse social consequences as a result of the bust and the attendant publicity than Zappa, partly because Zappa wanted attention and publicity, kept the Ontario *Daily Report* cutting, and doubtless decided that in the long run there was no such thing as bad publicity – and partly simply because she was a woman. Imagine how the good citizens of a 7,000-population town in the early sixties regarded a 19-year-old who made a Dirty Tape with an Odd-Ball like Frank Vincent Zappa. Zappa's father loathed her from the moment the whole incident first came to his ashamed attention. He decided that she must have lured poor Frank into the whole nasty business.

3. Goodnight Ruben & The Jets:

The Metamorphosis Into The Mothers of Invention

Following Zappa's involvement with The Muthers, he at last made it across the gulf from Ontario to Los Angeles and played guitar in The Soul Giants – his first introduction to Ray Collins, Roy Estrada and Jimmy Carl Black*. The move to LA meant an inevitable increase in Zappa's propensity to weirdness, and thus a temporary kind of goodbye to whatever aspects remained of the fifties punk pop group mentality which later reappeared on the back cover of the *Ruben & The Jets* album:

'Ruben Sano was nineteen when he quit to work on his car. He had just saved up enough money to buy a 53 Nash and four gallons of gray primer. His girl friend said she would leave him forever if he didn't quit playing in the band and fix up his car so they could go to the drive-in and make out. There was already eleven other guys in the band so when he quit nobody missed him except for his car when they had to go to rehearsal or play for a battle of the bands at the American Legion Post in Chino. They are all still good friends even today. The other main guys in the band: NATCHO, LOUIE, PANA & CHUY still come over to Ruben's house on Tuesday or Wednesday to listen to his collection of Richie Valens records and also "Eddie My Love". Generally speaking, they save "Cherry Pie" and "Work With

* This band – its line-up completed by David Coronado on sax – promptly changed its name to Captain Glasspack and His Magic Mufflers (now *there's* a sign of the times). The sax player left. They re-named themselves The Mothers (with an O, at last) on Mother's Day, 1964.

Me Annie" till the late part of the evening so they can have something to hum on the way home or to Burger Lane. Some of them continue to hum and pop their fingers even the next day, working in the car wash. . . . All the guys in the band hope that you are sick and tired like they are of all this crazy far out music some of the bands of today are playing. They hope you are so sick and tired of it that you are ready for their real sharp style of music. They are good socially acceptable young men who only want to sing about their girl friends. They want everybody to start dancing close back together again like 1955 because they know that people need to love and also want to hold on to each other. Even holding hands is okay to them. They want you to hold hands and dance the bop and fall in love to their music. One of the main guys in the band was telling me a couple of weeks ago; when we were talking about how only about half the guys in the band ever show up at rehearsals most of the time . . . "IF THE PEOPLE WOULD JUST HEAR MY PLEA I WOULD GIVE EVERYTHING JUST TO SING THE SONGS THAT WAS TURNING ME ON IN HIGH SCHOOL." Ruben has 3 dogs. Benny, Baby & Martha.'

Zappa in Los Angeles, 1965, turned to pursuing that crazy far out music, get away from the guys who worked in the car wash, and become more socially acceptable to LA's freak scene by becoming even less socially acceptable than in the days of Cucamonga.

This LA freak scene was just opening out as Zappa arrived in it. Clubs, coffee-houses, folk-rock music, drugs, and a whole parade of soon-to-be-supergroup bands being showcased in small, dark, atmospheric, tacky clubs. Ciro's. The Trip. The larger Whiskey A Go Go. A mass of new noises, new costumes, new in-people, all smeared colourfully across the magnifying glass of an essentially small and inward-looking in-crowd.

Zappa did not find it easy to get in. While he was forming the first Mothers, a whole gang of now-name musicians passed quickly in and out of Frank's range, including Jim Fielder, Henry Vestine, Van Dyke Parks, Jim Guercio and that rarity, a female Mother – Alice Stuart (who later made solo LPs for the Arhoolie and Fantasy labels in the States and played with a band named Snake). From Alice Stuart's description of her involvement, given in an interview years later, it comes across very strongly that Zappa was, back then, hardly disentangled from the Ruben & The Jets-type persona: 'Frank was starting a group. He had nothing to his name but a very good guitar and a very beat-up old car – yet he knew exactly what he wanted to do. We got a group together that consisted of Jimmy Carl Black, Ray Collins, Roy Estrada, Frank and myself, playing great beaters like "Midnight Hour". I went beserk after about three months with Frank doing his Chicano rap, so I split . . .'

Even when The Mothers was more or less finalized as Elliott Ingber, Estrada, Collins, Jimmy Carl Black and Zappa, and they were beginning to be booked to play The Trip, Frank was not sufficiently 'in' to get free admission to the club on nights when he wasn't performing. The hip rock scene is as rigidly hierarchical as the English class system, and Frank Zappa might have been pretty outrageous in his adolescent outbacks, but for LA he was going to have to work on it. Which he did.

Zappa's own later descriptions of this LA freak scene have tended to omit any mention of the snobbery and self-aggrandizement that was at work in determining who was in and who out; he describes it all, rather, as if it were a totally open and open-minded new order, and stresses the infinite superiority of LA freaks over San Francisco hippies. 'There is a generic difference,' he told the Salvos. 'The origins of hippies as per "San Francisco flower power Haight Ashbury" is quite a different evolution from the LA "freak movement" of which I was a part. There was just a difference in the concept of it. I was never a hippie. I never bought the flower power ethic . . . Most of the people in the LA freak scene around 1965 were getting their costumes together, dancing a lot. The real freaks weren't using any drugs at all. Then there were the weekenders who used to come in and stick anything in their mouth that they could find. And you were hearing about people freaking out on acid all over the place. And it was quite colourful . . .

'Vito was the leader of the freak scene and Carl (Franzoni) was sort of like his lieutenant. Vito was about 60 years old and was married to a 20-year-old ex-cheerleader, and they used to have this place down by Cantor's delicatessen and he would train people in how to be a freak.'

That's a pretty dewy-eyed account from someone who prides himself on being the unmyopic rock star.

Perhaps there *was*, for a short while, a kind of artsy freak scene only tangentially involved with the LA rock biz, and relatively pure in heart. But the rock biz, like capitalism generally, has a talent for co-option, and within a few months most freaks were caught up in the never-ending hustle for in-ness with the new rock 'n' roll musicians who passed through the LA clubs and the older, more established rock people – like Phil Spector – who lived in big houses up on the hills and hung around Cantor's and The Trip and The Whiskey looking cool. In the end, every one of us on the sidelines of rock becomes a groupie of one sort or another, and the LA freak people were not immune.

Neither is Zappa very accurate about the drugs situation. It is wishful thinking when he says that the real freaks weren't using drugs at all. Zappa himself has always been very hostile to the whole drugs influx – frightened of taking drugs himself, despising dope's ability to reduce relatively sensible people to long periods of giggling inanity, and hating the more damaging effects of stronger stuff. However much he disliked the fact, the LA freak scene was oiled as much by drugs as by anything else. In many respects, the picture of that time and place that comes across from Pamela Zarubica is a lot more accurate than Zappa's.

Pamela Zarubica was a white teenager with long hair and short skirts who went to Pepperdine College, a liberal arts college on the corner of Vermont and 79th, verging on a black section of Los Angeles. She lived in Inglewood but came into LA to explore Sunset Strip one day and never looked back. Through a long and painful process she became accepted as part of the rock hangers-on scene. Half groupie, half I-just-wanna-be-friends-with-you. She says she started out in love with Phil Spector, and ended up in love with Frank Zappa.

She did indeed become Zappa's friend, and had a long day-by-day relationship with him that she says was all the better for being platonic. Subsequently she felt sad for Zappa, she said she felt he never became what he could have become; indeed that he hasn't done anything since the late sixties.

Zappa has 'placed' Pamela Zarubica, too: at a distance as well as back in time, as in this discourse on the identity of Suzy Creamcheese in the interview given to the Salvos: 'She was a girl named Jeannie Vassoir . . . the voice on the *Freak Out!* album. And the myth of Suzy Creamcheese, the letter on the album which I wrote myself – there never really was a Suzy Creamcheese. It was just a figment of my imagination until people started identifying with it heavily. It got to weird proportions in Europe. In 1967 when we did our first tour there people were asking if Suzy Creamcheese was along with us. So I procured the services of another girl named Pamela Zarubica who was hired to be the Suzy Creamcheese of the European tour. And so she maintained the reputation of being Suzy Creamcheese after 1967.'

Ms Zarubica resents that. She particularly resents the phrase 'procured the services of' and the suggestion that she was a complete outsider just hired for the job. In fact almost from the beginning of Zappa's time in LA she was around him – having long heart-to-hearts with him, cleaning his house for him, being a private audience for his new songs, introducing him to the girl who later became his second wife, Gail Sloatman, and being there at the *Freak Out!* recording sessions.

Her account of Zappa's life in LA as he metamorphosed into the leader of a nationally publicized, outrageous and record-contracted band captures very well both the freak scene – sordid, chaotic, compulsive – and Zappa's gradual admission into the upper echelons of that narcissistic hierarchy.

At The Trip, says Zarubica, there was in the early days 'a Frank Zappa who had to pay admission because he hadn't yet become famous. There was a decrepit Arthur Lee and associates, then managed by . . . Herbie Cohen, far from the first record. Why even James W. Guercio could be found there sometimes, playing rhythm guitar with the Mothers . . . Phil Spector . . . beady little eyes, no chin . . . He always wore white Levi's, a navy peacoat and a little cap. He was also the owner of a Cadillac limousine with a pumpkin in the back. The most devastating deviate I was ever to meet . . . Carl Franzoni – the freak of all time . . . dressed in black tights and caps from head to foot and electric hair . . . with an undescribable goatee that rivalled only his tongue in length.'

Meanwhile the personnel of The Mothers finalized itself as follows: Zappa on lead guitar and occasional vocals; Jimmy Carl Black on drums; Ray Collins on lead vocals and harmonica; Roy Estrada on bass and Elliott Ingber on lead and rhythm guitars.

Ingber joined The Mothers after getting out of the Army, staying in the band from toward the end of 1964 till late 1966. After he quit he formed a flower power band called The Fraternity Of Man with, amongst others, drummer Richard Hayward, both later to be included in Little Feat along with original Mother Roy Estrada.

Estrada joined The Mothers after ten years or so as a bass player in Los Angeles rhythm 'n' blues bands. He remained a Mother through the first four main line-ups, number four being disbanded by Zappa in October 1969. It was while in Mothers number four that Estrada worked with Lowell George, who was a Mother for about a month and a half and played on one track of the bits-and-pieces album *Weasels Ripped My Flesh*. When Mothers number four got disbanded, Estrada joined Lowell George's new band Little Feat. In 1970, however (if you're still with this), Estrada quit Little Feat to join the fourth line-up of Captain Beefheart & His Magic Band – which reunited him with that other original Mother Elliot Ingber, who was by then a Magic Band man himself, though re-christened Winged Eel Fingerling by the Captain. Estrada briefly rejoined The Mothers in the mid-seventies and can be heard on the *Zoot Allures* album of 1976. He also played on the 1976 tour of Japan.

Ray Collins, of course, had long been a friend of Zappa's, had done lots of recording with him at the Cucamonga studio, had co-written that Penguins' record 'Memories Of El Monte', and more. But he had also been a singer in various non-Zappa r'n'b bands around LA for at least a decade prior to joining The Mothers, including the details-lost-in-the-mist-of-time band Julian Herrera and The Tigers (or at least, so says the redoubtable Pete Frame of *Zigzag*, July '72). Ray Collins stuck around through almost to the end of the fourth batch of Mothers in 1969, disappearing after 1968's *Uncle Meat* album. He re-surfaced on the 1974 album *Apostrophe (')* as a guest artist, performing alongside what was by then the eighth

Mothers Of Invention. I asked Zappa what had happened to Ray Collins in the interim – where he'd disappeared to?:

'He went back to being a carpenter – which is what he'd been before he was a full pro musician in the first place.'

Jimmy Carl Black, the original drummer with the Mothers, again stuck with it until Zappa disbanded the fourth line-up, though from the second line-up onwards he added trumpet to his drumming duties, along with congas and then vocals. After the fourth Mothers were disbanded, he and Bunk Gardner – who joined the second Mothers and stayed through the third and fourth – together formed a band in 1970 called Geronimo Black. Jimmy Carl Black reappeared on one track of Zappa's *200 Motels* film soundtrack album, and again, years later, doing 'guest vocals' in 1980; these surfaced on the 1981 album *You Are What You Is*.

Meanwhile, back at The Trip, 1965 – Pam Zarubica first saw these first Mothers this way:

'They were rivalled by nothing we had seen to that date . . . this Indian drummer that was never without a bottle of beer in his hand . . . The lead singer looked like an ex-hell's angel that would bash your head if your even talked to him, [though] he turned out to be the most peaceful person I know . . . The bass player was a Mexican who never said anything and [on this occasion] the rhythm guitar player was Henry Vestine (later of Canned Heat) . . . They played one song that lasted about 20 minutes, and they also did "My Babe" . . . As soon as their set was finished Frank was standing in front of our table . . . "Good evening ladies, I'm really glad you're here. Would you like to come down to the dressing-room?" He looked terrifying . . .' Or, as Zappa himself said later in his fictitious Suzy Creamcheese letter on the first album cover: 'One guy wears beads and they all smell bad.'

Gradually, Ms Zarubica zoomed in on Zappa's personal life – just as, very shortly afterwards, producer Tom Wilson and manager Herb Cohen were to zoom in on Zappa's professional life.

Zappa's apartment at that time, Ms Zarubica recalls, was 'one tiny room with kitchen and bath for which he paid $75 a month. It was thick with dust, old posters about El Monte

Legion Stadium dances, music sheets, and records. He asked me if I would like a job cleaning it for him some time, and I agreed to when he could afford to pay me five dollars, a nominal fee. All the kids in the neighbourhood, which was predominantly Mexican, use to pass by the window and call him Beardo Weirdo . . .

'I don't believe he always thought so much on a glandular level in those days. We shared a lot of what we had. Lots of times I would have to give him fifty cents for gas to drive from his house to Laurel Canyon. He used to come to my house all the time, bringing me those Chinese cookies from Greenblatts – the ones with the big chocolate drop on top . . . I would fix instant coffee – thank God he drank it black because we couldn't afford milk . . .

'He was all the advice I could have needed . . . He tried to teach me that sex didn't have to be dirty and that drugs were pointless . . . we used to have fun together, there was time to talk about things . . . My God, the boy had talent, was obviously brilliant yet warm and close.'

Herb Cohen was impressed by other qualities in Zappa. Cohen was a hustler from New York, born there in 1933 and growing up there till he left at the age of 17. He survived through the Merchant Marines, the Army, union organizing and general entrepreneurship and in the 1950s, via a relationship with Odetta, got into the clubs side and management side of the folk business. By the time he first saw Zappa and The Mothers – which was, he says, when they played at a Hollywood party sometime in 1965 – he told Mick Watts:

'I was managing the Modern Folk Quartet and a girl called Judy Henske, both extremely popular in the USA during that folk boom period. I was also involved in a lot of production things. I had signed Love to Elektra. I also owned a bunch of coffee-houses in California. A place called The Unicorn that was the first folk music coffee house on the West Coast. We opened in '58 – and I was in management a few years before that, basically dealing with the folk area.'

Herb Cohen is an absorbing man. He is very interested indeed in money; his past has attached to him a hint of the hoodlum from somewhere down the long line of his hustling;

yet he was involved in, and committed to, the folk thing in America not just when it was profitable – when the boom came – but also earlier than that, when McCarthyism made it positively unwise.

Of the change to rock music, he says:

'I made the transition to pop music when the music made the transition. Those who survive – not only in a business sense – are those who survive in terms of developing with the culture.'

It didn't take him long to realize that Frank Zappa and The Mothers represented something interesting in 'the culture'.

'I saw Frank,' he told Mick Watts. 'It was basically r'n'b, but original Zappa r'n'b material, which was a little different. And then I spoke with Frank the next day and then we had a couple of meetings and he sat down and explained to me what he wanted to do in terms of music. I didn't quite understand at the time what he was talking about. Because no one had used those frames of reference – at *all* – so it was a little hard to explain.

'But it was obvious that *he* knew what he was talking about – and that was hard to find. Not only did he know what he was talking about but he had a good background and was an excellent musician.'

Cohen decided to move in on Zappa's career, and Zappa decided it wouldn't be a bad move. So the old friend of Frank's, Mark Cheka, who at that point had been landed with the role of struggling to get The Mothers bookings, was relieved of that role.

Herb Cohen's first act as The Heavy Manager wasn't impressive. The Mothers had appeared, as an example of how weird everything in Hollywood was, in a nasty little movie called *Mondo Hollywood*. They had not been paid for their appearance, and Herb Cohen tried to lean on the film's producer for some money. The result was that the Mothers' sequence was deleted from the film.

Frank, meanwhile, continued to live on the fringes of the freak scene – performing occasionally at The Trip and the Whiskey, getting liked and disliked fairly strongly by different sections of the audiences, and living in a pinched apartment sharing gooey cookies with Pamela Zarubica and a fast-changing series of her friends.

It must have been very difficult for Zappa. He wanted freak acceptance, he wanted rock success, yet he found he had to climb up through innumerable creeps, had to write with no privacy and had to resign himself to tolerating an increasing drug use, of which he disapproved intensely, among every one of his acquaintances.

Pam Zarubica remembers first confessing to him that she, too, Brutus, had succumbed to the dreaded pot. Phone conversation between Ms Z and Mr Z:

> 'Guess what I did.'
> 'What?'
> 'Promise you won't be mad?'
> 'What did you do?'
> 'I smoked some grass and got high, but it made me dizzy and I passed out.'
> 'Well, I guess it's okay that once, but you shouldn't do it anymore.'

She also remembers a cameo of a Hollywood party which again features Frank Zappa, 1965, as a kind of social isolate – having to be there, but hating it just the same:

'It was a party up the hill, at a house on top of Rosilla Place . . . when we walked inside I saw a dark figure lying on the floor. I could tell by the hair and coat that it was Frank . . . He asked me if I wanted to leave.'

By November of 1965, the other important person had come into the Zappa picture: Tom Wilson. That month, this black economics graduate from Harvard took up the post of East Coast director of A&R for MGM/Verve. A few months before that, he had been Bob Dylan's producer – producer, in fact, of the first album on which Dylan had 'gone electric', *Bringing It All Back Home* (which had included the innovative AM radio hit 'Subterranean Homesick Blues').

When Wilson got the MGM/Verve job on the *East* coast, the first thing he did was fly over to the *West* coast to check out what was happening, see if he could predict the next trend, and look out for some fresh talent he could discover out West and bring back East in due course. He also had some production work to do for MGM in LA – including the Animals' album *Animalism*, on which Zappa was to have a job as arranger.

So Wilson found Zappa, seeing The Mothers for the first time at the Whiskey at the end of November '65. He only watched and listened to them for a few minutes on that first occasion, and Zappa has subsequently described his impression of *Wilson's* first impression like this:

'He stayed just long enough to hear one song, which happened to be about the Watts riots, and he must have walked away saying, "Hey, a white rhythm'n'blues band. We've got the Righteous Brothers, now we're getting the Mothers Of Invention."'

In the same interview (with Jim Smith for the *NME*, January '74) Zappa went on to maintain that even when the band was signed up, MGM had no idea that The Mothers – The Mothers Of Invention, as MGM made them call themselves, because they thought just The Mothers sounded rude – were anything more than a straight r'n'b group:

'MGM gave us 2,500 dollars and we went into the studio. The first song we recorded was "Any Way The Wind Blows" and they must have thought, "Hey, that's kind of a nice tune". The second song was "Who Are The Brain Police?". And at that point the eyebrows started going up. The music kept getting weirder and weirder.'

There may have been a few record company execs hanging around who *didn't* know what they were in for at that point, but Tom Wilson certainly did. He saw them a number of times before he signed them, and the go-ahead for Frank to prepare material for an album didn't come until 1 March 1966. At least, that's the chronology as Pam Zarubica recalls it.

So from late November right through till the album's eventual release and the consequent national publicity, life meandered chaotically on with Frank attended in different ways by Tom Wilson, Herb Cohen and Pam. During these months, Zappa's status at the freak school started to rise; he even started pulling a few groupies; he got busier, and life with Pamela got complicated. For one thing, she went in for a marriage of convenience, to a guy named Bobby, in order to avoid, it seems, being dragged home by her father. Frank got a frantic phone call from her about how she had to run away and get wed, and had to rush around getting five dollars together to leave in the mailbox for her. She got married, came back to Frank, and rarely saw her husband. She lived a hectic life, but can, apparently, recall it in detail.

'The first of March [1966],' she wrote years later in a still-unpublished manuscript, 'set the wheels in motion. It seemed MGM became interested in The Mothers and it looked like Frank was at last going to have his chance . . . Frank and I started spending a lot of time together while he began working on the material for *Freak Out!*

'I remember the first time he showed me the words to "Who Are The Brain Police?":

'Where'd you get it?'

'I don't know – it just sort of walked in here last night.'

But Zappa didn't yet look like an imminent star.

'One time my husband paid me one of his rare visits,' Ms Zarubica wrote, 'and Frank had fallen asleep in the bedroom. I answered the front door and Bobby came in and started rapping. By this time Frank woke up and came walking out of the bedroom saying "Think I'll go out and get a little action". People always used to look strange when they saw Frank at the house until the first record . . . That was when Omar' – she called him Omar because he had this huge and filthy old Zhivago-type coat (referred to on the first album cover) – 'became Mr Zappa . . . Not that he was decidedly different back then, just untouched by the success that can surround a person . . . Frank was a friend, and that was the most important thing in my life at that time.'

The coming of success – he could scent it by now – was the most important thing in Zappa's life. He decided he had to live somewhere better, and arranged that as from 1 May, he would take over half the rent of a $200 a month apartment where Pam had been living as a guest of Bob Green, a 30-year-old doorman at one of the clubs. Pam says that Zappa was by this point getting accepted – was known to be about to make an album – and yet financially, he and The Mothers were just as badly off as when they had first played at The Trip on sufferance, and had been thrown out of the gig for saying 'Fuck' on stage. Frank and Pam were still rummaging through their pockets to try to come up with enough cash between them to buy a hotdog from Orange Julius, while Jimmy Carl Black was threatened with having his drums repossessed by the Laurentide Finance Co.

Then Herb Cohen managed to fix up a no-details-known 'tour' of Hawaii, and at the end of that, things were beginning to pick up. Pamela Zarubica recalls: 'By the time Frank returned from Hawaii, a few dollars had started to roll in, and also a few groupies. First there were the infamous Cherry Sisters, two entirely freaky chicks that made our lives more colourful for the time that they were there. And then . . . Sally Anne Mann, who was just beginning in her all-time career. I was glad to see Frank enjoying himself, even if at short intervals.

'Aside from the new girls on the horizon, Frank had been speaking about some of his business associates. The most frequent names were David Anderle, who was at that time some way connected with MGM in the talent department . . . Tom [Wilson] . . . an enormous negro who loved to do the boogaloo. Billy James, at that time working for Columbia, brought The Mothers to Columbia but Clive Davis decided that they had no commercial potential.'

Zappa seized gleefully on that phrase 'no commercial potential' for the cover of the first album – along with other similar misjudgements by people in the record industry, like the noted LA disc-jockey who told them: 'I'd like to clean you boys up a bit and mould you. I could make you as big as The Turtles.'

Zappa and The Mothers became, of course, bigger than the Turtles – not in record sales in the early days, but in significance and public affection and critical esteem. And the twain did eventually meet up. The Turtles started out as a sort of high school rock group, picked up on the folk-rock vogue of 1965 and had a massive hit with a rock single of Dylan's 'It Ain't Me Babe' inspired by The Byrds' record of 'Mr Tambourine Man'. The first Turtles album, also called *It Ain't Me Babe*, was issued in September of 1965, and their second, *You Baby,* in March '66 in the USA. They had a complicated time of it, another huge hit with a song called 'Happy Together' and split up seven managers and myriad law-suits later, in 1970. At which point two of The Turtles joined The Mothers – The Mothers number five, that is, which Zappa got together in May 1970. The ex-Turtles

Right: Frank Vincent Zappa, aged 18 months, in the garden of 15, Dexter Street, Edgewood, Maryland.
Below: The Zappas at home (well, they all look at home except Frank anyway); lower-middle-class suburban California, 1953. Left to right: Frank Zappa Senior and Junior, Carl, Bob, Candy and Mrs Zappa Senior.

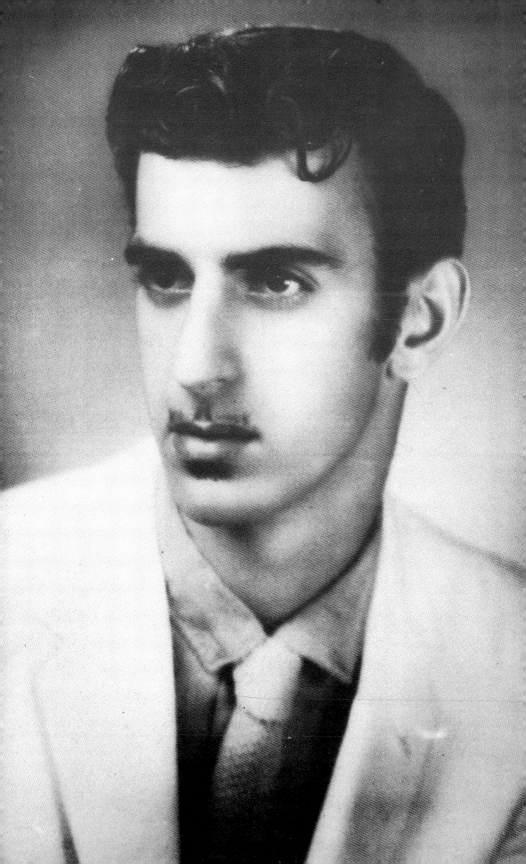

Left: Zappa as a 1950s adolescent – a shot used later for the early album Cruisin' With Ruben & The Jets.
Above: Mothers Of Invention Group 1. Left to right: Roy Estrada, Jimmy Carl Black, Billy Mundi, Elliott Ingber, Zappa and Ray Collins, plus a 'friend'.
Right: Mothers of Invention Group 2. Back row: Zappa and Don Preston; Middle row: Ray Collins, Roy Estrada and Billy Mundi; Front row: Bunk Gardner and Jimmy Carl Black.

Above left: Mothers Of Invention Group 4, with artwork maestro Cal Shenkel. Back row: Art Trip III, Jim Sherwood and Cal Shenkel. Middle row: Buzz and Bunk Gardner, Don Preston and Ian Underwood. Front row: Aynsley Dunbar, Ian Underwod and Frank Zappa.
Above: Mothers Of Invention Group 5. Back row: Mark Volman, George Duke, Howard Kaylan and Jeff Simmons. Front row: Aynsley Dunbar, Ian Underwood and Zappa.
Right: A 1967 promo-shot used in ads by MGM/Verve Records for the 'Absolutely Free' album.

Shame. . . . .
You didn't trust your mothers.

The Mothers of Invention go 'ABSOLUTELY FREE' on Verve records

*Above: Zappa pioneers
the Docklands redevelop-
ment scheme: London,
September 1967.
Left: An early concert
with The Mothers of
Invention, Birmingham,
1967.
Right: Zappa and the
mothers, London,
September 1967.*

*Left: 1968, outside the Royal Albert Hall
where The Mothers Of Invention concert
was to include ten members of the
London Philharmonic Orchestra. It was
Zappa's second visit to London.
Above: Conservative libertarian Zappa
discusses politics with the revolutionary
socialists of the London School of
Economics, 27 May, 1969 – the occasion
of his famous remark, 'Revolution is just
this year's Flower Power.'*

Above: Zappa at the Pauley Pavilion, L.A., taking part in 'Contempo 1970', a festival of contemporary music. Zappa and The Mothers Of Invention performed some orchestral music with the Los Angeles Philharmonic Orchestra conducted by Zubin Mehta.
Right: Frank with his wife Gail at the Oval, London 1970.

Above: Newts heading for the nightclub in the United Artists film 200 Motels, *1971. This scene was discussed in the Zappa v. Royal Albert Hall court-case in April 1975:*
'QC: Are you sure that 'newts' just means newts? That there is nothing at all suggestive about that?
FZ: Anyone who is disturbed by the idea of newts in a nightclub is potentially dangerous.'
Right: Ringo Starr and Zappa on the set of 200 Motels, *1971.*

*Above: On stage in Paris, December
1970: Zappa and jazz violinist Jean-Luc
Ponty.*
*Right: Frank Zappa in New York,
Hallowe'en 1974, with Louise Varèse,
widow of Zappa's hero the modernist
composer Edgard Varèse, originator of
the phrase so often quoted by Zappa,
'the present day composer refuses to
die!'.*

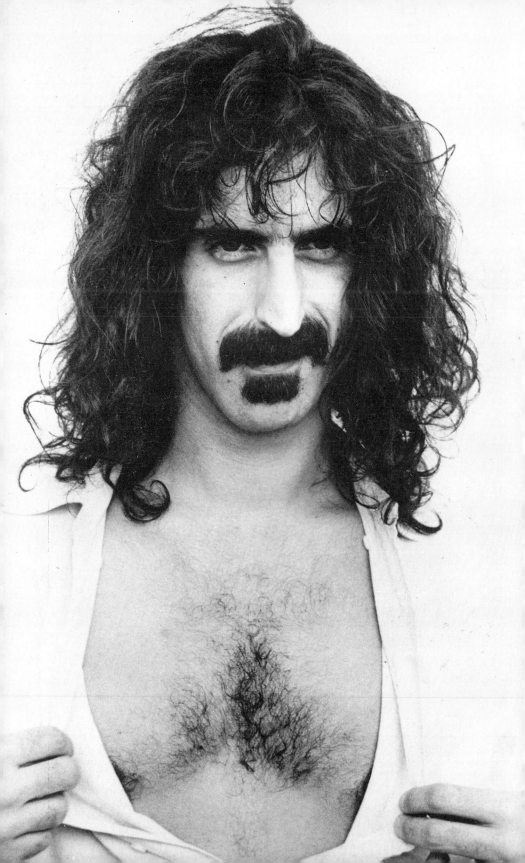

in the band were Howard Kaylan, vocalist, and Mark Volman, vocalist – known on the subsequent *Chunga's Revenge* album as 'The Phlorescent Leech & Eddie'. For the *200 Motels* film soundtrack, they and the other Mothers of the time were joined for a guest appearance by another ex-Turtle, bass-player/vocalist Jim Pons. In the early part of 1971, Jim Pons became a fully-fledged member of The Mothers number six. And on the first album made with this line-up – *The Mothers/Fillmore East, June 1971* – they all swooped into a performance of the old Turtles' hit 'Happy Together'.

Two other things happened in 1965 which affected what Zappa felt himself to be aiming at by the time he finally got to do the *Freak Out!* session. One was that Dylan had had a hit with his own version of 'Like A Rolling Stone', and the other was that Edgard Varèse had died that November. The latter event galvanised Frank into a stronger-than-ever determination that he was not going to just make records, but change the face of the music. If not the society as well. At a stroke. As for the Dylan hit, that wasn't folk-rock – it was a new kind of rock, and it seemed to Zappa that for a six-minute rock song with surrealistic/political lyrics to win AM radio airplay and reach the charts was a major breakthrough. He told me:

'I liked the lyrics to it because I felt that they were fairly direct, and I was encouraged by the fact that lyrics like that were on AM radio – and also by the fact that it was a *long* selection for AM radio. I said if this is on – if it's popular and if it's selling, then it's setting up an important trend. But, I didn't see it fulfilled in the way I'd hoped.' (Sometimes Zappa has instead credited the earlier Dylan single 'Subterranean Homesick Blues' with the same importance.) Zappa at the time felt that something was happening, that the time was fast coming when the old straight pop scene might be destroyed and replaced by socially, politically, musically *good* rock music. Music that would break boundaries both in what it said and in how it said it. He determined to contribute significantly to that destruction and renewal.

To this end, he started to prepare provocatively quotable remarks for when the music press would acknowledge his existence. He had not lost his flair for publicizing himself, and though it was much more arduous a task to make himself newsworthy in freaky Los Angeles than it had been in Cucamonga, he kept at it. As early as January 1966 he managed to crop up in an article on Vito which Jerry Hopkins published under the title 'Big Mike At Ben Frank's' in the *LA Free Press*.

Pamela Zarubica insists that she used to help Frank plan these juicy quotes that he was getting ready for the music press – and indeed that she was influential in the whole development of his calculated Image of Outrage. I think he could have managed it without her. Either way, what Frank saw in the spirit of Dylan's 'Like A Rolling Stone' was a theme he took to heart in these early planned quotes. 'Kill Ugly Radio!' was one such slogan he devised for himself, to magnify and dramatize his chosen stance as some kind of cultural leader. And when later in 1966 the press did come to talk to him after the record came out, he repeatedly avowed his intention to decimate Top Forty radio programming.

Nine years later, I asked him about these arresting declarations: 'Yes, well. There's no way that I could have done that. And I knew that right from the start. But nobody had ever *questioned* it before. So just to make the statement "Kill Ugly Radio!" was a step in the right direction. Just to alert somebody that there was something else to watch out for.

'Most of the stuff that I did between '65 and '69 was directed toward an audience that was accustomed to accepting everything that was handed to them. I mean *completely*. It was amazing: politically, musically, socially – everything. Somebody would just hand it to them and they wouldn't question it. It was my campaign in those days to do things that would shake people out of that complacency, or that ignorance and make them question things.'

It was also Zappa's campaign to shake people into noticing Zappa. Despite his talent and his flair, he never made as much headway as he thought he deserved, even among the close community of musician/freaks in LA, until MGM came up with some studio time and he was able to invite people down to *his* session, to have them being parasitic on *him,* to be seen to be about-to-be-a-star-and-perhaps-even-a-genius.

Finally, MGM did come up with that studio time. Tom

Wilson told Zappa he could 'do something big' – and Zappa didn't have to be told twice. He didn't just have The Mothers in for the session. He had literally hundreds of people in. Rock musicians. Friends. Freaks. Orchestral players. The lot. They all packed into the TTG Studios, with FZ right there in the middle, standing on a podium, *conducting* it.

'Frank gave it the full Toscanini and conducted their asses off,' Tom Wilson later told David Walley. As Ms Zarubica remembers it: 'Frank was in the studio all week with enormous amounts of studio musicians who were forced to play his arrangements. Frank would be pleased to death when one of them actually liked the music . . . The session, including about 300 of the freaks including Vito, Carl Franzoni (the model for Zappa's song 'Hungry Freaks Daddy') and numerous other names in the music business, took place on a Friday night.

'Frank came and picked me up. At that time he always drove a Chevvy stationwagon that we eventually had painted taxi-cab colour. We went to a restaurant called The Shack on Caluenga Boulevard; but we got there at closing time. David Anderle and his wife Cheryl were there, along with Danny Hutton . . . [later] of Three Dog Night fame. We drove in David's champagne pink . . . Cadillac to the Skillet, a greasy spoon just across from the CBS building.

'During dinner Frank and I wrote obscene words on the paper machine, and David talked about some guy named Al Kooper, that Bobby Dylan thought was a great piano player.

'They drove us to the TTG Studios on the corner of Sunset and Highland. It wasn't long before the studio began to fill up with people, all the freaks, and Mark Cheka – who always scared me . . . he looked like a werewolf – who was past manager of The Mothers. And there was Billy James [and his] wife named Judy . . . Tommy Flanders was there with his troll Maxine, sure ones to make any event . . . The Mothers played and the freaks danced and sang. Kim Fowley was up front doing his monologue, and Carl and Vito were screaming in the background.'

(Kim Fowley ought to be the subject of a book himself – an amazing hustler who has been involved with more hit records, in one capacity or another, than almost anyone alive;

his participation on the *Freak Out!* session was followed by live appearances with The Mothers at the Whiskey and the Cafe-A-Go-Go, and it is interesting that as he recalls it there was, around the same time that *Freak Out!* was recorded, 'a *Mothers Live At The Whiskey* album too, but it never came out.')

Eventually, as the night wore on, the freaks were cleared out of the studios so that the musicians could concentrate. Pamela Zarubica was not pleased to be included in those asked to leave: 'Herbie [Cohen] . . . told me I had to leave the studio part. Fat chance of that. Herbie is the kind of person that always has to be giving orders. Pushy.'

At the end of the session and for what was left of that night, Zappa slept fitfully on Ms Zarubica's couch and prepared, next day, for an evening gig at The Trip. Pam remembers that after the gig, she and Sally Anne Mann got very high in the living-room while Frank looked on affrontedly:

'He said we started talking really stupid once we got high.'

Shortly afterwards, The Mothers had some out-of-town gigs again – first at a barn-type place in Hayward, California, and then in San Francisco. When Frank left LA for the San Francisco weekend, he took Sally Anne Mann with him. Now that he could get groupies, he was going to. As Pam recalls it, 'she only lasted about one day. They disagreed about the dope.'

When Zappa got back from San Francisco, he moved house. Them were playing the Whiskey that week, and one of that band, Ray Elliott, was picked up by Pam and brought along to the house just in time to help Frank move in a grand piano. By the middle of the week, there was not only FZ, PZ, Ray Elliott and the grand piano, but all The Mothers, Carl Franzoni, John Judnich – installing a stereo system: money was beginning to be available – a friend of Frank's from San Francisco whose name was Stephanie and whose job was being a hooker, and for much of the time there were the Cherry Sisters too.

With that many people came that much more dope, and Zappa put up with it so long and then called a halt. From then on, people were not allowed to smoke dope in Frank's place. (From then on, a lot of people spent a lot of time sitting in their cars just outside the house.)

Ray Elliott stayed in the house a week, by the end of which, according to Pam, his drinking problem and the smell of his socks had become altogether too much. He was asked to quit the house but stayed on in town because Them were still featuring at the Whiskey. At the same time, Jim Morrison and The Doors were debuting in LA, and one night that May week both Morrisons – Jim and Van – jammed together on stage at the Whiskey. Characteristically, Frank Zappa missed them: he was too busy working.

One of the things that kept him busy was his rather intense round of business discussions with Herb Cohen, Tom Wilson, David Anderle and others. Pamela used to be on hand to serve up the coffee, and to listen afterwards to Frank outlining schemes and ideas.

A typical evening at the house back then had Jim Morrison, Frank, all The Mothers and Pamela. Morrison got stoned, Frank didn't, Pam cooked hamburgers, more people arrived: the Cherry Sisters, Tom Wilson, minor singer-songwriter Bobby Jameson, Phil Turetsky, the future second wife of Frank Zappa, Gail Sloatman – up at the house for the first time – all milling around the living-room and the hall while Frank stayed deep in business conversation with Herb Cohen. Pam remembers everyone finally leaving except her and Jim Morrison and Frank, and a current girlfriend of Frank's called Shelley, 'who was hot after him at that time'.

Pam was 'hot' for Jim Morrison, but Frank disapproved. He said he thought Morrison was 'kind of a spoilt high-school type'. He was further aggravated by almost everybody else's dope-smoking, snapping at Pam on one occasion after an evening she'd spent at the house with Morrison again:

'If you have to smoke your dope, would your please not leave the papers on the table so I have to find them!'

Zappa also had a hard time when he wanted to talk to Tom Wilson back then – because Wilson, being a big record company man, always stayed in a hotel when he was in LA, and the hotel he always stayed at was the Continental. Later they were to have many music people there, but in 1966 they had a more 'discriminating' policy and they did not like the look of Frank Zappa walking through their lobby.

Was it to get more attention from Tom Wilson that Zappa

engineereed a situation in which, Pam says, she had no choice but to make it with Wilson? Frank manoeuvered it, Pamela complied and wrote afterwards: '. . . next morning . . . cooked breakfast for Frank and Tom and listened to them discussing business'.

Such was the lot of the female of the species.

Frank ate his breakfast and then flew off to San Francisco again. He returned at the beginning of July with a session-player friend named Billy. This may or not have been Billy Mundi, who sometime in 1966 drummed in an obscure band called Lamp Of Childhood with ex-Mugwump James Hendricks and others, and who subsequently joined the line-up of The Mothers number two in late '66 and quit in December the following year after the 1967 European tour. As with other early Mothers, he re-appeared later: as a Mother at the UCLA gig of 15 May 1970, with the Los Angeles Philharmonic Orchestra.

Anyway, Frank came back with friend Billy, moved him into the house and gave him and Pamela to each other. She gave this account of the episode: 'Exactly two days when . . . he told me that I had given him a dose of the clap . . . I knew different . . . After he visited the doctor he decided that perhaps I hadn't been the culprit, but now he discovered he had the crabs too. Which, of course, I must have given him. It turned out Frank was the one in that case – he had been nurturing the little devils for some time without being aware of it, and he always used to sleep in my bed with his girlfriends. It took months to wipe out the epidemic, Frank wrote some delightful songs about it, and a lot of our dear friends got to share in something together. At first I was horrified, but it soon passed. I remember it as some sort of comedy.'

So this was the glamour of Hollywood. A cross-reference: interviewed by *Teen Set* magazine in '66, and asked what advice he would give young people wishing to become rock stars, Zappa replied: 'The first thing you do is get vaccinated.'

On 4 July Tom Wilson flew back into LA from New York, this time to produce the new Animals album, *Animalism*. Zappa was engaged to do some arranging work on it.

'Eric Burdon and the boys arrived about two hours late as

usual,' the ever-present Pamela recalls. 'Billy was playing harp on some of the sessions and Frank was doing some arrangements. They were in the studio for about five days . . . Chas Chandler' [their bass player, who at the end of that year spotted Jimi Hendrix in a Brooklyn Club, took him to England and made him a superstar] 'was constantly reading a book . . . and Barry asked Frank if he had any LSD. A fatal error.'

In the end, due to a mixture of the Animals' inefficiency and Zappa's hostility to what he saw as the cause of that, he only contributed arrangements to a couple of the tracks on the finished album.

Nonetheless, Eric Burdon and the others turned up at Frank's place just like everyone else. The ubiquitous Ms Zarubica provides a nice cameo of one such July evening:

'Zappa was playing oldies but goodies, and showing home movies, and Eric Burdon was there with Cynthia, waitress from the Trip – of course, black, as was his preference at that time – drinking beer and laughing and Chas Chandler was sitting reading . . . Dewey Martin was playing the piano and singing Ray Charles songs; Frank was about to vomit. All of Them showed up . . . Tom was running around somewhere . . . Billy James . . . Assholes hanging from the rafters! Frank Zappa was finally in vogue.'

The Animals' sessions ended with Eric Burdon singing Ray Charles songs till everyone got tired of it and left. Tom Wilson was off to catch a night-flight back to New York after going to a Samurai movie. Frank was still trying to sit him down and talk some more business with him, with Tom rushing off saying 'I'll call him from the hotel'. David Anderle and Pamela sat outside Frank's house in the car, getting high till the sky got dark. Frank sat inside the house, not getting high with one Lee Zeigon. They all sat around talking.

Zappa still has the tape he made that night of all of them sitting around talking, including the bit where Billy James burst into the room singing 'Who put the snatch on the Lindberg baby?'

Pam says that everything went into a decline from then on. Maybe part of that feeling was her sense that she was inevitably losing him. Things were surely looking good from where he stood. The album came out. Francis Vincent Zappa Jnr, ex-proprietor of Aleatory Music and of Studio Z, the black sheep of Ontario, the movie king of Cucamonga, had at last become Frank Zappa.*

* In fact Zappa's own book *The Real Frank Zappa Book*, Frank Zappa with Peter Occhiogrosso, Poseidon Press, New York, 1989 (Picador, London, 1989), reveals that late on in life Zappa discovered that he had *not* been christened Francis – he'd been Frank all along.

4. Freak Out/Overnite Sensation:

Into The International Rock Scene, Smelling Bad And Armed With Vegetables

The first album finally came out – and it looked good, a triumph of instant image-build packaging, for which Zappa can take more or less all the credit. Right there on the front cover was the filthy old Omar Sharif coat, along with the ugly faces of The Mothers in a lurid psychedelic specially treated photograph, while on the back cover another photo in similar style included a neater, more purposeful-looking Zappa with a cartoon bubble coming out of his mouth to introduce the catch-phrase 'Suzy Creamcheese, what's got into you?' Directly above this photograph was the letter Zappa dreamt up as coming from Suzy Creamcheese and with a facsimile signature to that effect. The letter read:

> 'These Mothers is crazy. You can tell by their clothes. One guy wears beads and they all smell bad. We were gonna get them for a dance after the basketball game but my best pal warned me you can never tell how many will show up . . . sometimes the guy in the fur coat doesn't show up and sometimes he does show up only he brings a big bunch of crazy people with him and they dance all over the place. None of the kids at my school like these Mothers . . . specially since my teacher told us what the words to their songs meant.
>
> Sincerely forever,
>
> (Suzy Creamcheese)
> Salt Lake City, Utah.'

In what is actually just a few short sentences, Zappa gets across everything he could want to – except for any information about the music. He focuses straight in on *weirdness* – appealing to a whole range of non-conformity-made-easy; clothes, school, naughty words, unpredictability. Zappa manages to press all those buttons, and in addition to create this fictitious character with the vaguely obscene name whom one is invited to envisage as being the personification of a classic fantasy-figure – The Broad-Minded Schoolgirl.

The inside cover of the double album serves as swift and definite a purpose, and between them they almost manage to tell the reader exactly what to think about The Mothers. Conquering indifference, the album cover demands a partisan approach, and people reacting favourably to the cover are thus halfway to fighting for Zappa's music, before they've even heard it. Anything they don't quite understand or identify with when they actually listen to the album becomes positively a point in the album's favour – a proof of its weirdness, and by association a proof of the perspicacity of the listener in having latched onto it in the first place. We can all be made to line up behind what we know we don't understand.

Zappa would justify this strategy on the grounds that everyone else had always told these kids how to think, feel, respond, behave, and in order for him to offer, through his music and socio-political comment, any real alternative, it was necessary for him to employ equally coercive tactics. And, granted how the business worked, the way to get wide attention for what he regarded as serious work was to concoct the most blatant possible images for The Mothers Of Invention and himself in order to make sure the media knew how to publicize their endeavours. There is no way that the media's idiocy could have been dismantled by one unknown Frank Zappa trying to get his musical talent across unaided by image-building or mind games or self-promotion or packaging skills.

So that's how it was done – though if anything about the *Freak Out!* cover betrayed any faltering on Zappa's part, it was that the inside cover squeezed in so much self-promotion, so much image-building and the like that it seemed as if he didn't quite believe he might ever have another opportunity to say it all. Just as that squeeze-it-all-in, every-last-bit-of-it is commonly a feature of a rock band's first album, so in Zappa's case it was also a feature of the packaging. There were eight different sets of information, plus photographs, on the inside cover alone.

Zappa knew he'd have trouble getting radio exposure for the album, and that he'd have to sell it entirely through press hype. He certainly got that. He got the underground press, the music press and the straight press – and what's more, he got them all to respond just right: that is, they all *took sides*.

It was summer 1966 and the world was still naive and excitable about all the trivial ingredients Zappa had pressed into the service of his image-building. Lorraine Alterman could begin her first article on them like this (*Free Press*, Friday 15 July): 'Mothers and fathers, you thought the Beatles were bad. You got up in arms about the Rolling Stones. Sonny and Cher made you cringe. Well, as the man said, you ain't seen nothing yet.'

In fact the press response to the *Freak Out!* album and to the discovery that there was this new group called The Mothers of Invention was so ideal, as far as Zappa was concerned, that the ads he persuaded MGM to let him design and place in papers like the *Los Angeles Free Press* were often more or less simply collages of the press-cuttings his launch had achieved.

In this way, he drew on the Lorraine Alterman article, and a number of others including a real gem by Bob Levinson of the *Herald Examiner* headed 'Mothers Invent Sounds Worse Than Music'. Meanwhile Ralph J. Gleason weighed in with an initial judgement on The Mothers that was both right and wrong about what they encompassed: 'Hollywood hippies full of contrivance, tricks and packaging; a kind of Sunset Boulevard version of The Fugs. They are really indoor Muscle Beach habitués whose idea of a hip lyric is to mention "LSD" or "pot" three times in eight bars.'

That was perhaps the only piece of initial press response that Zappa did not feel pleased by.

He didn't feel pleased by MGM's efforts on the album's behalf either, as he has said repeatedly in retrospect. Herb Cohen explained in more specific terms to Mick Watts what they felt was unsatisfactory about MGM's early handling of the group:

'We had a lot of very large battles with MGM. They would put out advertising copy that was totally disastrous – you know, sort of "hep": what they considered underground advertising. And they would say things that were so inane that it would turn off anybody. Anybody under fifty, let alone under twenty.

'One of the great things they did, I remember, not to us but to Pat Sky, was they put out an ad to the college press: Get High With Pat Sky. And I gotta tell you, y'know, I don't know how much money they lost by that ad, but there are enough colleges that did not book Pat Sky because of the connotation, the drug connotation, involved in that ad.

'And so that was the kind of thing we were dealing with; so we had constant fights with MGM over that kind of thing.'

Nevertheless, MGM did not, at least, sign up The Mothers and then just stick them in the drawer. And from the promotional effort MGM did make on *Freak Out!*, Zappa got the benefit of yet more reportage – this time in the trade papers. *Record World*, New York, July 9, 1966:

'MGM Goes Way Out For *Freak Out!*: New York – MGM is massing a major promotional campaign, already well under way, to boom their new *freak-out* music pactees, The Mothers Of Invention.

'Bud Hayden, exec in charge of album pushing, and Tom Wilson, who produced the two-records-for-the-price-of-one introductory package *Freak Out!* have already been to see distribs in a number of markets who have been extremely receptive, and the MGM men are readying a further push for this week's MGM meetings.'

What was Zappa doing while this publicity launch was under way? He returned from his short tour of Texas in July. He phoned Pamela Zarubica and asked her to meet him at the airport. She, in his absence, had befriended Gail Sloatman, who'd just been made a secretary in the same office Pam worked at. Pam asked Zappa if she could bring Gail with her to the airport to pick him up. No, said Frank. Pam brought Gail along anyway.

'Jim Black's wife, Loretta, was there . . . the first time I had met her and seen his kids. He had four at the time. Truly beautiful . . . We drove to the store and bought some steaks and went home to eat. Frank and Gail crashed in my bed . . .' Gail told Pam next day that no, she had not balled Frank Zappa yet.

On Tuesday 12 July, Zappa and The Mothers appeared on the afternoon TV show hosted by Robin Seymour in Los Angeles. Then Motorhead – James Euclid Sherwood – arrived. He was an old friend of Frank's from way back, the one who had attempted to play sax back in Sun Village in '64, and whose mother had given Frank a place to stay after his fall from parental grace in the Cucamonga Porn King Incident. He would shortly thereafter join The Mothers. In mid-July '66, however, he merely moved into the Zappa house.

(Jim Sherwood was a Mother Of Invention from the time of the second album, *Absolutely Free* – recorded in 1966 though not released till the end of May 1967 – through to the *Burnt Weeny Sandwich* and *Weasels Ripped My Flesh* albums issued at the end of the decade. He also appears, as himself, in the *200 Motels* movie of 1971, though not on the soundtrack album. He parted from the Mothers some time between 15 May 1970, when he took part in the UCLA concert by the Mothers and the LA Philharmonic Orchestra, and 18 June 1970, when he didn't take part in a Dutch TV 'documentary' gig. Yes, you guessed: he was to return later – as tenor sax player and 'guest vocalist' on Zappa's *You Are What You Is*, recorded in the summer and autumn of 1980 and released in September 1981.)

Bobby Jameson moved out. Gail was clearly on the way in. As Pam saw it: 'Gail was gradually becoming freakier and Frank was happy, in love even. Gail was really fun to be with.'

On Saturday 16 July, The Mothers again appeared on TV, this time on Dave Prince's Club 1270 show on WXYZ. After that, the band took a quick trip across the States to Washington DC, where they appeared on Scott Kerby's Dance Party on WDCA-TV and put in a surprise disruption visit to a Georgetown night club called the Roundtable. They came back to Hollywood, and Gail Sloatman moved in permanently to the house.

Being at the centre of a substantial amount of press, Zappa was by now able to control who came and went in the house far more authoritatively than at any time in the past. He decided he wanted a whole gang of people. Pamela objected when one of the people Zappa moved in was a groupie called Pepper, who soon had a whole stream of boyfriends drifting through: 'The Sagittarian was bringing his menagerie together under the same fucking roof I lived under.' Sometimes it was OK; most times, as far as she experienced it, it was a question of piles of clothes and dirty dishes. Zappa's non-comprehending response was: 'Why should you do the dishes? Look, everybody serves their purpose. Gail is here to fuck me; you work for me; let the others do the dishes.' The atmosphere in the house deteriorated, and Pamela and Gail fell out.

'The trouble began,' according to Pam's tight-lipped version of events, 'when Gail's roommate fucked him [Zappa] and Gail made the mistake of telling me. Relationships were completely severed. Gail had stopped taking her birth control pills and had failed to tell Frank. I felt compelled to make him aware of the situation. It was over this issue, plus the living condition, plus a few lies that were thrown in from an outside source which severed our association at that time.'

Pepper started trailing around after Arthur Lee; Pam and her friend Vicki started planning a big trip to Europe; Gail and Frank were turning into a couple; Pam, feeling squeezed out for a while, started going out with Johnny Rivers. But if things were crumbling from Pamela's point of view, she didn't blame Zappa: 'Throughout all . . . that went down during this time, Frank had been the person most directly responsible for keeping my head together. He knew how not to let me be wimpy, could make me happy even when I was really grouchy. I was happy with Frank alone in the sense that we had a home and a family.'

By mid-July 1966, however, nothing any longer seemed quite what it had been. Zappa had become famous and changed, tangibly and intangibly, as a result; Pamela Zarubica couldn't quite cope with Gail; she decided she was itching to go to Europe and get away from an increasingly claustrophobic LA freak scene. Zappa was too busy to get claustrophobia. He and The Mothers were booked to do a Friday and Saturday night at the Fillmore Auditorium on the same bill as Lenny Bruce. A French biography of Zappa suggests that he knew Bruce well and actually wrote some musical accompaniments for him. Certainly they came across each other: Bruce was tangentially involved in the same social round as a lot of the LA rock people, knew Pamela Zarubica and Herb Cohen and Phil Spector and John Judnich, and so on.

In fact there's an interesting parallel between Spector's 'involvement' with Bruce and Zappa's. Phil and Frank were both, of course, ambitious as rock producers, both had their own labels (Zappa setting up Bizarre-Straight in 1967 and 1968, Spector having had Phillies in the early sixties) and both were to put out posthumous Lenny Bruce albums. Yet neither came across Bruce until the last months of his life.

Danny Davis, Spector's special assistant, told Richard Williams (*Out Of His Head/The Sound Of Phil Spector*, Abacus Books, 1974): 'To tell you the truth, Phil was a bit of a Johnny-come-lately there; Phil only really got into him in his last days. He put out an album by Lenny on Phillies, with the famous cover picture of Lenny sitting on a john in a graveyard. It didn't sell much . . .

'Phil put Lenny into a theatre in Hollywood, on LaBrea, and took a tremendous beating. Lenny had asked him to sponsor a one-man show, but it was in Lenny's last days and it was tragic. It wasn't funny at all.'

That was in the spring of '66; Pamela Zarubica remembers it well: 'Lenny . . . live at a theatre on the corner of LaBrea and Hollywood Boulevard which no longer exists . . . I remember Gene [Clark, of the Byrds] being pissed off because he had to pay for all of us to get in because Lenny really did need the money . . . It was the first time that I had ever heard the truth live on stage.

'Lenny always wore this black trenchcoat, and just stood there for the world to see . . . The next night [Phil Spector] left for New York. He was gone a few days. Frank and I sat home working the Ouija board to find out things about him.'

It was around three months later that, in mid-July, Zappa found himself on the same bill as Bruce at the Fillmore Auditorium. Then, 27 July, The Mothers Of Invention appeared at the *LA Free Press* Great Underground Arts Masked Ball And Orgy, as it was billed, at the Danish Center in Los Angeles. Less than a week later, Lenny Bruce was dead, bowing out from a morphine OD on 3 August.

Spector and Zappa – to complete the parallel – were both in that awkward situation of not knowing quite what the seemly response was from people like themselves, who hadn't actually known Bruce all that well or for very long but who were aware of his place in their social scene and aware too of Bruce's contribution to their own cultural roadmaps.

'When Lenny killed himself,' Danny Davis recalled to Richard Williams, 'Phil [Spector] and I went up to see the body laid out in Lenny's home. It was one of the most unsavoury nights of my life. Going back, Phil took the wheel of the Cadillac and went down the canyon looking in the air and carrying on . . . I don't know whether it was genuine grief or just for show . . .'

Zappa's response was the opposite of Spector's melodramatics. Pam recalls: 'Frank asked me why I was crying. I guess he didn't think it did any good to cry. I told him that I cried because Lenny had wanted to talk to Frank and he never got the chance.' Frank went even quieter and more embarrassed after that.

The funeral was on the Friday. Zappa had no intention of going, and was getting ready to go to a business meeting when John Judnich called and asked Frank and Pamela to attend. Pamela was in a very fraught state and likely to be embarrassing again. Frank still didn't want to go and Herb Cohen disapproved of either of them going. As Pam recollects it: 'Herbie didn't think we should go, but then I was crying again about the whole scene, so Frank cancelled his appointment and we drove out to the valley.

'By the time we got there all there was was the dirt on top of the coffin, which was already in the ground. Frank, John, Herbie and I all just stood there for a while. Then Frank and I went back to the car.

'As we were walking up from the grave Phil arrived . . .'

Zappa and Pamela sat in the car in silence for a while; then Frank reached into the glove compartment and handed Pam a small rock that had 'I Love You' painted on the top of it.

'That rock,' says Pam, 'made a lot of people happy.'

Straight after the funeral, Zappa had to attend another cere-
monial occasion: Pamela's graduation from Pepperdine College.
Frank turned up with Gail and Carl Franzoni. Afterwards they
all went back to the house to find that Pepper was having a
party. Frank, stony-faced, stood in the middle of the room and
said: 'If anyone is holding they'd better take it outside.' A lot of
people did.

Frank left the party with Carl Franzoni, and after a while
Johnny Rivers phoned up to ask them over to *his* party. Zappa
arrived back and they decided they would go to Rivers', despite
the fact that they all despised his semi-cabaret style of success –
which included, like Phil Spector, having everything in his house
monogrammed. On the way over, they called in at Lenny
Bruce's house, but they didn't linger there long.

Eight days later, on Saturday 13 August, The Mothers Of
Invention did a concert at the Shrine Exposition Hall in Santa
Monica. It yielded some more ideal press for Zappa, including
this from Stan Bernstein in the *Times*: 'Necessity is the mother
of invention, but The Mothers Of Invention proved Saturday
night that a *Freak Out* will never be a necessity. P.T. Barnum
said there's a sucker born every minute and about 500 wan-
dered into the Shrine Exposition Hall.'

The Mothers replayed the Shrine on 17 September, this time
with the admission price up to $3. All the same, gigs were not
as easy to come by as might have been expected for a band so
sensationally publicized and with such a long-established local
following around LA. They played at places like the Lindy
Opera House, but they didn't play as often as they or Herb
Cohen would have liked. They also had other problems.

On 5 October they cancelled out of a gig – a concert at the
Earl Warren Showgrounds in Santa Monica – 'due,' as they
announced in ads, 'to a critical acoustic problem and virtually
no P.A. facilities'. Two weeks later these problems had been
solved and they did the concert on 29 October. Keeping up
Zappa's image-building promotion tactics, the ads this time
around were headed 'Legalize Therapeutic Abortion With The
Mothers'.

If there was, all the same, a disappointing lull in the pace of
their gigging, back at the house Zappa was having a quieter

time too: Pamela and Vicki had gone off to Europe. Pam's recollection of the scene at the time of her departure indicates that Zappa was looking forward to a quieter domestic environment: 'Frank and Gail were in love . . . Uncle Phil was getting ready to marry Veronica from the Ronettes, Tom Wilson was boogalooing in New York . . . Uncle Phil gave me 100 dollars, Vicki and I sold everything we owned and bought two one-way tickets for Europe . . .

'When it was time to go in the morning, Pepper borrowed Frank's car to drive me to the airport where I would meet Vicki. Frank and Gail were awake, but they never came outside the bedroom to say goodbye . . . Frank and I had said our goodbyes long before that, the first moment when we began to doubt each other's word. Everything good can't last forever.'

In November, Zappa and The Mothers began recording their second album, the brilliant *Absolutely Free*, back at Sunset Highland Studios in Hollywood. The producer was again Tom Wilson, but the line-up of The Mothers for the album was much expanded. The Mothers Of Invention number two comprised: Roy Estrada, Ray Collins (who might or might not, as Pete Frame suggests, have quit and re-joined the band five times around this period), Don Preston on keyboards (who might or might not, as Pete Frame also suggests, have been a computer programmer before Zappa picked him up, but had in any case been involved in music since the 1950s), Zappa, Jimmy Carl Black, Bunk Gardner on saxes, Billy Mundi on drums and – Motorhead. Motorhead was brought in partially as a roadie and partially as a Mother allowed now and then to play auxiliary saxophone. (He wasn't very good at it but he was an old friend and he was ideal Mothers material.) Herb Cohen's daughter was brought in to be the little girl who says 'What would you do, Daddy?' three times on one of the album's songs.

November was occupied in the studios, but outside on the street things were deteriorating. The police mounted a prolonged and vicious crack-down on 'freaks'. David Walley cites the culmination of this activity as being the turning of Pandora's Box into a fortified stronghold surrounded by a picket fence. 'Eventually this incident would find its way onto The Mothers' album *We're Only In It For The Money*'.

When the album was done, by the end of November, it was time to move The Mothers away from their home territory. Just like an English band which has to go to London eventually before it is deemed truly to have 'made it', so The Mothers and Frank Zappa were going to have to go and conquer New York. With the continuing gigs shortage around Los Angeles, this seemed the right time to try it.

The gigs they landed were at The Balloon Farm and the Garrick Theater in Greenwich Village. Walley says Zappa thought they'd only have to stick in New York for a few weeks and that they could come back to LA for Christmas. In fact what happened was that they did several weeks of gigs at The Balloon Farm and then moved to the Garrick Theater for a gruelling stint of 14 shows per week, for several months.

Perhaps ironically, New York received The Mothers a great deal more respectfully than Los Angeles had ever done. New York critics didn't try for a quick dismissal, even when they could spot the packaging element a mile off. Within days of opening at The Balloon Farm (a venue aimed at hippies that had only recently opened, at 23 St Mark's Place, where The Mothers' show ran until New Year's Eve) they were getting this kind of notice: 'The Balloon Farm became much more than a discotheque last weekend, and the resident combo became much more than a pop music ensemble. The occasion was the first New York appearance of The Mothers Of Invention, from deepest, freakiest L.A. They are the perfect embodiment of *all that is super-hyped* and stunningly creative about West Coast rock' (my emphasis).

The same notice continued: 'Forget that one Mother wears a sweat shirt which advertises "Folk you" in bright buttonese. These eight musicians made The Balloon Farm a concert hall. They seized the stage and belted the world's first rock'n'roll oratorio at an audience that was either too engrossed or too confused to do anything but sit and listen.

'The show was a single extended number, broken into movements by patter, and fused by repeated melody themes. Especially notable was the use, as leitmotif, of music from *Boris Gudonov*, sewn into the fabric of the song so that it became an integral part of the melody and not a sequin pasted on for class.

On another evening – I have it by word-of-ear – the group lit into Stravinsky, with a rocking beat.

'The Mothers use the secondary technique of pop parody with devastating effect. They goof brilliantly on the bass falsetto hang-up of '50s teen music, and on the cocktail-clinking orchestration of the '40s. Their lyrics leave the Fugs gnawing scraps.

'The whole show – call it a theater piece and tell Beck and Malina to tail it back from Europe to catch this one – is surrounded by a pulsating lightscape . . . It all flows freely, and for once, in sync with the music.

'The Mothers Of Invention haven't arrived yet, but they strive with out-stretched fingers toward something perceptively unique. Their first album, *Freak Out!*, is the most poorly produced package since the Hindenburg Zeppelin, but don't let this baby-dribble fool you. The Mothers Of Invention are to be watched, and leader Frank Zappa deserves your attention, and your three bucks.'

I think he liked it.

Zappa didn't get home for Christmas, but on Xmas Day he got a special present, from the *New York Times*. They published a long piece by Robert Shelton, the man who had first given Bob Dylan a review – and a rave review at that: a review which Dylan had carried around in his pocket gleefully afterwards and which contributed to Dylan landing a contract with Columbia Records, which had never before picked up on any of the Greenwich Village folk artists.

Shelton's piece on Zappa and The Mothers was headed 'Son Of Suzy Creamcheese', and ran alongside a stylishly repulsive photograph of the FZ face captioned 'Frank Zappa, Dada of The Mothers Of Invention: "No one knows for sure who plays the drums".'

'The most original new group to simmer out of the steaming rock'n'roll underground in the last hour and one-half is an audacious crew from the West Coast called The Mothers Of Invention . . .

'The Mothers Of Invention are primarily musical satirists. Beyond that, they are perhaps the first pop group to successfully amalgamate rock'n'roll with the serious music of Stravinsky and others. . . Compared to The Mothers Of Invention, such earlier big-beat groups as The Beatles and The Rolling Stones emerge as Boy Scouts with electric guitars.'

(Balloon Farm, incidentally, got itself a little extra mystique back then from the rumour that Bob Dylan had christened it; certainly Albert Grossman, then his manager, had a hand in managing the place, and his assistant, Charley Rothschild, wasn't denying that rumour. Who knows?)

Zappa and The Mothers finished at the Balloon Farm at the end of their New Year's Eve Show, and went up to Montreal for two weeks of gigging there. They didn't like the cold. They flew back from Montreal to LA – to warmth and home and their good old local following.

It was mid-January. Jimmy Carl Black and his wife had their four kids to support, and were sorely in need of a lot more money than the Mothers' thin gigs-schedule was bringing in.

Worse, the *Absolutely Free* album, which was supposed to be released towards the end of January (1967), was going to be delayed. One of the troubles was that Zappa wanted the album package to include the 'libretto' of the songs, plus notes and so on. MGM didn't like the naughty words – they didn't so much mind selling them on the vinyl but they didn't want to see them there in cold print inside the sleeve. When, later that year, Frank Zappa Music, BMI, put out the libretto separately, under the title *Absolutely Free, The Mothers Of Invention American Pageant*, he included this introductory comment:

'. . . the reason for the delay? Partly because of this libretto. The original plan was to include within the album the words in this brochure. The record company attempted to censor the words and a long discussion ensued. We were forced to manufacture this product.'

The delay was for four months, the album finally emerging in May. Herbie Cohen gives another reason for the delay:

'We had a fight with MGM's legal department. On the back of the album cover was a small little notice on a billboard in amongst a whole back cover montage, and it said, in very little letters, "War Means Work For All". And we had a battle with MGM because their legal department felt that there was something wrong in saying that. And they refused to let it out. So in the end it came down to where they agreed to let us use it if we printed it in half tones! So it came out grey instead of black.'

The Mothers struggled on in LA, waiting for the album to emerge, waiting for the gigs to pick up, right through until just before Easter. Jimmy Carl Black had the worst time of it, because money was most pressing a question for him; Zappa at least had Gail and was in love; and Motorhead had picked up this strange new girlfriend who hung around the house for a while.

Zappa recalled this relationship when he talked to me eight years later, in April 1975: 'Yeah he picked her up in New York some place and brought her to the house. And I remember her sitting in the corner, playing guitar, singing to herself; she had a beret on the first time I saw her and she was leaning over the guitar and she was drooling. That was before she had a record contract.' Her name was Joni Mitchell.

(I said I found it hard to imagine the 1967 Frank Zappa and Joni Mitchell being compatible kinds of people. Zappa said: 'No. That's not true. Actually I have a great respect for what she does. The thing I like is her melisma – I think that it's well executed and I think that it's interesting, from a musical standpoint. I'm not too enthralled by the lyrics, because I'm not into love songs.')

In February, though, the LA gloom was lifted for some of the band: Frank was doing a solo album project, which was to end up being called *Lumpy Gravy*. The term 'solo album' is a little misleading – it didn't mean Zappa performed alone: on the contrary, he used a 51–piece orchestra; what it did mean was that it wasn't to be a Mothers Of Invention album – although when it came to it, the 'chorus' ended up including Roy Estrada, Motorhead, and Jimmy Carl Black.

They all went back to New York and recorded it in February, at Apostolic Studios, which was then new, unconventional and the first anywhere, reputedly, to have installed a 12-track machine. These were the first Zappa sessions produced by FZ himself.

At Easter weekend, having been back to LA in the interim, The Mothers were again in New York, this time opening at the Garrick Theater in Greenwich Village. They remained there until the summer.

This long-running gig, which ran variously under the name 'Pigs And Repugnant' and 'Absolutely Free (An Entertainment)' went down well; the critical notices were good – consistently respectful, in fact – and since May saw the release of the *Absolutely Free* album, at last, it worked out very nicely as a promotional exercise.

Not that Frank left the press to do the promotional job he wanted by themselves. He found time not only for interviews, but for contributing directly to the underground papers himself. On 3 May, for instance, the *East Village Other* ran a cross between an ad and a letter that they'd received from FZ the week before. It ran: 'I was born in Baltimore December 21, 1940. Then lived in the country for a while . . . Then moved back into the city. That didn't last very long. Then moved back to the country and my father made poison gas for the government during World War II. That was a lot of fun. Then moved to California. Lived in California for a while. Kept living in California over and over and over again until I started making poison gas for our government. Hopefully Capitol Records will help me distribute this poison gas. DID YOU GET ANY ON YOU?'

Despite the steady Garrick gig (which wasn't actually much of a money-maker: the Mothers ended up with about 200 dollars a month each, reportedly) Frank still wasn't happy. He didn't much like his audiences; he didn't all that much like New York.

'There wasn't,' he says, 'too much going on in the Village that interested me. The people who came to see us at the Garrick mostly had short hair, they came from middle class white Jewish environments, mostly suburban. They came to see our show because we were something weird that was on that street and we were a sort of specialized recreational facility.

'The reason they were shocked in those days was that they hadn't seen or heard anything that came close to what we were doing. Now, after so many groups imitating various aspects of what we did, they've seen it from other sources. Take, for instance, Alice Cooper. Basically what they're doing is a cosmeticized version of the same thing we were doing in 1967.'

You see the force of Zappa's adjective 'cosmeticized' if you contrast the formularized Alice Cooper show with a Mothers night at the Garrick such as the one when some US Marines came along. What happened that night was spontaneous and showed that despite Zappa's desire to have a pretty tight hold on the reins of whatever his band was doing, he could at times hold them loosely enough to let real unpredictability gallop in. The incident is described in David Walley's book like this: 'One afternoon, when the Mothers were rehearsing, three Marines in full dress uniform walked in. About a week before, a Marine had been killed in the Village and there were rumours that every Marine within striking distance was aching for revenge. Frank was a little miffed at the time but politely invited them to sit down. After the rehearsal the Marines said, "We just bought your album and we really like it." Frank said, "Well I'm glad you do. Hey listen, how would you guys like to work with us tonight?" Frank asked them what they could sing; they said they knew 'Everybody Must Get Stoned'; (i.e. Dylan's 'Rainy Day Women Nos. 12 & 35') and 'House Of The Rising Sun'. They adjourned across the street, and while Frank and the band ate, the Marines rehearsed their big number. When they came back after dinner, fully rehearsed, Frank said, "Now look, there's one little thing I want you to do. When I give you the signal, I want all three of you guys to lunge for the microphone and start screaming 'Kill!'"

'During the preformance the Mothers played some dissonant jazz reminiscent of Archie Shepp. The Marines lunged forward on cue screaming "Kill!" The audience couldn't believe it. When it was all over they clapped. Then Frank said, "Thank you." Ray Collins said "Thank you". When it got to the Marines, the first one said, "Eat the apple, fuck the Corps." The audience couldn't believe it. The second one said the same. More confusion. The third Marine capped it all with: "Hey, you know I feel the same way as my other buddies: Eat the apple, fuck the Corps, some of us love our Mothers more!" And that was only the first show.

'Frank was astonished. "Don't you guys realize you could get court-martialed for that?" The Marines said they didn't care – the Corps could only court-martial them once anyway. Frank had another brainstorm – he told Gail to run home and get a doll they'd been given as a present. Frank opened the second show with: "Hey ladies an' gennelmen, the guys are, uh, going to sing "Everybody Must Get Stoned". The Marines did as they were bid, then Frank said, "Now we're gonna have basic training. Uh, ladies an' gennelmen, this is a gook baby; and the Marines are going to mutilate it before your very eyes. Kill it!" Frank tossed out the big, plastic doll. The Marines ripped it apart, pulled its arms off, tore it to shreds. After they were done, with music and lights low, Frank held up the mangled doll by its hair and pointed out to the audience all the damaged parts as if it were alive. Frank reminisces: "There was one guy in the front row, a Negro cat just back from Vietnam, was crying. It was awful; and I ended the show there."'

In the summer, the Garrick show finally closed. The Mothers did not return to LA but stayed on in New York for the large number of recording projects that Frank Zappa was getting under way.

Ian Underwood had seen the Garrick show, been impressed and so, one day in August, he located Zappa in the Apostolic Studios in New York City, introduced himself and asked if he could work with FZ. FZ listened while Underwood explained that he was a bachelor of music from Yale with a Masters Degree in composition from Berkeley, a pianist whose speciality was Mozart and an accomplished alto saxophone player – not to mention that he could also play organ, clarinet and flute, and he could read music. When he'd said all this, Zappa just leaned over and gestured expansively at the studio full of instruments and said 'Okay, whip it out.' Underwood demonstrated a few bits and pieces and was hired. Zappa knew a good thing when he heard it; Underwood's ability to read music was a very big advantage so far as Frank was concerned; multi-instrumental ability was pretty handy too; Ian Underwood was an asset, no doubt about it.

So the second Mothers became the third Mothers, simply by the addition of Ian Underwood. And from then (August '67) until October, the Mothers set to work recording the album *We're Only In It For The Money*, oddment tracks such as 'Oh No' and 'Dwarf Nebula Processional March & Dwarf Nebula' which were eventually to surface on the excellent album

Weasels Ripped My Flesh in 1970, an attempt at a hit single (it flopped, of course) called 'Big Leg Emma', and more besides.

At the same time, Zappa was also patching up a solo album project. This had come about because Zappa had signed a contract with Capitol Records as an arranger and producer, despite his contractual obligations to MGM. Eventually this solo album – *Lumpy Gravy* – was purchased from Capitol by MGM, after much legal dispute. Which is why it didn't get released till long after the *We're Only In It For The Money* album, despite being recorded before it. (It eventually came out in May '68.)

It used a studio orchestra, which Zappa called the Abnuceals Emuukha Electric Symphony Orchestra and consisted of 51 musicians. In addition, there was a chorus, comprised partly of Mothers and partly not: Louie The Turkey (Kuneo), Cucamonga friend Ronnie Williams, Roy Estrada, Spider, Motorhead, J.K. Adams Tony, Gilly, Monica, All-Night John Killgore, John Nie, Cal Shenkel (the guy who designed Zappa's album covers), Larry Fanoga and Jimmy Carl Black.

The album consisted simply of 'Lumpy Gravy Part 1' and 'Lumpy Gravy Part 2'. But getting it ready for release was hardly a simple process.

The original tapes recorded way back in February 1967 were with Capitol and Zappa first had to get them back. When they came, they were in, apparently, an unbelievable mess. Very nearly unsalvageable. As David Walley reported it, 'It was discovered that Capitol engineers had their own way of editing and splicing: one day's guitar track would be next day's percussion track. They had no standardized way of making splices; there were even holes in the tape. The job of putting them all together was monstrous, especially for a qualified engineer. It was tougher for someone who didn't like Frank's music.'

That person was Gary Kellgren at Mayfair Studios, where the re-assemblage was booked to take place. He moved later to the Record Plant in LA, which was the studio complex Zappa used most often in the mid-1970s and by coincidence his apartment in Hollywood was just across the road from Zappa's manager Herb Cohen's. He also engineered some of the *We're Only In It For The Money* album and it is his voice, on that album, which whispers 'I know he's sitting there in the control room listening to everything I say but I sincerely don't care. . . . hello, Frank Zappa!'

The recording of *We're Only In It For The Money* was interrupted by the first European tour lined up for Frank and The Mothers in September. New York had established Zappa as a national star – written up, critically praised and by now sought after as a producer by other rock artists, even if actual sales of albums were not what they might have been and never got radio airplay. The Europe tour was to put Zappa on the music map as an *inter*national star.

The timing of the tour, though, was awkward. Not only did it interrupt the recording sessions at Mayfair Studios (New York), but it also meant that Zappa would be away from home while Gail was having their first baby.

Pamela Zarubica sailed back into the picture on that cue. She'd been down and out in Europe all through 1967, and finally returned to California, full of misgivings as to whether any of her old friends would remember her, disappointed to find that Zappa and family were 3,000 miles away on the East Coast, and, though she didn't mind this part, pregnant.

She'd been back a couple of weeks when the phone rang: 'and a recognizable voice, none other than that fave of all raves, the girl who had used my friendship and taken my man, getting ready to blossom his child, Miss Gail Sloatman . . . to bring me hellos and tidings that the master would like to talk to me.

'"You don't sound happy to hear from me."

'"I just woke up."

'"Do you want to talk to Frank?"

'"No, I really want to talk to the President but if he's the best you can do put the fucker on the phone."

'Zappa came on:

'"Why hello you old devil, I see what you've been up to. Did you get the *Newsweek* article on McCartney? And how does it feel to still be five years ahead of your time?"

'He told me he was getting ready to go to Europe with the Mothers and would I come to New York to stay with Gail while she had the baby. Whoop-dedoo! My ticket to ride right away from [some people in LA], well maybe I'll come.'

91

Then Zappa told her he was 'looking for some freaky chick to take to Europe as Suzy Creamcheese'. Pamela was nonplussed. 'How could you take anyone but me?' she screamed down the phone, adding: 'I mean, after all, I'm the only one with the brains for the job and besides I'm the only chick that knows what you really wanna do!'

Three days later, she got her ticket sent by FZ.

'Vicki's advice was remember this is only round two and there are going to be a few more before this thing is finished, but we had to quell all our plans to kick Gail in the stomach.'

She flew to New York and found both Zappa and Gail somewhat changed.

'I don't remember whether I first noticed Frank's scrawny body or the size of Gail's stomach and the fact that most of her dress appeared to be missing.' Frank Zappa *was* thinner than he'd been a year earlier. Then he'd lived on poor food, nervous energy and ambition; now he was living on poor food, nervous energy, frustration and overwork. He was too busy – and after he came back from Europe he was to become even busier – and it wasn't good for his health.

Pam describes Frank's Charles Street apartment in New York like this: 'what I thought would be some kind of a hovel . . . turned out to be a real Frank Zappa delight with a garden in the back that actually boasted a scrawny cherry tree . . . they had just moved in and Gail hadn't fixed up the bedroom yet . . . to my horror I then realized that I would be sleeping on the couch at the foot of their bed . . . in the front room . . . oh sweet privacy goodbye. Not even a closet to turn on in, and besides, I wasn't the only other inhabitant, there was also Calvin Shenkel, talented boy artist from Philadelphia, whose main fetish was his unusual love for eggs and his ability to pile dirty dishes in the kitchen until there wasn't any room for people.'

(Poor Pamela – gone a year and what does she come back to? The same old dirty dishes.)

They sat around playing the sections of *We're Only In It For The Money* that had been finished or nearly finished, caught up on all the local poop and then Zappa and Gail slept. Later, Herb Cohen and his wife Suzanne dropped in. Cohen was not pleased to note the return of Ms Zarubica. He was even less pleased to learn that she was going to Europe with Frank to live out the role of Suzy Creamcheese.

That Sunday morning they all drove around the city 'shopping for antiques' and ended up at a party at The Tin Angel, where they bumped into Billy Mundi. Then they went on to Herb Cohen's apartment where they dutifully listened to a Tim Buckley album that Cohen rated pretty highly.

Things were, in these few pre-Europe days in New York, a little tense in terms of the personal relationships involved.

'Suzy Cohen,' as Pamela reports it, 'hated Gail and Gail hated Suzy and I wasn't quite sure who I hated at the time. And then Gail was . . . looking cute and pudgy, and . . . I just felt sorry for her under the circumstances and wanted to protect her.'

Not enough, however, to stay behind. And it was that evening that it was finalized that Pam would be Suzy Creamcheese, would consciously talk with 'that Sarah Lawrence dropout accent' and would get some suitable clothes for the job.

It was in this period, pre-Europe, that Pamela got used by Frank for bits of the *We're Only In It For The Money* album. They went over to the studio in the rain one evening. Jimmy Carl Black was there: 'As usual he [was] upset about money which he just never seems to have enough of – but you have to take into consideration that he [had] a wife and five kids – well, Geronimo [the fifth] was on the way at the time – so of course he was distraught. He wanted me to go up on the roof and get high, but I was afraid Frank might find out.'

Ian Underwood was there too – 'then billed as the straight member of the group . . . really short hair' – Tom Wilson was there (no longer the producer of The Mothers' album: *Money* had Zappa as producer proper, with Wilson billed as 'executive producer', which means he was the theoretical boss but didn't actually do anything) and engineer Gary Kellgren, who wasn't ever a Mother but who was credited as an 'auxiliary' on the album when it came out (as was, among others, Eric Clapton).

Kellgren was the guy who invented the Suzy Creamcheese line of dialogue on the album that ran 'I'm not going to do any more publicity balling for you' – a line that Zappa discovered was missing the word 'balling' when MGM/Verve released the record.

While they were at the studio, Gail phoned up and told Pam to phone Vicki right away because Pam's father 'had the FBI after me and they were about to arrest Vicki for withholding information on my whereabouts.'

So Pam phoned Vicki, Zappa tape-recorded part of the conversation – and yes, that's what the prelude to 'Bow Tie Daddy' is an extract from.

After that was done, Tom Wilson went home early, Zappa got Pam to do some singing on the song that bore the same title as the previous album, *Absolutely Free*, and Pamela was pretty happy all round: 'I had no idea any of this would be used, it was just joking around with Frank in the studio just like back at TTG in the days of *Freak Out!*, and the Zappa wheels were in motion again, and I was there and part of it once more, which was all that I had ever wanted or believed in up to that time of my life.'

Pam took the subway home with Ian Underwood after that, and decided he was 'a secret lunatic'.

Just days before the European tour began, Frank Vincent Zappa and Adelaide Gail Sloatman were married at New York City Hall. Instead of giving Gail a ring, Frank bought a 10–cent ball-point pen bearing the motto 'A Present From Mayor Lindsay' from a machine on the desk and pinned it to the front of her dress during the ceremony. The proceedings were rushed through just before closing-time by an official who punched in their card on a time-clock sitting on top of what Zappa described as 'a cheesoid Formica *replica-pulpit*'. Two days later, Moon Unit was born.

The day before the band and entourage left for England and the Royal Albert Hall concert, there was a briefing meeting: 'The boys were briefed on the dope situation, how they definitely weren't supposed to be holding anything in Europe, and also that Frank was the spokesman for the group, and no-one else was supposed to be doing interviews.'

When they flew into London Airport, they were met by reporters. (So far so good.)

'Miss Creamcheese, are you and Mr Zappa married or something?'

Frank answered:

'We're or something.'

There were two public relations people on hand for the band – Michael Goldstein and Danny Halperin, but within a few days Goldstein was removed as unsuitable. Halperin proved to be OK.

They went from the airport to the Royal Garden Hotel, checked in, and then went straight to Piccadilly Circus (one country's Mr Cool is just another country's tourist) where Zappa bought a bowler hat, a Homburg and some other sort of hat as well.

That night they went to the Marquee and saw The Crazy World Of Arthur Brown. Zappa was delighted to find that in England he was regarded as a bona fide rock star. His presence was noticed as soon as he arrived; a buzz went round. He turned to Ms Zarubica and whispered, 'Frank Zappa is here!'

Pete Townshend came up and introduced himself and later on they went, inevitably, to the Speakeasy. There they bumped into Noel Redding and Zappa got picked up by Jimi Hendrix's girlfriend Cathy Etchingham.

Within 24 hours, Zappa had succeeded in becoming the centre of attention among the London equivalent of his old LA freak in-crowd. Pam remembers that the rest of The Mothers stayed in their cheaper, separate hotel while Zappa and herself found their room at the Royal Garden filled up with Beautiful People: 'a room full of groupies, a photographer who was supposed to be making a movie of this whole thing but whose main interest is taking shots up girls' dresses . . . Hendrix was there too.' Later that evening it was back to the Speakeasy where Frank stood at the bar drinking scotch with Jeff Beck.*

The rest of that week was spent, as Pamela reports it, 'with The Mothers rehearsing in a bingo parlor outside of London,

* John Peel met Zappa there that night, too. Peel was, at the time, the most highly regarded of the 'pirate station' DJs. Radio One was about to start up, supposedly in place of the pirate stations, and Peel didn't yet know whether he'd be acceptable to the BBC. But in the meantime he had a regular column in the British underground fortnightly *International Times*, and in the edition dated 31 August-13 September, which came out in mid-September, he reported on the meeting with Zappa – making it clear just how often Zappa was on the self-promotional *qui vive*: 'I exchanged persecution manias with Frank Zappa at the Speakeasy (trendy!) during the showcasing of an extraordinary film he'd made and to the accompaniment of the Mothers' latest recorded idyll called *We're Only In It For The Money*.' Marc Bolan and Steve Peregrine Took were the performers that night, but Zappa, rather than just dropping in, brought with him the extant tapes of *Money* and a film.

and making the movie which consisted of shots of the group in front of Buckingham Palace, and driving all over town in search of London Bridge.'

Zappa also spent a fair amount of time working on publicity for himself. He was photographed with Claudia Cardinale: and the dividends were coming in also from a brief pre-tour visit to London he had made in the third week of August. Then he had posed for *Melody Maker*'s photographer in a flowery dress and with his hair in bunches. That truly did look revolting. Revolting enough to make a good front cover photo, which is exactly how the *MM* used it. *MM* reported: 'Have you seen your Mother, baby? Or is it Suzy Creamcheese? In fact it's boss Mother Frank Zappa, leader of America's own Mothers Of Invention who'll be in England sending up the nation in their own freaky way in September. Negotiations are going ahead for ten members of the London Philharmonic Orchestra to join The Mothers in their only British concert which will take place at London's Royal Albert Hall on 23 September.

'Mother Frank . . . told the *MM*: "We'll come into London about a week before the concert to do some promotion and things. I may bring six, eight or 15 Mothers with me – it depends how many cats want to come to England."

'Promoter Tony Secunda . . . told the *MM*: "The group are flying in 1000lbs of equipment. They're bringing in a new member of the group, Motorhead, and they may bring the original Suzy Creamcheese, and another chick called Mother Meat.'

'The group's second album *Absolutely Free* is to be issued by MGM in October.'

Why MGM in Britain had to release the album five months later than in the USA I don't know – nor why they didn't have the sense to tie in its release with the Albert Hall concert.

The *Melody Maker* front page caused quite a reaction – Zappa was in his element, of course: it was just like a re-run of all that obliging press he created when *Freak Out!* was first released in America. *Melody Maker*'s readership was as obliging as any of the LA pressmen had been. The Letters Page of the *MM* for the issue of 9 September (two weeks prior to the Albert Hall concert) included all this:

'Frank Zappa must be joking! Lipstick and a handbag were

all that were missing, or do *MM* readers fancy him as he is? What a pathetic state the pop scene has got to when you have to look like him to sell records. Flower power is only another craze started up by the Yanks and as usual our gullible fans and groups have fallen for it. Thank God for Tom Jones. – E.H. Tull, Abingdon, Berks.'

'Own up Zappa! You are part of that rotten, commercial and crumbling society in America. The US younger generation was formed by that society and you are as much a product as any crew-cutted college kid. Thank heaven English society is not yet American enough to need "flower power". – Paul St Claire Johnson, London NW10. LP WINNER.'

'I have never in my whole life seen such a horrid, vile and disgusting picture as Frank Zappa's . . . Effeminate flower power has turned our pop scene into a charade of rubbish. – Mike Wade, Berners Street, London.'

That same week – just to provide some chronological bearings – MGM was advertising a new Connie Francis record, as if it were still 1960; Cilla Black was talking about Brian Epstein's very recent death; the *MM*'s reviewer was predicting another hit for The Turtles with their third single; and Harold Wilson had just got his injunction against The Move, stopping them from issuing a 'controversial' postcard.

Zappa's ability to save things and use them later is one of the ways in which his self-publicizing ability and his musical composition methods fit together. Music examples of this neo-recycling process are innumerable (for example, a track on *One Size Fits All* includes a differently orchestrated repeat of the theme from 'Peaches En Regalia' from the album five years previous, *Hot Rats*) but a fine example of the same process at work in the Zappa image-building is this: that one of those photographs of Zappa outside Buckingham Palace on his first London trip of September 1967 – a photo that featured the bowler hat – was destined to be saved up by FZ and to emerge on the inside cover of the *Hot Rats* album in 1970.

Apart from rehearsing The Mothers, and the ten members of the London Philharmonic who were to perform with the band at the Albert Hall concert, Zappa was also concerned to meet a band called Tomorrow, who, with Keith West, were involved at the time with a much-publicized but ill-fated teenage opera.

Tomorrow were, in Pamela Zarubica's phrase, 'tight friends with Hendrix', so a meeting was easily arranged and Zappa and Pam and Jimi Hendrix and Jeff Beck went round to a flat Tomorrow lived in at the time.

'All I remember for sure,' Pam reports, 'is that . . . everyone was getting high, except us, and for once Frank didn't seem to mind. When we left the place Frank's first comment was, "I never met such a nice little group of junkies before."'

She adds: 'Not that they were [junkies], it's just that Frank is so totally unfamiliar with the drugs scene that I doubt that he could tell the difference between hash and heroin.'

Zappa got depressed about the rehearsals; he also, according to Ms Zarubica, got the clap again, from a groupie encounter. Then they visited Middle Earth at the Roundhouse, where Zappa's entrance caused a flattering stir again; but within minutes they decided to leave – too many hippies for Frank's liking – and as they were leaving, an incident occurred which really turned FZ off:

'On the way out some typical type came running up to Frank seemingly to shake his hand. Instead, he placed a small object in it which I immediately recognized to be hash. I should have grabbed it and marched out the door, but all these people were standing around waiting to see what Frank would do. He just looked down at the hash and said, "What is it?" . . . The numbers of freaks stood around in complete shock, trying to figure out how the freak of them all could not only not want the hash but not even know what it was.'

They retreated to the plush calm of the Royal Garden Hotel and the infinitely preferable treat of peach melbas.

The next day was the day of the Albert Hall concert. It was an unqualified success, endorsing Europe's consensus view that Zappa was a true international star.

It was written up graphically in both the music press and the 'straight' press. *Melody Maker* reported:

"There is the mighty and majestic Royal Albert Hall Pipe Organ," said Zappa cooly as the audience fell about. Mother Don leapt from the stage and like a mischievous ape clambered up the balconies high above and settled into the organ nook. He fumbled about in the darkness – got a rousing ovation when he found the light switch and settled in.

'Zappa hitched his breeches and drawled into the mike: "Play something for the kids, Don, play something that'll really sock it to 'em – like 'Louie Louie'!" And lo – true to his word – the giant Royal Albert Hall pipe organ burst forth with life and "Louie Louie". Ad lib laughter for the rest of the concert.

'During the evening very few people can have avoided Zappa's verbal or musical axe. The Supremes and "Baby Love" was the subject of much hilarity, so too the Doors, so too most of American society, flower power, and finally the Mothers quite happily send up both themselves and their audience.

'As a colleague said, "They're about two years too early."'

Suzy Creamcheese was on stage that night too (as she was on the other European dates that followed the London gig) – and she sang, without knowing the words, a version of Donovan's 'Mellow Yellow'.

She remembers that evening more or less as the highlight of her life: 'Albert Hall. The second half of my dream come true. As I said then and could still say, if I die after this show is over my life will be complete . . .'

Her on-stage recollections are understandably hazy: 'By the time we walked on stage everything was very mellow, almost unconscious, truly tremendous. All the acid heads were there in droves, plus the basically curious, the sceptical, the few supporters, and reporters. They didn't expect the musicianship, the humour, the realism, or the people from the London Philharmonic accompanying The Mothers and making fart-like noises through their sheets of music.

'We were surrounded by people on all sides, even behind us, smiling faces and glazed eyes. . . . Frank telling me to sing "Mellow Yellow"; I didn't know the words; so what? Mothers Ray and Roy with their arms around each other singing "Baby Love", a few familiar faces in the crowd. So you still want to be a pop star? Want to stand there in front of those thousands of people psychologically jerking yourself off because they're there to see you, oh and how great you are because the people in the front row clap and everyone else follows them, because no matter what kind of shit you shove down their throats your PR man has assured your fame, and read about yourself in the centre spread of tomorrow's papers . . . Why the Hollies were there, and even Jimi Hendrix . . . and they liked it, yes folks, Frank Zappa was vogue, in, accepted and sought after in the world-renowed London pop scene.'

Quite what occasioned that sudden swerve from starry myopia to cynicism Ms Zarubica doesn't make clear.

After the concert, Zappa went back to the Royal Garden Hotel and ensconsed himself in his room with a secretary called Pauline, who had worked for him when he'd made that brief London promo trip the month before the gig. Pamela went back to the hotel too, and tried to capture both Jeff Beck and 'a darling little munchkin by the name of Ronnie Wood'.

By five in the morning they all had hangovers, except for Frank, who never drank that much. They had to get packed to go to Amsterdam, the next concert city on the tour.

They arrived there and Zappa was delighted to find that the Dutch kids took him pretty seriously, not least as a politico. The concert hall was next door to the hotel. After the concert Frank and Ray Collins had a fight, and Ray, on the point of quitting as so often throughout his Motherhood, was threatening to fly back home to the States right then and there. Tom Wilson hovered diplomatically in the background.

Next day, The Mothers and the entourage flew on to Copenhagen while Tom Wilson and Zappa darted out for a brief visit to Italy, to investigate the possibility of being commissioned to write the music for Vadim's movie, *Barbarella*. Frank flew back to Copenhagen for the third European concert.

After that concert, just as they were about to leave for Gothenburg, news came through from New York that Gail had given birth.

On the plane to Gothenburg, Zappa felt ill. He staggered through the press conference held at the hotel on their arrival, and then went to rehearse at the concert hall. Tom Wilson flew back in from Italy.

What happened next Pamela remembers graphically:

'Then [after the concert, which was the first that wasn't full] Frank came down with the chills and fever, shaking and sweating – and of course Herbie told me I was getting too upset.

100

Getting too upset? You motherfuckers would stand around and let him die if you thought you could get a marginal profit off of selling tickets to his wake. We spent the night after the show with Frank going from freezing and shaking while I would jump in bed with him and hold him tight as I could . . . to five minutes later when he burns up with fever and I jump back into my own bed so he can cool off. . . . six (a.m.) rolls around and we're supposed to be on the plane to Stockholm. I called Herbie's room and told him Frank couldn't make the plane trip. "Just get him on the plane, I've called ahead for a doctor to meet him at the Stockholm hotel" . . .

'We get on the plane, so cramped, economy class . . . Frank's passing out on my shoulder . . . I wake up wondering why we aren't in Stockholm yet, turns out the airport was fogged in and we're on our way to Finland to wait. Frank's laid out on a bench at the airport trying to get down a cup of tea and keep it down, three more hours and finally dead on our feet to Sweden. Twenty miles to the hotel, I get stuck for the cab fare, a usual Cohen trick, get Frank situated in the hotel, and of course no doctor. Frank hates doctors, doesn't want to even call one, and I'm left arguing with the clerk at the desk to get one. He arrives, diagnoses appendicitis, tells Frank he should go to the hospital, can't possibly do the show, gives him some pills, takes two autographed pictures for the kids, $20, and leaves me to argue with Herbie, who of course takes it all as a joke. . . . Of course Frank kept getting worse and insisted on doing the show anyway.'

The show was particularly important to Zappa because it was being televised*. Nonetheless, during the second part of the concert, he had to give up and leave the stage. The audience didn't like it. The Mothers did what they could without him, which wasn't much but included their inimitable 'Baby Love'.

Back at the hotel the doctor Herb Cohen had called in the first place arrived, and he diagnosed food poisoning, gave Zappa some more pills and ordered him to rest.

Zappa got really ill that night, fell out of bed and cut his mouth open. There was supposed to be a Copenhagen show next day, and The Mothers duly took their 7 a.m. flight.

* This may have been only a radio broadcast. A re-broadcast in the 1970s led to the bootleg 'Tis the Season To Be Jelly.

Mid-morning, a car was ordered to take Frank and Pamela to the airport for a flight that would still get them to Copenhagen in time for the concert. Pam was enraged at the idea of making Frank do the show, but he told her to be quiet, took the car, took the plane, arrived just in time for the show and lay down in a special dressing room.

The band's equipment failed to arrive, so they borrowed John Mayall's. It wasn't such a bad concert either, considering the circumstances.

Next morning they took a bus and a ferry boat to Lund for the only college gig of the tour. That night, Pam and Frank stayed up late talking. Pam was struck by how frightened Zappa was of the weight he had successfully placed on his own shoulders: 'He was scared and he wasn't ready to leave the times we had in Europe.' Her reaction was unsympathetic: 'Why how dare you be scared you motherfucker, I mean I gave up a lot just to come and go with you because you were the one who knew how democracy could work and who could be President, and now when the responsibility is yours and all these people look to you for the answers you realize it isn't an easy job, that you're tired and that it could cost you more than your security.'

In other words, they both in their different ways came face to face with the fact that there at the end of the Europe tour, Frank Zappa had indeed become an international rock star.

Next day they flew back to New York City.

5. What Will This Evening Bring Me This Morning?/Would You Go All The Way?

More Of The Frank Zappa & The Mothers Chronology And A Court Case

Zappa was back in New York, after the European debut tour, in October 1967.

That month The Mothers started recording what ended up as the *Uncle Meat* double album. In November, while still recording, Zappa had a walk-on part, as a sort of critic-cum-cowhand, in the first feature film made around the Monkees, who were then bidding for a public acceptance less teenybop than before. The film, intended to help change the Monkees' image, was by Bob Rafelson and was to end up being called *Head*. It's easy to see why, granted the intentions of the film, Zappa was invited to appear in it. Zappa's comment was less clear: 'They're trying,' he said, 'to make a heavy out of me.' And while he was at it, he also took part in one of he Monkees' TV shows. The film *Head* didn't emerge until over a year later. Similarly, the album The Mothers were concurrently working on, *Uncle Meat*, didn't get completed till February '68; the mixing down was still going on in April '68 and it didn't get released till April '69. One of the main banes of Zappa's creative life has been this inevitable delaying process from recording to release. (All the same, he has capitalized on it: it all ends up as part of his continuity-scheme, his re-arrangement of time methodology.)

In December 1967, not content with simply getting on with *Uncle Meat*, Frank was still fiddling about with *Lumpy Gravy*. Billy Mundi quit The Mothers, and was replaced by Arthur D. Tripp III, who had spent two years with the Cincinnati Symphony Orchestra and was consequently just the sort of new Mother Zappa wanted – as the similarly qualified Ian Underwood had been when he'd turned up in the summer. Billy Mundi went from The Mothers to Elektra, which in January 1968 was putting together a studio band. Pete Frame says they backed various Elektra people like David Ackles; they were 'unbelievably good live but never captured on record' and they made three albums. They were called Rhinoceros and their albums were called *Rhinoceros* (issued late '68), *Satin Chickens* (late '69) and *Better Times Are Coming* (1970) – though Billy Mundi had left them and moved on again by the time of that third one. He was one of the two drummers on the Bob Dylan album *New Morning*, issued 1970.

Once Arthur Tripp was in the band (December 1967) Zappa decided to get on with yet another album project, while the others were still in progress. The new one was to be *Cruisin With Ruben & The Jets*, which David Walley aptly calls 'an experiment in cliché collage'.

While all this was going on, The Mothers were still trying to get suitable gigs, and that same month landed a set of weekend concerts at New York Town Hall.

The anonymous reviewer for the *East Village Other*, writing up one of these gigs in the 5 January 1968 edition confirmed Zappa's view of what kind of people made up Mothers' audiences back then. He wrote: 'Just sweet little carefully groomed boys and girls – teen America out for its big night out in New York, out on daddy's money for a Friday night in Manhattan to see The Mothers Of Invention, and, later, sitting around stoned in daddy's car out along Queens Highway and into Long Island; yeah man, The Mothers . . . they're really boss. With tickets running from three dollars fifty to six dollars, there just didn't seem to be many people I knew there and I began to feel a little guilty in my six dollars reviewer's seat surrounded by all that well scrubbed, miniskirted teenage flesh.'

Then he describes the first half of the concert. In the intermission, he turns his attention back to the audience:

'Turning around again, I'm met by hundreds of absolutely stoney eyes; it's unbelievable – the kids aren't grooving on it.

'It was different after the intermission. Zappa came out and put the audience down, very cool . . . very subtle. All right boys and girls, a little teenage medley for all of you. The band went through some of its older material; a parody of The Supremes and other recent rock favourites, lots of falsetto singing and rolling eyes, and the audience ate it up. Between numbers, Zappa talking to the kids. Like Stokely, he almost doesn't deserve his audience and vice versa, but the audience wants to be condescended to . . . wants to be put down. And Zappa knows it, is learning what he can get away with and still make it . . .'

Recalling this sort of circumstance years later, Zappa told me – as he has similarly told many other interviewers down the years: 'Most of the stuff that I did between '65 and '68 or '69 was directed toward an audience that was accustomed to accepting everything that was handed to 'em. I mean *completely!* . . . Somebody would just hand it to them and they wouldn't question it. It was my campaign in those days to do things that would shake them out of that complacency, or that ignorance, and make them question things.'

He went on: 'We used to do things at concerts like I would say "OK, everybody, start clapping your hands!" – which was what a lot of groups did and people did it and it was like real robot-moron behaviour – and then when they were doing it I'd say "Do you know how stupid you are to be doing this?" and they would look around.

'In fact one time in Berkeley – which was supposed to be a *very* avant-garde, hip scene – I had 3,000 people in the Berkeley Community Theater standing up and doing calisthenics. Doing jumping jacks! And these were the intellectual student types. So while they were doing it I was saying "Do you *realize* what you're doing?" And you know what? They got mad at me, because I spoiled their fun. They enjoyed doing it. And I found that nine out of ten times when you alert an audience to a phenomenon like that, and imply that they're being duped or they're the victim of their own ignorance, they take it out on *me*. They think that I'm doing them some harm. They should thank me for reminding them that they've been chumped off.'

In contrast, he told me: 'Today our audiences are surprisingly young, younger than they used to be. But they have heard a much wider range of rock music than the people who were listening to our first few albums. They have an appreciation of things that are a lot more subtle. That audience wasn't around when we did our first three albums. It's a different world, and it seems that the audiences have grown up, musically speaking.'

January 1968 saw the release of the third album, *We're Only In It For The Money* (from which Ray Collins was missing); the same month Zappa was voted 'Pop Musician Of The Year' in the 5th Annual International Critics Poll in *Jazz and Pop* magazine. A far cry from the initial critical response to the first Mothers' album.

In February, The Mothers collected another accolade of sorts. They were invited to play at the National Academy Of Recording Arts And Sciences dinner in New York. Why they'd been invited was a source of both puzzlement and some hostility among many of the Academicians. The Mothers' performance – described as being of 'psychedelic music' – did nothing either to enlighten these people or to lessen their hostility. Zappa deliberately aimed at insulting them with an introductory speech: 'All year long you people manufactured this crap, and one night a year you've got to listen to it! . . . your whole affair is nothing more than a lot of pompous hokum, and we're going to approach you on your own level.'

The same month, the recording of *Uncle Meat* was completed, though the task of mixing it all remained. Typically, Zappa condescendingly hinted at how complex a job this was in his sleeve notes for the album: 'Things that sound like a full orchestra were carefully assembled, track by track, through a procedure known as over-dubbing.' You would think no-one except Zappa had either the slightest clue as to how recordings were made nor the least experience of other albums that were in any way the product of comparable studio care. Yet by the time those sleeve notes emerged with the album – in April 1969 – the Beatles' album *Sergeant Pepper* was past history and a recognized classic; and unlike Frank Zappa, who had, for *Uncle Meat*, a 12-track machine at his disposal, George Martin and the Beatles had achieved their impressive production with a simple four-track board. Moreover, the influence of that album's production had already been widely felt in other people's work by the time *Uncle Meat* came out.

One reason for his snappishness at the time was that his battles with his record company seemed endless. Not only did they censor things without telling him, not only was there the additional mess created by having to transfer the *Lumpy Gravy* tapes from Capitol to MGM because MGM disputed the validity of his Capitol contract, but on top of that MGM hadn't actually given the band any royalties at all. Eight years later, Frank was still pursuing these royalties and suing MGM in a Los Angeles court.

By the end of 1967 he had decided that something had to be done, and in March 1968 something was. He and Herb Cohen set up Bizarre, his own record company.

Cohen explained what happened like this:* 'The contract with MGM expired in '68, and so we decided that what we would do was, instead of signing directly with a company, we would build an independent structure, where we would have total control of everything, and all that a major company would do for us would be to distribute the product.

'We talked to a few labels and finally decided that Warner/Reprise would be the most flexible situation for us. Warners at that time had just acquired Reprise – before that it had been Sinatra's label – and I had known Mo Austin for a number of years, I had done business with Warners before and they were very nice people. They understood to a great degree what we wanted to do and they were willing to give us the facilities – and the money, ah ha! – with which to do it. And they were willing to accept the idea that Frank was capable of designing his own projects.

'As to the money, I don't think I better say how much was

* Cohen was talking in 1975. His *theme* is how fast things change: no better illustration of how right he was than the way his account of then is *now* riddled with irony.

involved, first of all because it doesn't mean anything any more and secondly because it wasn't that kind of Big Deal deal. What we signed was a contract for them to distribute Bizarre Records; it wasn't like them signing the artist to their label. But they gave us enough money for us to start a project for our label.

'The distribution deal was for four years. And it meant, of course, that Frank got to own his own masters – no-one can put out crummy compilation albums of his material against his wishes any more like MGM did – and still do.

'Will we keep on with Warners? Well you must ask me in a year from now and I'll be better able to tell you. Because nothing is permanent in this business. Since the time we signed with Warners, they've bought Elektra Records, they've bought Atlantic Records, and they've turned from what they were to an entirely different structure. They've strengthened the company enormously. On the other hand, Kinney just turned around and bought Warner Brothers. And Kinney also just turned around and sold all their mortuaries.'

(Ah, Americans! – terrified by the idea of a Welfare State; but happy with a situation in which it must have been perfectly possible, till they sold the mortuaries, to grow up watching Kinney-owned cartoons, go to work in Kinney offices, park in Kinney car parks, spend their money on Kinney albums, TV shows and movies, and go to the grave in Kinney's green and pleasant land plots.)

'Yeah,' Cohen says, 'because Kinney is a multi-billion dollar company. And they own a *lot* of things. Anyhow, I think they just unloaded thirty million dollars worth of undertaking parlors!

'So as to our long-term association with part of that empire, how can I say? They might turn around six months from now – a month from now – and sell part of it to someone with totally different ideas on how to run it. So I can only deal with the situation today.

'But I will say we've not been dissatisfied with Warner Brothers so far. There have been a certain amount of natural fuck-ups – that I would expect dealing with anybody – but it's a question of attitude. If someone screws up because they tried to do something great and it didn't work out, that's one thing. As opposed,' he adds darkly, with another company specifically in mind, 'to when someone screws up out of total ignorance and stubbornness.'

The same month that Bizarre started – which was designed as a way not just of handling Mothers albums and other Zappa project albums, but also of handling other artists (of which more later) – Zappa and The Mothers Of Invention number four appeared at a music festival in Miami on the same bill as the Jimi Hendrix Experience.

In April, *Rolling Stone* previewed the *Lumpy Gravy* album, referring to it, as usual conveniently for Zappa, as 'the suppressed record'; mentioned the existence of an *Uncle Meat* film – 'The Mothers' movie – a surrealistic documentary on the group'; and reported that Zappa was still editing the album of the same name. '210 tracks have been made,' they said, 'and are being mixed on a twelve-track machine.'

Lumpy Gravy was released, finally, in May, and simultaneously Zappa was declared, with humorous intent, Best-Dressed Rock Musician by *Hit Parader* magazine. They also gave him a Best Mustache Award and presented him with the Nostalgic Greaser Plaque.

By this time, the *Uncle Meat* mixing was finished, and so was the *Ruben & The Jets* album, which had been recorded in January, also at Apostolic Studios. (When it emerged, Zappa had, as ever, appended some inside sleeve-notes, and this time they ran as follows: 'This is an album of greasy love songs and cretin simplicity. We made it because we really like this kind of music. [Just a bunch of old men with rock 'n' roll clothes on sitting around the studio, mumbling about the good old days].' Then he added prophetically: 'Ten years from now you'll be sitting around some place with your friends doing the same thing, if there's anything left to sit on.')

David Walley notes in his book that Arthur D. Tripp never did believe that Zappa's profession of love for this old fifties r'n'b material was genuine. Perhaps there is a touch of the he-doth-protest-too-much about it all – and yet certainly when I talked to him his affection for, and knowledge of, that whole oeuvre was impressive. So too was the detail and thoughtfulness involved in what he said on the subject in the *Let It Rock* magazine feature 'Zappa's Top Ten' in 1975.

I had a specific discussion with Zappa as to his motives in doing the *Ruben & The Jets* album. He had several reasons – among them the challenge of combining fragments from a whole wealth of genuine fifties r'n'b numbers, and mixing them up with fragments of Stravinsky which are in there on the album too – check out the fade-out to 'Fountain Of Love' and you'll find *The Rite Of Spring*. I asked him whether the album was also made partly to educate the college audience to the delights of old r'n'b for its own sake, bearing in mind that those people had, in the late fifties and early sixties, either been interested in jazz or in folk – both of which were snobbish interests that went with an abhorrence of rock 'n' roll and its sources; student audiences were still booing rock as late as 1966 when Dylan did it in concert. So I asked whether *Ruben* was intended as an educative album for that sort of audience, just as what he called his 'music music' was intended to be educative in another direction:

'Yes, that's true . . . and prior to the release of that *Ruben & The Jets* album nobody in amplified music had even touched on that aspect of early rock 'n' roll. Their idea of early rock 'n' roll was a pseudo-Chuck Berry song; and the college students and the generation that was our audience at that time didn't know from nothin' about group ballad vocals and things like that, or the context from which that flowed. And I thought that it might be a valuable public service to show them that some of that could be entertaining to listen to and could even make you feel good.'

With *Uncle Meat* and *Ruben & The Jets* completed, Zappa was finished with New York for the time being. So he and The Mothers and Gail and the baby all moved back to live on the West Coast again. Zappa bought a house in Laurel Canyon that was supposed to have belonged to Tom Mix and to have his wretched old horse buried somewhere in the grounds. Pamela Zarubica moved in with them too, fresh from her own work on the *Uncle Meat* album. She says it wasn't really Tom Mix's old house at all, it was just his manager's.

Gail had flown to LA ahead of Frank to find a house; she'd found it; so Frank had followed and moved in. Pam says it was really vast, and really decrepid. Pam was given a room to herself, painted it red and got high a lot in it. By this time she'd had her baby – in a New York hospital – and had it adopted.

Pam says the house was known as 'the log cabin' and that Frank filled it with his 'usual entourage of freaks and phonies'. The GTOs (Girls Together Outrageously) moved in. Pam didn't like them, seeing them as 'a group of freaky dressing, hard-narcotics-loving young girls who feign lesbianism as their thing.' Miss Christine was one of them, and she became Moon Unit's governess at the house.

The same month they moved back to LA – June 1968 – they played a return gig at the Shrine Exposition Hall. A sentimental journey maybe, a triumph certainly. 7000 people packed the hall this time around, and even *Newsweek* took notice: 'A staggering figure since The Mothers' radical vision and raw language have cut them off from virtually all but underground radio exposure, the lifeline without which most groups sink.' *Newsweek* also noted that Jimmy Carl Black had grown a beard. He'd probably say it was because he couldn't afford razor blades at the time.

Zappa, working frenetically as usual, also wrote an article on the history of rock music for *Life* magazine, and in the issue of 28 June, it was published – though Zappa retained the copyright on it. His piece was part of a whole *Life* forum-teach-in heavy focus on rock, and by general consensus, Frank's piece was the only redeeming feature of the whole thing. The Oracle Has It All Psyched Out won him fresh respect as a contemporary figure – revealing, as it were, new talents all the time. 'There is still something to be said,' wrote a *Rolling Stone* reader, 'for a nation that lets a man like Frank Zappa write for *Life* magazine.'

A month later Zappa was on the cover of *Rolling Stone* – a semi-underground equivalent, back then, of making the cover of *Time* or *Newsweek* – and Jerry Hopkins, no longer just an *LA Free Press* freak writer, did a long and wide-ranging *Rolling Stone* interview with him inside the same issue.

Toward the end of that month – July – The Mothers went back to the Whiskey and gave a five-hour performance which was also, like every concert they did, a recording session.

In August, *Ruben & The Jets* was released, and Pamela

Zarubica finally quit Zappa. She seems to me to have remained in love with him ever since, but she got to the point where she could no longer tolerate his entourage, her position on the sidelines, or the feeling Frank gave her that he was opting out of his more radical social responsibilities. She'd thought he was going to change the world, but she found he'd postponed that project.

In September, The Mothers went back to Europe. They performed in the Essen International Song Festival in Germany (performing, among other things, one of their best combinations of music and humour, 'Prelude To The Afternoon Of A Sexually Aroused Gas-Mask,' a number that was to appear on the *Weasels Ripped My Flesh* album in due time, and which had been originally inspired, of course, by Zappa's recollections of dismantling a gas-mask as a child back in Edgewood Maryland). As well as performing, Zappa took part in a seminar organised as part of the festival, along with some of the members of The Fugs. Ed Sanders, a Fug, later commented: 'Zappa said a great thing to the audience at the Essen Song Festival . . . He said, "You must enjoy our concert."'

That was at the end of September, and they stayed in Europe for some German concerts scheduled for October. They did one in Munich on the 9th, which was billed as 'Total Music Theatre', and then moved on to do a concert in Berlin. Back in '66 on the *Freak Out!* notes, Zappa had said 'Sometimes there is trouble.' There was trouble in Berlin. It was one of those concerts where the audience is on all four sides of the stage, and Zappa found himself surrounded by left-wing students. 1968 was a much more political year than 1967 had been, and Western Europe a much more political place than Laurel Canyon. May 1968 had seen oh-so-nearly a revolution in France (betrayed, in classic manner, by the Communist Party). There were plenty of posters around declaring 'PARIS, LONDON, ROME, BERLIN, WE SHALL FIGHT AND WE SHALL WIN!'

Only a few months beforehand, at the return concert at The Shrine, Zappa had discussed politics with a *Newsweek* reporter, who noted that Zappa was merely hoping 'to counter-act what he sees as the rise of the herd instinct and mass passivity.' Zappa told him: 'Half of America is under 25, yet there is no real youth representation in government.'

Clearly, Zappa was no Marxist; his individual neo-anarchism had already tamed to hopes for 'youth representation in government'. The riot-experienced youth of Berlin were out for a great deal more than that. As usual, the activists' demands came across as crude, simplistic and naive. The audience at Zappa's Berlin concert demanded that he make some public declaration of intention to bring down capitalism. Zappa refused. The audience screamed 'Fascist!' at him and chanted 'Mothers Of Reaction! Mothers Of Reaction!'

It was not a nice concert. Frank was to run into similar trouble when he gave a lecture to students at the London School of Economics in 1969; and he was to speak sternly to his Royal Albert Hall concert audience that year when a section of the audience objected to security uniforms being in the hall.

'Everybody in this room is wearing a uniform,' he was to say, 'and don't kid yourselves.' Naturally, the tape of this moment was used on record later. The Berlin incident also provided him with a source of material for the same excellent album, *Burnt Weeny Sandwich*. When it appeared, two tracks were musical evocations of the October '68 Berlin 'unpleasantness': 'Overture To A Holiday In Berlin' and 'Holiday In Berlin, Full Blown'.

Back in the USA in November, Lowell George joined the band briefly. He was only in the band a few weeks, but in that few weeks The Mothers were, as ever, recording, and so George ended up on a track issued later on the *Weasels Ripped My Flesh* album, 'Didja Get Any Onya?'

Bizarre Records, by this time, had been busy signing other acts, and by the time December rolled around, some of these were ready to go on the road. So it was back to the Shrine Exposition Hall in Santa Monica again, for what was billed as a 'Gala Pre-Xmas Bash' on Friday and Saturday 6 and 7 December. The bill promised The Mothers, plus Easy Chair, the GTOs, Wild Man Fischer and Alice Cooper. Kim Fowley turned up and performed, but he didn't get signed to Bizarre. As to the others, the GTOs we've already glimpsed, if only through Pamela Zarubica's eyes; Easy Chair, which had featured Jeff Simmons, later became Ethiopia; Wild Man Fischer did make an album for Bizarre – a double, in fact, called *An Evening With*

Wild Man Fischer, which Frank Zappa spent months producing. The GTOs similarly made a Zappa-produced double
album, entitled *Permanent Damage*, on which Zappa also
played tambourine and inside the cover of which he published
his manuscript *The Groupie Papers*. And Alice Cooper, the only
one of those Bizarre acts 'direct from Hollywood' ever to make
a successful musicbiz career, made their first two albums for
Zappa's label and then transferred elsewhere to find fame and
fortune.

Bizarre was not, in other words, out to have streamlined, formularized hit records. As Zappa wrote on the inner sleeve of
Uncle Meat – the first of his own Bizarre albums – 'We make
records that are a little different. We present musical and sociological material which the important record companies would
probably not allow you to hear. Just what the world needs . . .
another record company.'

One week after the second of those pre-Xmas Shrine concerts, the Monkees film *Head* had its première, in New York
City, 14 December.

In January of 1969 Zappa and The Mothers appeared yet
again at the Shrine, this time sharing the bill with the Sir
Douglas Quintet (fronted by Doug Sahm) and Fleetwood Mac
(then an anaemic British blues band).

January was also the deadline set by publishers Stein & Day
for a book they had commissioned Zappa to write. As if he
wasn't busy enough. What they had commissioned was a political book, but Zappa said: 'I couldn't get into that . . . So I did
the groupie book.'

The groupie book was *The Groupie Papers*; whether Zappa
handed it in or not I don't know; either way, Stein & Day didn't
publish it and it was left to be published, as we've noted, as part
of the GTOs' album packaging.

January also saw Buzz Gardner joining The Mothers and Ray
Collins disappearing. February saw the publication of the
Rolling Stones Groupies Special Issue, in which it was no sur-
prise to find that Frank had a lot to say for himself.

In April Zappa turned his hand to some home-made ads that
were placed in Marvel Comics – which showed where Frank
thought part of his audience lay – though these ads were for the

We're Only In It For The Money album, and it isn't clear why he was still advertising that. Particularly since the same month saw the release of the *Uncle Meat* double album, along with other Bizarre products.

One of these was the double album by Lenny Bruce, called *The Berkeley Concert*, which was the first time an unedited concert performance by Bruce had been issued. It, like *Uncle Meat*, was issued in Britain through Transatlantic. At that time, Warners didn't have its own distribution network but was distributed through Pye, and Pye refused to issue *Uncle Meat* because, Herb Cohen says, it had the word 'fuck' on it. 'Transatlantic put it out instead,' says Cohen, 'but it wasn't exactly what we wanted – it was a small label, a small company – and we suffered. We suffered as a result of Pye refusing to put out the record.' It was like the old American battles with MGM. Which is why, when Cohen and Zappa added a new label, Straight, to go with Bizarre, the Straight label had a British distribution deal with CBS. Bizarre Records were all either spoken word records and/or records that Frank Zappa produced himself. Straight Records was initiated to put out stuff that Frank hadn't produced, wasn't spoken word albums and didn't fit into the kind of category suggested by the word 'Bizarre'. At least, that's what Herb Cohen says, but the GTOs were put out on Straight and they were (a) spoken-wordish (b) produced by Zappa and (c) decidedly bizarre. And (b) and (c) hold true for Captain Beefheart & His Magic Band also, yet their double album *Trout Mask Replica* was also issued on Straight.

Straight/Bizarre also put out a sampler album of its 'product' at the same time as *Uncle Meat* and the Lenny Bruce album were issued (April, 1969). The sampler was called *Zapped*, was available mail-order from Warner Brothers in the States, and was a real loss-leader, selling for just one dollar. It featured tracks from albums by Frank Zappa, The Mothers Of Invention, Wild Man Fischer, the GTOs, Tim Buckley, Tim Dawe, Jeff Simmons, Lord Buckley, Alice Cooper, and the redoubtable Captain Beefheart.

So all those peoples' albums came out around the same time. I don't know who Tim Dawe was, but, like Easy Chair, he disappeared and was never heard of again. As for the others, Tim

Buckley was an artist Herb Cohen had managed since the beginning of the former's career; he made interesting but hopelessly self-indulgent albums and died in 1975. Lord Buckley was a pioneering social commentator/entertainer – a kind of black prototype for Lenny Bruce – who had died in 1960 and been cited as an influence on The Mothers in the mammoth list Zappa compiled for the sleeve of the *Freak Out!* album.

Jeff Simmons, whose album for Zappa's label was called *Lucille Has Messed My Mind Up* and featured Zappa's guitar work, was later to become a Mother (in May 1970) and then resign in a huff during the rehearsals for Zappa's film *200 Motels*. He re-appeared on 1972's Zappa album *Waka/Jawaka* and as a Mother on the *Roxy & Elsewhere* album of 1974.

Another album released in April 1969, though nothing to do with Bizarre or Straight or Warner Brothers or Frank Zappa, was an interesting solo album called *Dr Dunbar's Prescription* by the English musician Aynsley Dunbar, who had been solidly immersed in the British blues tradition and had played with John Mayall and later with Jeff Beck, and later still formed his own band, Retalliation and then Blue Whale. Within six months of issuing this *Dr Dunbar* solo album, he was being used by Zappa for his solo album *Hot Rats*, and he went from that straight into The Mothers at the same time as Jeff Simmons. He lasted in The Mothers rather longer.

It was also in April in 1969, finally, that The Mothers returned to New York for a concert – their first in that city for nearly a year.

In May, the band came to Britain and for the first time played outside London. It was on this trip that Zappa had his contretemps with the students at LSE. These extracts from the British edition of *Rolling Stone*, describing what happened, are seeped in that magazine's deplorable late-sixties political wetness!

'LSE turned out in force to see Frank Zappa and . . . it turned out to be a display of the tight-minded, intolerant attitudes and political bullshit that one has come to associate with LSE over the past few years.

'First there was Zappa's film, *Intercontinental Absurdities* . . . Then, on came Frank, hair tied in a knot and shiny brown shoes – Florsheim's, at a guess.'

Zappa sat down and a long silence followed. He asked for questions. There was more silence. Then 'a flurry of irrelevant questions about the film to fill up the silence . . . very soon the students . . . were getting up-tight. He wasn't saying what they'd come to hear, namely "Up against the wall, mother-fucker!" . . . "I'm not big on demonstrations," he replied to a question about the recent Berkeley riots, and suggested that, rather than demonstrate, why not make movies or become a lawyer. "Infiltrate the establishment. That's the way it happens." Hisses, boos, anger from the auditorium . . . "Infiltrate until there's another generation of lawyers, doctors, judges – I don't think you should harm people."'

Then Zappa made his famous remark 'Revolution is just this year's Flower Power.' Or anyway, that's how the remark has become in legend. I think what he actually said, with less panache, was 'Demonstrations are just a fad.'

The meeting finished in mutual hostility. It has become a frozen moment in the history of the 1960s.

A couple of days later, on 30 May, The Mothers played their first provincial British date, at Birmingham Town Hall – a concert promoted, appropriately enough, by the proprietors of the 'underground' live music venue in the city, 'Mothers'. The day after, they played Newcastle City Hall. On 1 June, they played Manchester Palace Theatre, moving on to Bristol's Colston Hall on the 3rd, Portsmouth Guildhall on the 5th and finally the Royal Albert Hall on the 6th (where Zappa made the remark about how everyone wore a uniform). In retrospect, it is possible to see that Zappa's political life went into long abeyance after this last confrontation.

Zappa went back to the States with the band, and in August 1969 started two months of work on his *Hot Rats* solo album at three different West Coast studios: Whitney, good old TTG, and Sunset Sound. With Tom Wilson, he had also worked out an album owed to MGM, a best-of type compilation album called *Mothermania* which was issued in early September.

October was a very busy month indeed. *Hot Rats*, issued with uncharacteristic speed, came out to acclaim on the 10th. Zappa started negotiating with Playboy Records (oh how the bizarre are straightened!) for their company to release no less than twelve Mothers' albums by setting up a special Mothers Club, using the organization and distributive machinery Playboy already had for their Bunny Clubs.

Nothing came of this project, and Zappa had to wait many years before any such extravagant multiple-album sets came out. And then he had to do them himself.

Also in October Frank Zappa simply disbanded The Mothers Of Invention. On the 17th in the Warner Brothers Circular, he published a piece of writing called 'Whatever Happened To The Mothers Of Invention' . . . and a week later announced that he'd chopped them.

The reasons were several. I think he'd taken the various awards and accolades of earlier times as his by right, and he didn't like the critical 'carping' he'd come in for recently. It seems always to be one of the perils of rock eminence that the artist becomes surrounded by yesmen, and grows very poor at coping with adverse criticism of any kind. I think also that Zappa was frayed at the edges through over-work and frustration caused by all the various hitches and delays and squabbles that surrounded his projects. There had, in particular, been a lot of friction over the whole Straight/Bizarre relationship with Captain Beefheart, not least because Zappa saw just how good Beefheart was, and how good a performance he was getting out of the third line-up of his Magic Band. His own musicians, The Mothers, were berated regularly during the second part of 1969, with Zappa demanding to know why they weren't doing more and doing it better than Beefheart's crew. As well as that, there was the financial drain on Zappa himself. He was paying each Mother $250 a week and there were seven of them (Ray Collins and Lowell George had left) and that money wasn't coming from concerts – Zappa's band *lost* money doing concerts – and neither was it in any way coming from the non-existent profits made by Straight/Bizarre. It was coming from Zappa, and he just reached a point where he didn't feel like paying out any more. He also blamed his audiences for their lack of appreciation. 'Those kids,' he said nastily, 'wouldn't know music if it came up and bit them on the arse.'

He told Jerry Hopkins: 'It all started in Charlotte, North Carolina. We'd been booked by George Wein on a jazz concert date as bait to get the teenage audience. We went into a 30,000-capacity auditorium with a 30 watt public address system, it was 95 degrees and 200 per cent humidity, with a thunderstorm threatening. It was really horrendous.

'After that I had a meeting with the group and told them what I thought about the drudgery of grinding it out on the road. And then I came back to LA and worked on *Hot Rats*. Then we did one more tour – eight days in Canada. After that I said fuck it.

'I like to play but I just got tired of beating my head against the wall; I got tired of playing for people who clap for the wrong reasons. I thought it time to give people a chance to figure out what we've done already before we do any more.'

The notice Zappa had contributed to the Warners Circular had similarly said: 'It is possible that, at a later date, when audiences have properly assimilated the recorded work of the group, a reformation might take place.'

Just over a year later, looking back at his disbandment, Zappa was to explain: 'At first they' – The Mothers – 'were extremely angry at me for breaking up the band, not because they wanted to play the music but because I had been supporting them. Suddenly I had taken away their income. I said to them "Look, am I supposed to kill myself going out and doing this over and over again? Well, it's not any fun for me any more." I was really depressed about it, I couldn't do it any more.'

Zappa didn't hang around, to listen to the howls of outrage. He rushed off to the Festival D'Amougies in Belgium and played there on stage with the Pink Floyd. And he brought Beefheart with him. The festival was filmed by one Jerome Lapperrousax, and the film was to be called *Music Power*. It never came out.

He came back to the States and did a pilot TV show, and announced: 'If it works then I'll have my own weekly TV series. It will be syndicated.' It didn't work.

The same month – still October '69 – he announced that he'd booked the Royal Albert Hall for a concert on 25 April 1970 (in the event, the date used was the 26th); Bizarre/Straight announced plans to release four more albums; Zappa declared himself to be working on the script of a feature-length film of

Captain Beefheart vs. The Grunt People, which he'd originally written in 1964; he also announced that three short films – two of them documentaries about The Mothers in Germany – were complete and would be offered to colleges in lieu of cancelled Mothers gigs; and in addition to all of that he started working on the arrangements for an album of Zappa music to be made by jazz violinist Jean-Luc Ponty.

Frank finished the month with some more good press. On the 30th he was on the cover of *Down Beat*, while on the inside they published 'A Brand New Frank Zappa Score'. On the 31st, *Time* magazine came up with another great quote: Zappa was, their writer said, '. . . a force of cultural darkness, a Mephistophelian figure serving as a lone, brutal reminder of music's potential for invoking chaos and destruction.'

Zappa continued working on all these projects. The Mothers went their various ways. James Euclid Motorhead Sherwood, Zappa told me, 'got into scientology for a while and then recovered' and turned up again to take part in *200 Motels* the following year. Jimmy Carl Black formed his own band, named after his fifth-born child – Geronimo Black – and Bunk Gardner joined it with him. Don Preston collaborated with the dancer Meredith Monk in performing electronic music, and emerged on mellotron and moog on an album called *The Visit From Bob Smith* issued in America on Kent Records. Ian Underwood first intended to form his own jazz-oriented group with Ruth Komanoff (who had played marimba and vibes with Arthur Tripp on a substantial amount of the *Uncle Meat* album), whom he'd married; instead he decided to stick with Zappa, working with him on both Zappa's solo album *Hot Rats* and on the Jean-Luc Ponty album. Ray Collins had already disappeared. 'He went back to being a carpenter,' Zappa told me. Lowell George, who had left a while before The Mothers disbanded, had started his own un-Motherish band Little Feat, and now Mother Roy Estrada joined it too. (He later quit to join Captain Beefheart's Magic Band number five, and in the spring of 1975 everything came full circle when Beefheart himself appeared to have rejoined The Mothers – but that's another story.) And finally Arthur Tripp, who unloaded a lot of his frustration at having been a Mother and at having been disbanded, when he was interviewed by David Walley for his Zappa biography, did quit and go to join the fourth Beefheart Magic Band, in 1970 – but not before working with Zappa on his Jean-Luc Ponty album, on which Tripp played drums on two tracks: 'King Kong' the title track, and the long specially-written piece 'Music For Electric Violin And Low Budget Orchestra' which occupied more than 19 minutes of the album's second side.

The other people who worked with Zappa on those two albums were as follows. First, his own *Hot Rats* album: Zappa and Ian Underwood plus – Captain Beefheart himself; Don Sugarcane Harris; John Guerin; Paul Humphrey; Ron Selico; Max Bennett; Shuggy Otis; and Jean-Luc Ponty.

On the Jean-Luc Ponty album there was: Zappa, Ponty, Underwood and Tripp, plus – John Guerin again; George Duke (of whom more later); Gene Estes; Buell Neidlinger; Wilton Felder; Ernie Watts; Donald Christlieb; Gene Cipriano; Vincent DeRosa; Arthur Maebe; Jonathan Meyer; Harold Bemko; and Milton Thomas.

(Ernie Watts was to turn up again on the album of *Grand Wazoo* in 1972, though he wasn't on the Grand Wazoo tour; and when The Mothers were reformed in May 1970 – somewhat in haste – several of the others mentioned from those two albums were to become members of the band.)

In January 1970, Zappa was in London, being photographed with old ladies on park benches. The same month, the *Hollywood Reporter* noted that: 'An unpublicised screening of Frank Zappa's 20 minute film-montage *Burnt Weenie* [sic] *Sandwich* at San Fernando Valley State College had to be run five times in succession last week, when 2000 rain-soaked students materialized where only 200 had been expected.'

Zappa was there – the week after being in London – and during a question and answer session after the screenings he gave details about 'the feature-length film he currently has in production, *Uncle Meat . . .*'

In February, the *Burnt Weeny Sandwich* album was released, and got the good reviews it deserved; in March, Zappa was reported to be shooting another – yep, another – movie. 'It's not about The Mothers,' he said, adding helpfully: 'It's about something else.'

He was also reported simultaneously to be making a film that *was* about The Mothers for Dutch television, which included footage of The Mothers in concert, plus the GTOs, Wild Man Fischer, Zappa telling his own story, something about work towards the *200 Motels* project, and stuff about Frank's family.

And while he was over in Europe doing that, he also popped over to France and jammed and 'had fun' with various French 'pop groups'.

In April, the *Uncle Meat* film was reported to be at the editing stage in Los Angeles, and Zappa did his Albert Hall concert on the 26th.

The month after that, Frank was offered the opportunity of having his music played by, and with Zubin Mehta and the Los Angeles Philharmonic Orchestra – on condition that he form a new Mothers to do it with. He was reported to be looking around LA for a new organist and a new bass player.

He didn't have to look far. He gave up on the organist but brought in the jazz pianist who had worked with him on the Jean-Luc Ponty album, George Duke, and he brought in Jeff Simmons – who'd made the Bizarre/Straight LP *Lucille Has Messed My Mind Up* on which Zappa had played guitar. Along with them he got Ian Underwood (of course) on keyboards and winds; and Aynsley Dunbar, the British bluesman, on drums.

They didn't have long to rehearse – the concert was scheduled for 15 May – Mothers Day. It was to serve as the world première of Zappa's *200 Motels* music. One hundred and four members of the Los Angeles Philharmonic were to be involved.

Before the concert, Mel Powell, Dean of the School of Music at California Institute of the Arts, withdrew his own new work *Immobiles 1-4*, which was due to be performed, in protest at the Mehta-Zappa collaboration. 'The very hypocrisy young people abhor,' he declared, 'is at work ensnaring them, seducing them . . . Pop music . . . is manifestly in the wrong zone when set beside a symphony orchestra.'

Wrong zone or not, it happened, starting with Zappa shouting 'Hit it, Zubin!' and ending thus: 'Then, everyone in the orchestra suddenly screamed, one final frightening chord was heard, and with a giant blurp *200 Motels* closed down for the night.'

It wasn't, in fact, very good. There was mutual hostility and arrogance. The orchestra was haughty about The Mothers; Mother Jeff Simmons said afterwards: 'Those dudes are really out of it man. It's like working with people from another planet.'

In the audience were Mark Volman and Howard Kaylan, vocalists, who found Zappa afterwards, told them they loved him and that they were available for work now that The Turtles had split up. In June, therefore, they joined The Mothers. A lot of people welcomed their vocal skills; a lot of people thought, especially in retrospect, that they tended to encourage the banal side of Zappa's humour. The test, really, is whether you like the live albums *The Mothers/Fillmore East June 1971* and *Just Another Band From* LA (recorded August 1971, released May 1972) enough to play them more than once or twice.

The same month Volman and Kaylan joined, June 1970, Zappa was back in London and did a recording session at Trident Studios on the 6th. Sometime around then, he also managed to be in Indianapolis, giving an interview to *Down Beat* magazine. On the 19th, The Mothers were in Amsterdam and Zappa was in Hanover – and they all flew into London. The Mothers checked into the Kensington Palace Hotel. Zappa checked into the Inn On The Park with Gail. On the night of the 21st they did some more recording at Trident, and the next morning Herb Cohen flew in from New York and joined the Zappas at their hotel.

On the 23rd, Zappa left London at 4.30 pm and checked into the Birers Hotel in Climping, West Sussex in order to be at a reception held in his honour the next day. Zappa's finances had looked up considerably, not least because United Artists had by this time apparently come up with something over half a million dollars for his film of *200 Motels*.

In case the reception had taxed his strength, Zappa had been booked to stay at the Climping Hotel till the next day, when he returned to London. The day after that, the 26th, The Mothers did some more recording at Trident; and the day after that Zappa went to Bath and checked into the George Hotel, ready for The Mothers' appearance on the 28th at the Bath Festival.

The Festival schedule, as so often, was in a complete mess by the 28th (a Sunday). By early afternoon, none of the bands seemed ready to go on stage; so Zappa and The Mothers did. I remember their performance well – from my vantage point about a mile off across a field full of cold, polythene-covered people. The crowd numbered 150,000. Hours later, queuing wretchedly for deplorable hotdogs round near the side of the stage, I saw Zappa leaving. He was sitting all by himself in one of the middle seats of a 52-seater coach. It inched its way through a mass of frozen hippies and took him, presumably, back to the warmth and comfort of the George Hotel, Bath. On the 29th he returned to London and subsequently flew back to New York.

Zappa spent the rest of the summer pre-occupied with *200 Motels* and various other odd projects; *Hot Rats* and Jean-Luc Ponty's *King Kong* were released; Zappa recorded *Chunga's Revenge*, which sounds like a Mothers album to me but was billed as one of his solo ones; later in the year they did a concert which began with a midget lady tap dancer at the London Coliseum and in November a concert in New York sharing a bill with Sha Na Na. In December, Zappa collected *Down Beat* magazine's Pop Musician Of The Year award.

And Zappa announced, perhaps a little defensively beneath the humour: 'For those who can't stand The Mothers and have always thought we were nothing more than a bunch of tone-deaf perverts, *200 Motels* will probably confirm their very worst suspicions.'

1971 started breezily with Zappa writing a fictional interview with himself on the history of The Mothers, his continuity concept and the *200 Motels* project.

What Zappa couldn't control, in February 1971, were the people in charge of the Royal Albert Hall. At the last minute, they cancelled his concert of the 8th; The Mothers and the Royal Philharmonic Orchestra found themselves locked out of a lunchtime rehearsal and that was that.

The concert was to have been a sort of British equivalent of the previous May's gig with the Los Angeles Philharmonic Orchestra – another promotional concert of *200 Motels* material to increase public interest in the film that was still to come.

The Royal Albert Hall had requested that Zappa submit the lyrics that were to be used in the concert; Zappa had done so;

requests for changes were made; Zappa says he made the changes and re-submitted the lyrics and was given the go-ahead and then at extremely short notice the concert was inexplicably cancelled. The RAH says he didn't submit satisfactory replacement lyrics.

The cancellation got a lot of press. On 9 February, the *Daily Telegraph* published an editorial entitled 'NO MUCK AT THE ALBERT HALL', which began: 'No-one will much regret . . .'

On the 11th, the same paper published a letter explaining the policy of the Royal Philharmonic Orchestra as regards collaborations such as the one with Zappa and The Mothers: 'Sir – in view of the substantial publicity given to the cancellation of a recent concert at the Royal Albert Hall which involved the Royal Philharmonic Orchestra, I wonder if I could have the courtesy of your columns to clarify several points concerning the orchestra's policy towards "mixed media" events of this kind.

'May I say at once that under no circumstances would members of the orchestra do anything in the course of an engagement (or, indeed, in the production of any film) which we consider "obscene" and out of keeping with the professional standing of the orchestra.

'During the past eighteen months the RPO has given over 200 concerts of which only two have been with a pop group. The reason why we did so was because we feel the need to "build a bridge" between those young people who may never have seen a full-scale symphony orchestra at work and the more "conventional" concert audience. . . .

'From a financial point of view, however, the costs of maintaining the high artistic standards of an orchestra of international repute are rising continuously. The support we gratefully receive from the Arts Council, the Greater London Council and other "official" bodies is, unfortunately, still not sufficient to meet all our expenses. Consequently it is necessary for us to look elsewhere for additional income. We are making strenuous efforts to attract support from industry and commerce, but one of the ways the orchestra can help itself is by accepting profitable film and other work of a more "popular" nature – and this directly supports our main artistic objective, which is to continue to play the music of the great composers.'

That civilized letter from the orchestra's chairman, John Lowdell, was followed by many less civilized letters over the next two weeks, including one from the President of the Royal Albert Hall, Sir Louis Gluckstein, who wrote, among other things: 'It is time that a stand was taken against the production of what many regard as dreary and inartistic filth for money.'

Herb Cohen and Zappa sought legal advice and as a result, took legal action. It took more than four years for the case to reach the courts. The bookings manager for the Hall and the person in charge of contractual dealings with promoters, a Ms Herrod, had cancelled the concert, at the last minute, despite the relevant contracts having been signed. Zappa sued for breach of contract, loss of earnings and damages. No-one disputed that the Albert Hall had in fact reneged on the contract, but Mr Ogden QC, for the Hall, claimed that such a course of action had been fully justified – indeed, had been obligatory – granted the obscene nature of much of the material to be performed. Not only was this material in very poor taste, he alleged, but there was, in addition, the possibility of audience participation in the concert which would put the Hall itself at risk, so far as damage was concerned. Ms Herrod maintained that after reading the amended lyrics submitted by Zappa she had decided that the concert could not possibly be allowed to go ahead. There was by that point insufficient time to ask reasonably for further revisions to the lyrics submitted, and cancellation was unavoidable in these circumstances.

Zappa's counsel, Mr Campbell QC, argued for the artistic merit of his client's music, comparing it with that of Shostakovitch and Stravinsky, and contended that further revisions to the lyrics would have been possible in the short space of time available after Ms Herrod decided the first revisions were unacceptable, and argued that in any case Zappa had offered to do the whole performance entirely instrumentally, without lyrics at all, if need be, and that there was no justification for breaching the contract by cancelling the concert. He pointed out that Zappa had lost a great deal of money through the cancellation, had lost what would have been the favourable publicity resulting from a good concert from a musician of established repute, with whom such 'serious' musicians as the members of the Royal Philharmonic Orchestra and guitarist John Williams would not have associated had they not considered Zappa a musical figure of any consequence. He also pointed out that Zappa had used the Royal Albert Hall in previous years without any damage being done to the Hall, either physically or in terms of its reputation.

Ms Herrod gave evidence, saying that on several other occasions she had refused bookings for the Hall, but had never before been obliged to cancel a concert after a contract had been signed. She had nothing personal against Mr Zappa and, while she didn't recall his previous concerts there, she remembered having been not entirely happy with the content of his 1969 programme either; however, she had hoped that the Royal Philharmonic Orchestra's influence this time would raise the tone of the whole affair. She said she had very little knowledge of the pop scene and that the Hall had perhaps 280 functions a year, of which possibly ten were pop concerts.

Witnesses for Zappa included Derek Taylor of Warner Bros. Records, George Melly, and the pop columnist closely involved with the making of the *200 Motels* film, Tony Palmer.

Palmer was asked whether he would have expected songs 'of that calibre' in 1971. Certainly, it was commonplace. Did he find the lyrics objectionable for a pop concert audience? Certainly not. He considered some of Zappa's lyrics feeble but songs like two of those objected to, 'Penis Dimension' and 'B'wana Dik', he would have been happy to include in a television programme had he been making one.

Zappa was called to the stand early in the proceedings, since he had to be back in America for concerts a few days after the opening of the case.

I had thought the days of dessicated manic magistrates gaoling Rolling Stones and judges incongruously poking their way through *Oz* and *IT* sniffing for obscenity, had gone out with the 1960s. April 1975 at Court No.7, The Law Courts, The Strand told a different story. When Zappa stood up in the witness box, no-one walking in and sitting down in the spectators' gallery would have thought that an established musician and composer was suing an established concert venue for breach of contract.

The overwhelming impression was of an underground hippie-type up there on an obscenity bust.

Smelling strongly of *déjà vu*, even at the time, the following is my transcript of part of what took place on two days during the case:

'Tuesday afternoon, 15 April:

> FZ: Do you know what a score is?
>
> QC: I know what a score is but you must assume we know almost nothing.
>
> FZ: Well, it's the musical equivalent of a recipe: it lists all the ingredients . . .
>
> QC: What do you mean by the term 'social games'?
>
> FZ: Social games are a sophisticated social charade [pronounced the American way as 'charaid'] by which –
>
> JUDGE: – Charade!
>
> QC: Would you not say that any young woman who seeks to contact a member of a rock and roll group in order to procure sexual intercourse – that such a young woman is in a very sorry state?
>
> FZ: Er, no. I would not.
>
> QC: I don't think you can have heard the question. I will repeat it. Mr Zappa, I ask you again, would you not say that any young woman who seeks to procure sexual intercourse from a member of a rock and roll group, whom she has never before even met! – that such a young woman is in a very sorry state?
>
> FZ: No. I would not.
>
> QC: You really don't think so?
>
> FZ: I do not. . . .

'Wednesday morning, 16 April:

'At 10am I am waiting, with Zappa, Herb Cohen, a man from Warner Brothers Records and a young mustachioed lawyer, an assistant to Mr Campbell QC, who is armed with *Webster's New Collegiate Dictionary* which includes useful definitions of "groupie" and "freak out". One or two reporters hover around. The corridor is like some hideously venerable public school hallway. Herb Cohen is smartly dressed in a neat dark suit. He looks discomfited and at the same time impressed, by the atmosphere of the court building. Zappa, tall and sun-tanned and clean, is wearing a restrained brown check suit and tan shoes. He would be looking respectable, quiet, low-key even, except that he is also wearing a pair of semi-luminous puce socks.

'Someone who looks like a prison officer on plain clothes duty comes down the corridor and opens the door to the court. I go in and sit down in the press benches, which are cunningly situated so that whoever is on the witness stand is directly behind you.

'The professionals drift in at 10.23 am. "It takes me ages to get my stuff together," the Royal Albert Hall's QC remarks chattily. The judge comes in; all rise.

'There are microphones all over the court room, but no-one switches them on, so that at least 45% of the day's proceedings is taken up simply with people being asked to repeat what they just said because no-one can ever quite hear anyone else properly. The judge cannot hear what counsel says, counsel cannot hear what Zappa says, Zappa cannot quite catch what the judge says. Another 10% of the day is taken up with recurrent adjusting of the sun blinds. Somehow, in amongst all this genteel and snail-paced English bumbling, the evidence proceeds, and Zappa continues to be cross-examined in detail about the obscene nature of his lyrics.

'The lyrics are organized into bundles – Bundle A, Bundle B, Bundle C. Zappa waits patiently in the witness-box, thin hands on the sides, leaning forward, giving every appearance of being perfectly at ease with himself, while the judge tries to sort out which bundles are which. Whenever, as the case proceeds, Zappa is called upon to read out names of songs, he uses a heavily sober tone of voice, strong and clear. The more bizarre/Zappaesque the title is, the more soberly and solemnly he says it. The effect, though entirely lost on the judge and the counsel, is highly comic. Jane Golding (Warner Bros Records UK Special Projects) finds it as hard as I do not to laugh out loud.

> JUDGE: Which songs in Bundle A were not in the film?
> FZ: "Babette". 'Would You Go All The Way'. "B'wana Dik" . . .

QC: Now. 'Lonesome Cowboy Burt'. This cowboy, Burt,
is saying that he wants to have sexual intercourse with a
waitress. Is it not? [sic]'

(There is a long wrangle about whether they are discussing
the original or the amended version of the lyric. Counsel says
scathingly that surely Mr Zappa can remember his own lyrics
sufficiently to answer so basic a question. Zappa asks cuttingly
whether there is any reason why he should answer a question
about a lyric without having the opportunity to examine that
lyric, since it is, after all, a part of the submitted evidence and is
readily available. Counsel concedes that Zappa indeed has the
right to read through the lyric before answering. Zappa reads
it through and finally concedes that a forlorn desire to have
sexual intercourse with the waitress might possibly be one way
of summarizing Lonesome Cowboy Burt's intentions. Mr
Ogden QC mutters under his breath 'It's like extracting teeth.'
Zappa tries to explain that the song illustrates Cowboy Burt's
character, which is not the same as approving of it, and that the
phrase queried by counsel, 'You can sit on my face', originated
from a real bar of the type a Lonesome Cowboy Burt would
frequent, where Zappa had taken the phrase from actual bar
room graffiti.)

'JUDGE: Did he say "perfidy"?
QC: No, "graffiti", m'lud.
JUDGE: Ah.
QC: Now. "Would You Go All The Way". That means
having sex, does it not?
FZ: It is an expression that was used in America in the
1950s to mean having sex. It is an archaic expression,
intended for laughs.
QC: Well whatever its intention that's what it means.
Now, m'lud, I turn to "She's Painting Her Face" . . .
[Counsel reads through the lyric aloud, finding *double
entendres* everywhere, misreading as he goes.]
QC: . . . "to break her parts in". Would you please explain
what that means?
FZ: It doesn't say "to break her parts in"; it says "to break

her pants in". It means she's going to wear some new pants.

QC: Oh. "To break her pants in." Well, once one starts reading this kind of script, one finds oneself making these mistakes . . . Now this next song –

FZ: – It's about unhappiness.

QC: Hm. Well, be that as it may, do you not consider it objectionable for boys and girls of 14 to hear this song?

FZ: No.

QC: Twelve?

FZ: No.

QC: Eleven?

FZ: No.

QC: Nine?

FZ: That could be problematical.'

(On it goes. At 11.52 a telegram arrives for Herbie Cohen, just as counsel for the Royal Albert Hall is calling Zappa 'a liar, yes, in set terms'. Zappa makes one of his very few retorts – it being characteristic of his manner in the witness box that he shows restraint and a quiet dignity at all times, and never resorts to the kind of easy insolence so many other rock stars would have hidden behind in similar circumstances. Noting the almost total lack of comprehension of Zappa's considered, intelligent answers throughout his evidence, I couldn't but wonder just how badly a more average rock'n'roller would have fared – someone less intelligent and less articulate than Zappa.)

'FZ: Your attempt is to direct all my lyrics into a sexual meaning, which is neither fair nor accurate.

QC: What does "pussy" mean? The pubic hair surrounding female private parts?

FZ: In the part of America that I come from, it means the private parts themselves . . . What I do find surprising is that you are dwelling on these lyrics, which we volunteered to change.'

(From here, the line-by-line examination of lyrics continues, with Zappa in each case steadfastly refusing to concede that any of his lyrics could be reduced *simply* to a sexual meaning without any other meaning being there just as integrally, and without taking into account the ironic intent of almost all the passages picked on – which is how counsel constantly attempts to reduce them. Counsel grows more and more weary of what he tries to present as pure evasiveness on Zappa's part. Consequently, he nearly falls over backwards in surprise at Zappa's immediate, clear answer in the following exchange:)

'QC: All right, Mr Zappa, I shall move on and try again. In the song "Daddy Daddy Daddy", what exactly did you mean by "dick"?
FZ: Penis.'

(Counsel then passes on to ask about some stage directions in the screenplay, which calls for two newts to be featured in a night club scene.)

'QC: Are you sure that "newts" just means newts? That there is nothing at all suggestive about that?
FZ [permitting himself a rare hit-back]: Anyone who is disturbed by the idea of newts in a night club is potentially dangerous.
JUDGE: . . . What does a "send-up" mean? . . .'

'Wednesday afternoon, 16 April:

QC: You don't suggest that publicity from the concert's cancellation was more unsatisfactory than if the concert had taken place?
FZ: It *was* less satisfactory because I believe I write good music, the performance would have been good, and so as a promotion for the film good publicity resulting from a good concert would have been more beneficial. Yes.'

(Zappa's counsel then takes over the questioning.)

'QC: What age group did The Mothers Of Invention aim at in 1971?

FZ: I write my music for anyone of any age. But people in a younger age bracket are more disposed to buying albums and concert tickets.'

(Later, counsel gets Zappa to take one of the lyrics objected to by the Royal Albert Hall even in its amended version, and asks him to amend it again – to prove Zappa's contention that last-minute amendments would have been perfectly possible.)

'QC: Will you amend that lyric now, please.
FZ: So as to render it suitable for a socially retarded audience?
QC: Yes.
FZ: How long do I get?
QC: A very short time. Five minutes. Three minutes. [Aside:] I want to see him working under pressure.'

(Zappa, with pencil and paper, works away in silence in the witness box. By the time five minutes is up, he has completely re-written the lyric of the songs 'Half A Dozen Provocative Squats' and 'Shove It Right In'. Not only do the new lyrics he reads out contain nothing whatever for the Royal Albert Hall people to object to; not only do they make sense in a new and sustained way, standing up in their own right as lyrics; but they also fit perfectly the structure, the rhythms and the rhyme-schemes of the original versions. A buzz of begrudgery goes round the courtroom.)

'Original Amended Version:

Half-a-dozen provocative squats
Out of the shower she squeezes her spots,
Brushes her teeth,
Shoots a deodorant spray up her twot . . .
It's getting her hot.

She's just twenty-four
And she can't get off
A sad but typical case

Last dude to do her
Got in and got soft
She blew it
And laughed in his face . . .

5-Minute Court Room Version:

Half-a-dozen provocative dots
Out of the flower she cleanses her pots
Brushes her wreath,
Puts an elaborate spray on her hearth
It's getting her hot.

She's just twenty-four
And she can't grow up
A sad but typical case
Last night a boozer
Came in and he scoffed
She knew it
And covered her face . . .'

(Followed by more of the same, culminating in this masterly change:)

'Original Amended Version:

. . . Waiting for girls they can
Shove it right in!

5-Minute Court Room Version:

. . . Waiting for girls they can
Chuck on the chin!'

(After that, the last exchange of the afternoon I remembered to write down – another rare hit-back from Frank Zappa):

'QC: Sir Louis Gluckstein, the President of the Royal Albert Hall, a man of considerable eminence, has said that

you write "filth for filth's sake". What is your response to
that?
FZ: My only response to that is that if I were in his position, I would not make an irrational statement like that.'

Zappa lost the case. Anyone who attended it during the time
he was in the witness box would find it possible only to con-
clude that what had been on trial was not a matter of contracts
but of the sub-culture of dissent of the 1960s generation.
In other words, it was a quiet but clear example of a British
political trial.

6. Revised Music For Guitar And Low-Budget Orchestra/ The Duke Loses And Regains His Chops.

The End Of The Frank Zappa & The Mothers Chronology

Zappa returned to the States after the cancellation of the February 1971 concert at the Royal Albert Hall and rushed around all over the place getting ready for the actual filming of *200 Motels* which, when it came to it, was done in under a week.

During rehearsals, Jeff Simmons quit the band, unable to tolerate working under what he saw as Zappa's autocratic rule. Zappa hit back on the liner notes of the *200 Motels* double album with the line 'Special thanks to Jeff Simmons from all members of the group' and with mocking bits of lyrics in the song 'Dental Hygiene Dilemma' (where 'Jeff' hears his Bad Conscience asking him why he is wasting his life playing 'this comedy music' and he replies 'You're right! I'm too heavy to be in this group!') sung by Volman and Kaylan with Simmons' replacement, Jim Pons – another ex-Turtle.

Don Preston returned to the band to fill the gap left by the departure of George Duke, and Zappa simultaneously worked on a piece for the magazine *Stereo Review* about Edgard Varèse.

This was finished in the spring and published in the June issue of the magazine, under the title 'Edgard Varèse, Idol Of My Youth – A Reminiscence And Appreciation.'

On 5 June, The Mothers played at the Fillmore East in New York, which, like its West Coast sister venue, was being closed down by Bill Graham. A live album, *Fillmore East, June 1971*, was made of The Mothers' performance.

The same night, they also had John Lennon and Yoko Ono up on stage and jammed with them. The largely hideous results of this collaboration (the exception was a version of 'Well (Baby Please Don't Go') were released by Apple on the Lennon/Ono album *Sometime In New York City.*

The day after, Zappa, Lennon and Ono had lunch together in an Italian restaurant in New York and discussed the possibility of further joint concerts. Nothing conclusive was arranged or decided on, though, and for once it was not up to Zappa to take control of the situation. He was left with the distinct impression that it was up to Lennon to say yea or nay, and found himself wondering afterwards whether it had really amounted to any-thing more than 'pleasant Italian restaurant talk'.

While Zappa was in New York, he also appeared as one week's Mystery Guest on the American TV show *What's My Line?*. One of the guests eventually guessed who he was, but the others – and much of the audience – gave a strong impression of being none the wiser for knowing his name.

The *Weasels Ripped My Flesh* album came out, to a less favourable critical reception than it deserved. Despite being a ragbag of odds and end from here, there and everywhere, partly done live and partly in innumerable studios, it did achieve a cohesive identity and a very high standard. I find it evidence of Zappa's editing skill at its height.

On 7 August, The Mothers did another concert which was recorded for another live album – this time back at the Pauley Pavilion at UCLA (where the concert with Zubin Mehta had been held the previous spring). The album taken from it was *Just Another Band From L.A.* One side was devoted to the story of 'Billy The Mountain' and a film of this title and story was scheduled to start shooting at the end of the year.

While Zappa was back on the West Coast, for this concert

and his usual projects-in-progress-in-the-basement, *Life* magazine came around wanting to feature him in a spread about rock
stars at home with their parents. Zappa's parents, however,
preferred to be photographed at Frank's house. The photograph
and blurb were published on 24 September, and showed Frank's
hideous purple living room to be otherwise ordinary and suburban. Zappa himself perhaps felt a bit sheepish about it: when he
chose to include it in the pressbook *Ten Years On The Road
With Frank Zappa And The Mothers Of Invention* (1974) he
counteracted its conventionality with cartoon balloons, so:

'Mr Zappa: . . . And I worked my way through college as a
barber . . .

Mrs Zappa: That cat just farted.

Zappa: Re-strain yourself Gorgo.'

In October, The Mothers were off touring again, hitting
Boston Music Hall, New Haven Connecticut and Carnegie
Hall, among others, in the first two weeks of the month.

Melody Maker was at the New Haven concert, and reported
that after The Mothers' performance, a note from a member of
the audience was handed to Frank. It read: 'Frank, my balance
went of to were it seamed I should maby be dead except Greag
Lake said to SAVE every hair on his head. He's dead, it seamed.
Like The Moody Blues said it might fuck up the world's balance.
Black Queen Midnight – that's me. Please help. 326-6604 Gary.'

Zappa read it, re-read it, and said, 'That's what the great
drug culture has done to American youth.'

Zappa was playing to large audiences, high on cheap red
wine and downers, as were a large proportion of all rock concert audiences in America by the end of 1971. He didn't like
them much. *Melody Maker* reported that he would respond
by walking on stage, waiting a little while the initial applause
and noise died down, and then say: 'Will you children please be
quiet so we can tune up?' Later in the evening, he would follow
this up with commands of 'Silence!' and towards the concert's
end: 'Even though you people are extremely rude we like you.'

Jim Pons told *Melody Maker*, in the course of this tour, about
how tightly disciplined the band was under Zappa's leadership.
He said that before the tour they rehearsed six hours a day, six
days a week.

'It's very regimental,' Pons said, 'and sometimes, when Zappa walks out of a rehearsal without saying goodbye, then I start thinking "Is it worth it?"'

That same month, October, the *200 Motels* double album was released and by 10 November the film, by then out on limited release in the States, figured in *Variety's* listing of America's Fifty Top-Grossing Films. A week later in Britain, the TV rock show *Old Grey Whistle Test*, then hosted by critic Richard Williams, ran a special feature devoted to Zappa and The Mothers. The *Radio Times* reported that the programme would show 'rare film of the original Mothers blowing in London' (the original Mothers never came to London; Mothers number two was the first group that did that, back in '67). There was also an interview with Zappa and some clips from the *200 Motels* film.

Two days later The Mothers opened a new European tour. Everything seemed to be going fine, but disaster was imminent.

The tour opened on 19 November in Stockholm, moved on to Aarhuus (Sweden), Copenhagen, Düsseldorf, Berlin (no student protests this time), and Hamburg. By the 27th, it had reached Rotterdam, where The Mothers went down exceptionally well.

On 4 December, the tour hit Switzerland – the first time The Mothers had played there. The concert was held at the casino, Montreux – but was interrupted by the hall burning down. Zappa remained calm and asked people to leave in a quiet and orderly way, and there was little injury to audience or tour crew (one roadie was blown out of a window and injured his hand). But The Mothers lost £25,000-worth of equipment and concerts in Paris, Lyons and Brussels had to be cancelled as a result. (Deep Purple was in the audience for Zappa's concert, and subsequently wrote up the fire incident in 'Smoke On The Water'.)

On Monday 6 December, therefore, Zappa and The Mothers flew into London prematurely – they were due three days later, in time for their Rainbow Theatre concert on the 10th – to buy or hire some new equipment.

They played at the Rainbow – the first since the Montreux Casino gig – and at the end of the performance, a fan's boyfriend jumped onto the stage and pushed Zappa sharply in the back. Zappa fell forward, caught his foot in a lead, twisted and fell 12 feet down into the orchestra pit. He was unconscious for several minutes and broke his leg. His attacker was set upon by some of the audience but was dragged off before he could be seriously hurt. Zappa was taken off to hospital as the audience filed away bemused.

Frank was later transferred to an expensive Harley Street clinic and on the 12th had an operation, which a clinic spokesman said was for 'an adjustment' to his ankle. His condition was said to be, as they say, satisfactory. The day after – Monday the 13th – the rest of The Mothers flew back to America, leaving Zappa in the clinic. Later he was to say: 'I spent a month in hospital with a cast on my leg in a wheelchair.' Later still he was to say he'd spent nine months in the wheelchair, avoiding interviews for once, but getting on with other projects, including recording a new solo album *Waka/Jawaka – Hot Rats*.

The music press reported the immediate tangible consequences of the Rainbow attack. They were supposedly as follows: the cancellation of the rest of The Mothers' British tour and with it the plans to record the tour performances; the postponement of the shooting of the *Billy The Mountain* movie; and – this last being the reason for my 'supposedly' – the postponement of the 1972 release date for the nine-album set!

The long term, less tangible result of Zappa's attack at the Rainbow was on Zappa's attitudes. It affected him deeply, and for at least a couple of years afterwards he was markedly more of a loner, more defensive, more suspicious, less outgoing and less open-minded than he had been before. For a long time he was palpably bitter, turning his feeling into a generalized anti-British animus.

It was just six days after the Rainbow that the film *200 Motels* opened in London, at the Classic in Piccadilly Circus. Zappa remained in the Harley Street Clinic while his fans were bored, fascinated and bemused in more or less equal proportions by his film of what the life of rock 'n' roll stars was really like. The movie is the only full-scale feature film Zappa has made (so far). It was directed by him (characterizations) and Tony Palmer (visuals). Zappa wrote the story and the screenplay. The animation was by Chuck Swenson. It was produced by Jerry Good and Herb Cohen, and was a Murakami Wolf/Bizarre Production, distributed by United Artists.

Most critics and at least half The Mothers' audience considered it a lavish failure – 'the most indulgent home movie ever made'; 'an act of undisguised aggression against the audience'; '[they] overindulge in elaborate color effects that give the movie the touchingly antiquated look of a psychedelic record jacket'; 'the movie has the attention span of a speed freak'; etc. etc.

Yet Robert Hilburn, in the *Los Angeles Times*, argued the case for *200 Motels* being 'a stunning achievement' and 'a minor classic', and said it was uniquely important in being 'a movie that finally deals with rock music and the rock environment in a way that makes it as compelling as the best albums or concerts', adding that 'the film has a sense of vitality and excitement that is akin to some of the feelings generated by the early rock records'.

1972 was a difficult year for Zappa. 'I spent,' he said in August, 'a lot of time hobbling around on crutches before they replaced the cast with a leg brace . . . just recently I've been able to walk around without using the crutches so much.'

It was in those tetchy eight months of the year that he recorded *Waka/Jawaka – Hot Rats*, a solo album which, as the name suggests, was a sort of follow-up to the first *Hot Rats* album. That had been a landmark recording for Zappa: it had taken a lot of people by surprise – among the public and within the music business – in showing just how fine a *guitarist*, as well as producer/composer, the ex-freak was. *Waka/Jawaka* never got similar recognition but it was a fine album, and made with every bit as much meticulous care.

The music world, and its 'counter-culture' – which was still considered to exist, in 1972 (we were still, existentially, living through the 1960s) – had nevertheless changed, slowly yet emphatically, since the time of Zappa's early albums. Rock music made by increasingly complex bands for those who, in Bob Dylan's phrase, 'accepted chaos'; the psychedelic-ignited movement of things, especially after the failure of the 1968 revolution in Europe, towards the baroque-thru-to-rococo – from *Sgt. Pepper* through to Crosby Stills Nash and Young and from

20-minute guitar solos through to four-hour Grateful Dead gigs before quarter million audiences; the cultural roll back, if not spotted till later, after Woodstock; indeed the very processes which turned Woodstock from a mass coming together of the Alternative Society (1969) into a big-grossing movie for those beginning to be the affluent young professional class (1970-73) – all these aspects of the *context* in which rock artists worked had changed visibly.

Album artists (as opposed to singles pop stars) had become, and Zappa was among them, a sizeable cultural elite. While this meant that a good deal of snobbery pervaded the rarefied air some of them breathed – including, for example, the affectation that they were uninterested in their sales figures – they were, after all, an elite of superstars. Their albums were not only taken seriously by a whole new breed of rock critic but were selling in millions and earning millions for artists who by now were often on far higher royalty rates than had ever been heard of in the history of the recording industry.

The fruits of the golden years were finally ripening into money. Rock stars no longer hung out at tacky clubs; now they bought country estates and bred race horses and specified in their con-tracts for concert appearances exactly what temperature they required their dressing room.

In the studios, extravagance on a similar scale became commonplace. Many artists and bands took to not writing the material for their next album till they turned up at one of the best, most expensive studios to begin recording it. Sometimes they stayed for months, waiting for the muse to emerge through the chemicals or imagining that it had emerged in the course of night-long stoned jams which somehow never seemed much good at all when played back a day or two later. It goes without saying that Zappa was atypical in these respects: he never earned millions and certainly by the start of the seventies did not toler-ate drugs or chaos in the studio when he was paying for it.

All the same, the studios grew rich in their turn – and being run by optimists and businessmen and music freaks, in whatever combination, much of their money was invested in ever greater ranges of recording and mix-down facilities.

In 1967, when you could say that Zappa was one of the first

round of people to be established as album artists, The Beatles' *Sgt. Pepper* was recorded. Florid and multi-tracked though it was, it was recorded on a four-track machine. When they made it, such a small machine was normal: but the boom-time in sales which that album helped to propel forwards meant that by the time the album was a steady old face in the middle reaches of the charts, such facilities already seemed archaic. As if in one leap, eight-track studios were now only good enough for making demo records. By the time Frank Zappa went into Paramount Studios early in 1972 to cut his *Waka/Jawaka* album, it had a 24-track facility.

There had been a brief moment when it had been imagined by some that these hugely increased facilities would speed up the process of getting albums recorded. For the album artist elite, it didn't work out that way. The odd exception, like Bob Dylan, *did* work faster, or at least, as fast – because he liked to record with everyone playing together, as if at a gig: he sought the spontaneity of feeling.*. Then again there were other people like Zappa. Just as expenditure rises with a rise in income, so too Zappa's exacting requirements expanded to push to the edge the state of the art in the studios.

Waka/Jawaka – Hot Rats was recorded at Paramount Studios in Los Angeles 'under the thoughtful supervision of Marshall Brevitz', say the sleeve notes, and engineered by Kerry McNabb, with 'thanks to Bob Moog & Co. for the use of their new frequency shifter.' (No doubt just one new toy among the many.) Sending out bad wheelchair vibes Zappa got it all organized, recorded and mixed down. It was by no means his only project in 1972; nor was his dependency on the wheelchair his only source of irritation.

Relationships between Zappa and Beefheart were at their nadir, as the result of Beefheart's distrust of Herb Cohen and dissatisfaction at the sales and general aftermath of the album he'd done for Straight/Bizarre, *Trout Mask Replica*. Beefheart told David Walley: 'Now I got along fine with him [Frank] until we got into this contract with this Herbie.'

* When Dylan and The Band got the *Planet Waves* album recorded and mixed in four days in November 1973, it was regarded as utterly extraordinary – and as an amusing indication of Dylan's cranky eccentricity.

Business soured their all-the-way-back-to-high-school friendship. Zappa says he got fed up with all the Bizarre/Straight
artists feeling he'd failed them when they didn't sell millions
of records and make millions of dollars, as if he'd somehow
cheated or tricked them, when in fact no other company would
have taken them on in the first place and no-one in his right
mind would have expected much commercial action out of
them. Beefheart didn't think that applied to him at all. He'd
been with other labels previously (even though he had never
been given anything like full artistic control of what he did with
those labels) and expected to get other labels in future (which
indeed he did) and he felt that Bizarre/Straight and Zappa had
only previously given him artistic control because they regarded
him as an amusing weirdo on the same sort of level as the GTOs
or Wild Man Fischer. I don't think it's true that Zappa thought
of Beefheart simply as a weirdo – in fact he respected what
Beefheart came up with on the *Trout Mask Replica* album
so much that he was actually jealous, and bullied his own
musicians, as noted earlier, because they weren't achieving as
much.

As for the part played in all this by Herb Cohen, well, there
are two sides to that. David Walley says Pam Zarubica saw
Cohen as interested only in money and whenever Zappa talked
to him about ideas – music, politics – Cohen would just say
'Yeah, Frank, sure Frank': not interested. Walley also quotes
Arthur Tripp as saying of Herb Cohen: 'The point is that
he's still punching it out on the streets of Brooklyn . . . How can
you do business like that? You can do business, it's like selling
pretzels, it's like cheating people out of pennies and dimes at the
carney – he's a carney cat . . .'

That's one side of it. The other comes across when you imagine what it must have been like for Cohen, whose responsibility
it was to look after the financial side of all these uncommercial
recording artists' work and deal with Warner/Reprise and keep
Zappa on the road – where the amount of equipment and personnel involved meant consistent losses from touring. Cohen
had to keep all this afloat and at the same time tiptoe his way
around all these hopelessly impractical, difficult artists. And,
because Zappa wanted it that way, and because that was the

point of Bizarre/Straight in the first place, Cohen had to try to balance the books while giving all these artists unprecedented freedom in the studios.

And when you listen to Cohen describing some of these problems, he comes across as sincere, not necessarily in having any devotion to those artists *per se*, but certainly in trying to organize and lay on what they wanted because Frank Zappa wanted it done that way.

This is Cohen talking, for instance, about Wild Man Fischer: 'That guy was on the streets, singing for dimes. You've heard accusations that he was ripped off? Oh yeah, well – he's totally out of his mind. See, it was not exactly what you'd call a successful album. I don't think we sold more than 6,000 copies – and Frank had been in the studio with the guy for three months. A lot of people in the business liked it, it got a good reputation, but it wasn't what you'd call popular. Even though there was a Wild Man Fischer Fan Club – and as a matter of fact there's even a Wild Man Fischer Baseball Team! With uniforms and everything!

'But he's an unfortunate victim of the culture . . . he'd been committed to institutions a couple of times, and the last time he beat up his mother they threatened to put him away again and so he disappeared. And so, you know, it was difficult. Unfortunately, you can't deal with him on any kind of logical basis. He got paid for doing it, though. He got money and so forth.

'I never paid him large sums of money, but what we did do was pay him every week for a long period of time. And the point is, whatever you paid him, it was gone the next day, so we tried to pay him some money in small doses. I mean, the first time we paid him, he went out and bought some silk shirts – some Mod clothes. But he was sleeping in the streets! So then what we did was we put him on a salary and put him in hotels. So he was living in a hotel room for a period of about six months. The only trouble is, you know, Bizarre/Straight [was] not as rich as Columbia or Capitol or Kinney or whoever it is, and we can't afford to subsidize indefinitely.'

And Cohen on dealing with Captain Beefheart: 'Oh! Well! – I hardly know what to tell you! Beefheart is in a class by himself.

First we spent some time trying to get him out of a previous bad contract, and unfortunately Beefheart is not what you'd call an astute businessman. I don't think Beefheart is a nut or anything, at all. . . . Beefheart's thoughts are very clear to him. He knows exactly what he's saying. Now whether it has the same meaning to you, or to me, or how we interpret it in terms of how we understand things, that's our problem – it's not his problem.

'I think Beefheart's lyrics are *incredible* – that's sheer poetry; his music I find a little difficult to understand, or to take . . .

'When we did the album with him, Frank said, "Hey, let's get into the studio and you rehearse the group and we'll put down exactly what you want." It was the first album he ever made where he had total control of everything that went down – he picked the musicians and the studio, I mean everything. Frank sat behind the board and recorded it for him, but it's all his. And I really like it.

'The way I got involved, though, was that Frank called me one day and said Beefheart was up at the house and needed some help. So I got him round to the office and he sat down – and first off it took us six months to get him out of all the legal entanglements he was in. So we spent a *lot* of time and money just on the legal end of things before we could even start with him properly.

'And then what he was doing at the time was not particularly commercial. I mean, his band, d'you realize, were not professional musicians. They were not musicians *at all*, his band at that time consisted of five guys who were *not* musicians, and what he did was assign each one of those guys an instrument and he taught them how to play the specific *sound* that he wanted out of those instruments. Those guitars are not tuned – it's all just recreations of sounds that Beefheart wanted to hear.

'So partly from that and partly from the fact that he is a little strange, Beefheart was a little difficult to deal with on a certain level. When we went in to do the album, I asked him how much it was gonna cost, to give me a budget for rehearsals and production and so on, and he gave me a list of expenses, and in there he had 800 dollars for a tree surgeon. And when I asked him what the tree surgeon was for, he said, well, the band rehearses out at his house, and there's this tree out in the front yard that overhangs the house and he wanted to make sure that the vibrations from the amplifiers didn't disturb the tree so the tree would get angry and the overhanging branch would fall on the house in retaliation. And so I, er, I told him that I felt, er, they could surely turn the amplifiers the other way or something, because I felt that was a bit extraneous as an expense – but I'll be goddamned if I didn't get a bill for 240 dollars which I *paid*, which was for a tree surgeon, at the end of that session. Y'see.

'Another thing that he asked me for – when we went into the studio he called me and told me what he needed, and he needed some guitars and a bass and an amplifier and some drum heads – and "20 sets of sleigh bells". And I asked him what he needed them for, I mean being that there was only five people in the band and one producer and one engineer, that's only seven people in the studio! And if each person held one set of sleigh bells in each hand, that's only 14 sets – assuming each person in his band had only two hands (which with Beefheart, y'know, is hard to tell . . .), so I said, "Well at the most, that's only fourteen. What happens to the other six sets of sleigh bells?" And he said "We'll overdub them!"

'So I gotta tell you, dealing with him on a certain level is – well, it's not difficult, but it's just not the clearest-cut situation in the world. I mean, I got him 20 sets of sleigh bells. I couldn't argue with that logic.'

By February 1972, Beefheart had changed his band slightly from the *Trout Mask Replica* line-up, had done two more albums – *Lick My Decals Off Baby* for Straight and then *The Spotlight Kid* for Reprise – and had brought two ex-Mothers into his Magic Band: Arthur Tripp and Elliott Ingber (one of the original Mothers). Arthur Tripp was renamed Ed Marimba while Ingber became Winged Eel Fingerling. By February, also, Beefheart had reached the height of his long anti-Zappa phase, and was blasting out at Zappa in every interview he gave.

So there was his old friend, helper and producer, sitting around in his wheelchair just two months after being assaulted at the Rainbow, picking up the music papers and reading this sort of thing from Beefheart (February '72): 'Zappa was an oaf. All he wanted to do was make me into a horrible freak. I'm not a freak. I am an artist . . . it was disgusting and totally degrading that Zappa should do this to me. Zappa uses people.' He added what anyone who knew Zappa's attitude to drugs couldn't possibly find plausible: 'He used me by making it appear that I advocated the use of hard drugs . . . the epitome of an acid-head.'

He went on: 'Because Zappa couldn't really understand me, he was afraid of me . . . The trouble with Frank is that he's not a good artist or a writer and by surrounding himself with good musicians and exploiting them he boosts his own image. If I hadn't been so pitifully poor at the time, I might have been able to do something about it. . . . People have always held me back.'

This kind of public slagging went on for a long time and other disgruntled musicians – ex-Mothers like Arthur Tripp – joined in. Zappa put up with it in relative silence for a long time. Eventually he started hitting back in *his* interviews. He said he got extremely fed up when all these people whose records he'd spent time and effort on all turned round and blagged him, and he wasn't going to do it any more.

He couldn't resist, though. It was all part of work to him, and work was something he never stopped. In fact one of the first things he did while still in the wheelchair period was round up a band, give them the name Ruben and The Jets, and fix up a deal for them with Mercury Records. They made an album called *Ruben & The Jets: For Real* which Zappa produced, wrote for and did some arranging work for. Subsequently, two of the band, Ruben Ladron De Guevara and Robert 'Frog' Camarena, appeared as back-up vocalists on the live 1974 album *Zappa Mothers – Roxy & Elsewhere*. De Guevara also appeared two years later on the *Zoot Allures* Zappa album.

Meanwhile, on 26 February, *Melody Maker*'s poll results showed that Zappa had, as usual, succeeded in bringing musicians from beyond the mainstream of rock into public and popular focus: in the Violin section of the poll, the Number One slot went to Jean-Luc Ponty and the Number Three slot to Don Sugarcane Harris. They owed their inclusion to Zappa's use of their talents.

In March, Zappa's Rainbow attacker was jailed for 12 months. Frank made no comment.

A month later, a 14-hour unedited version of the *Uncle Meat* film was booked into the New Yorker Theater in Manhattan. The soundtrack consisted of four Mothers albums played over and over and over. Tickets were stamped with the moviegoer's time of arrival and departure, so that patrons could be charged fifty cents an hour with a maximum price of three dollars. The film was distributed by Paradigm.

In May, the album *Just Another Band From L.A.* was released, and while some reviewers thought it pretty funny, and one even called the long epic of 'Billy The Mountain' a 'masterpiece', just as many gave it a firm thumbs down, thus making for Round Two of Zappa sitting in his wheelchair reading nasty things about himself in the music press.

I think the critics who didn't like the album were right – and that the 'Billy The Mountain' saga was so far from being a 'masterpiece' as to make one wonder what it would take for them to recognize a bad Zappa track if, to use Frank's own phrase from a different context, 'it came up and bit them on the ass.'*

When *Just Another Band From L.A.* came out Frank Zappa was in no mood for taking criticism, whether benevolently meant or not. He was also trying to oppose publication of David Walley's biography of him, *No Commercial Potential*, and it was that same month – May – that the press got wind of this and reported that Zappa and Herb Cohen were involved in an attempt to suppress the book.

In fact, Zappa had given Walley a tremendous amount of co-operation. The writer had been able to hang around Zappa's house, talk to him and his family, over a considerable period of time. Quite why Zappa changed his attitude isn't clear. He could not reasonably have expected that in exchange for his co-opera-

---

* But then I tend to zoom into content and take less notice of technique. Charles Shaar Murray, writing calmly about the album, advanced a more balanced case: it represented, he observed, the 'total triumph of style and technique over content. The incredibly precise musicianship of the Mothers and the virtuoso vocal abilities of Kaylan and Volman made it possible for Zappa to create a very fair approximation of the jump-cut editing of *We're Only In It For the Money* in a concert situation, with the result that 'Billy The Mountain', a 25 minute epic that takes up the album's first side, is composed entirely of musical, verbal and vocal one-liners. Technically, it's extraordinary . . . but it has no real content – presumably because Zappa has absolutely nothing to say . . .'

tion, the book would be totally uncritical of its subject; and I don't think Walley ends up in any way trying to do a hatchet job. Anyway, the book was delayed but did in the end get published, and in spite of Cohen's and Zappa's opposition, did succeed in getting the right to quote from many of Zappa's songs.

It was also in 1972 that another book came out which in a sense connected with Zappa: W. W. Norton & Co. of New York published Louise Varèse's biography of her husband, *Varèse: A Looking Glass Diary, Vol. 1*.

By August, Frank Zappa had assembled what had been announced as 'a new 20-piece electric symphony orchestra . . . including six reed, six brass, two concert percussionists . . . synthesizers and an electric cello.'

This was the Grand Wazoo, and it replaced The Mothers number six. The intention was to tour Europe, and America, and issue an album, using this very large line-up: Zappa conducting, and on guitar and vocals; Tony Duran on slide guitar; Ian Underwood on piano and synthesizers (years before the synth boom); Dave Parlato on bass; Jerry Kessler on electric cello; Mike Altschul on piccolo, bass clarinet and 'other wind instruments'; Jay Migliori on flute, tenor sax and more besides; Ray Reed on clarinet, tenor sax and ditto; Earl Dumler on oboe, double bass and more; Charles Owen on soprano sax and alto sax; Joanna McNabb (whose husband was the engineer; an unusual partnership) on bassoon; Malcolm McNabb (another relative) on D trumpet; Sal Marquez on B-flat trumpet; Tom Malone on B-flat trumpet and tuba; Glen Ferris on trombone and euphonium; Ken Shroyer on trombone and baritone horn; Bruce Fowler on trombones; Tom Raney on vibes and electric percussion; Ruth Komanoff Underwood on marimba and electric percussion; and Jim Gordon on 'electric drums'.*

This large, costly and unprofitable orchestra did a try out/launch gig at the Hollywood Bowl and then started the European Grand Wazoo Tour. For this, Frank and Gail Zappa

---

* A veteran session player, Jim Gordon became one of the, as it were, superstars of the elite, and has drummed for Clapton, Jackson Browne, Joan Baez, Joe Cocker, Roger McGuinn, Nils Lofgren, Yoko Ono, Alice Cooper, Steely Dan and a thousand others. In 1984 he was arrested in the States and charged with the murder of his mother. No pun intended.

flew into London in late August to do the usual pre-concert promotion work and then flew back to the States.

By the 15 September this striking couple was back in London, being photographed (not only in the music press but in papers like *The Guardian* too) at the Oval, where the Grand Wazoo European debut concert was to take place the next day.

It was around this time (to set a context again) that the new Sundowns were opening in London as large rock venues, with concerts by Slade, Wizzard, Vinegar Joe, Stackridge, Status Quo, Brinsley Schwartz, Man, Quicksilver Messenger Service and Steppenwolf.

The Oval gig was a success and a comparatively contented Frank Zappa flew out from Luton Airport next day, 17 September, destination Berlin, for the second of eight European gigs. From Europe he went back to the States, decided the orchestra was just too big to lug around any further, and so after one concert in New York and one in Boston he pruned it down to the following line-up: Zappa, Earl Dumler, Malcom McNabb, Gary Barone, Tom Malone, Bruce Fowler, Glen Ferris, Tony Duran, Dave Parlato and Jim Gordon. The name The Grand Wazoo was retained – despite the reduction in size, the changes in personnel and a shift in repertoire – and thus transformed, the tour continued through America and Canada, ending up with a final gig in Boston before Zappa flew back home to LA.

Meanwhile, in London, an interview Zappa had given to, of all things, the magazine *Punch* was published on 27 September. It included one vividly true Zappanswer and one palpably false one. True: 'It all finally comes down to one thing,' he said, talking about the pressures of taking a band/orchestra on tour and the responsibilities he felt as its figurehead, 'I am their employer.' And False, talking about what had happened at the Rainbow less than a year before: 'I am not bitter about that.'

On 9 October, in the *Warner Brothers Circular*, Zappa returned to print with his 'The Complete History Of Last Week's Mothers Of Invention/Hot Rats/Grand Wazoo' and the text for 'the ballet The Adventures Of Greggery Peccary'. (The song 'Greggery Peccary' finally emerged on album on *Studio Tan*, 1978.)

Meanwhile the album, *Grand Wazoo*, featuring yet another line-up, was immeasurably better than previous releases like *Fillmore June 1971* and *Just Another Band From L.A.* and the subsequent *One Size Fits All*, with Zappa's orchestration oddly sensitive to the old world quality the instruments themselves evoked. The line-up that achieved it was: Zappa, Janet Neville-Ferguson (previously called more simply Janet Ferguson), Sal Marquez, Mike Altschul, Earl Dumler, Tony Ortega, Joanna McNabb, Johnny Rotella, Fred Jackson, Malcolm McNabb, Bill Byers, Ken Shroyer, Ernie Tack, Bob Zimmitti, Alan Estes, Don Preston, Tony Duran, Erroneous, Aynsley Dunbar, George Duke, 'Chunky', Joel Peskin, Ernie Watts and Jim Gordon.

In November, the girl from the GTOs who had been on the cover of the *Hot Rats* album and had been the governess for the Zappas, Miss Christine, died of a heroin overdose, while visiting friends in Massachusetts. She'd been in dire straits for some time. By a wry coincidence she, like Zappa, had spent six months in a plaster cast in 1971, as a result of back trouble. (Coincidence was compounded by the fact that Pamela Zarubica also fell down a cliff at around the same time Zappa fell from the stage of the Rainbow. Soon afterwards they met by chance. You can picture Pamela and Frank both standing there on crutches, glaring at each other.) In the early months of 1972, Miss Christine had been trying to get a portfolio together as a step toward trying for a new career as a model. She died on 5 November, her portfolio incomplete.

Zappa spent the rest of that month at home in his basement, working on his projects.

By the end of the year, Zappa was itching for the road again. His music publishing company published the *Frank Zappa Songbook Volume 1* while Frank got himself a new Mothers together and a new tour lined up.

The new Mothers, number seven, comprised Zappa, Jean-Luc Ponty, Ian Underwood, Ruth Underwood, Bruce Fowler, Tom Fowler, Ralph Humphrey and George Duke. An excellent line-up.

The tour started in February (1973) and is described in groupie-ecstatic detail, through a bizarre aptness of fate, by a Nixonite lawyer called Craig Eldon Pinkus, whose name was to crop up in the outer ramifications of the Watergate opus. Pinkus ran a fanzine on Zappa called *The Mothers Home Journal*, and he managed to get himself invited along on the American lap of the very extensive tour the Mothers number seven undertook.

According to Mr Pinkus, the tour began in Fayetteville, North Carolina, where Zappa stayed at the Holiday Inn. Zappa was determined not just to play the major concert halls this time around but also a good many student campuses: he enjoyed being the famous man prepared to bring his music to the folks who live in out-of-the-way places. Witness his inclusion, on the Scandinavian lap of the tour, of Helsinki; not many rock 'n' roll stars played dates in Finland back then.

After the Fayetteville concert, Zappa sat in a Waffle House across the highway from the Holiday Inn and ate cream waffles. The band listened to their performance – the first the new line-up had given – on a cassette system. Zappa was very pleased with it.

'Listen,' he said, 'it's ten times as good as the debut gig from the last band.'

Next day, the entourage went by bus to Durham and gave a concert at Duke College that was especially good.* Then they flew to Atlanta, Georgia, and checked into another Holiday Inn where, to Frank's surprise and amusement, a sign hung up in the lobby declared WELCOME FRANK ZAPPA.

The Atlanta concert, on the 26th, was followed next day by a concert at the main State University of Georgia campus in Athens. Two days later, on 1 March, they hit Macon – still in Georgia. On the 3rd they did the first of two Florida dates, in Tampa; the second, in Miami itself, was on the 5th.

Following the same pattern, of one day on and one day off, they moved on to Memorial Hall, Columbus, Ohio, on the 7th, and by this time Zappa was sufficiently used to having Craig Eldon Pinkus along with them that he persuaded the lawyer to dance on stage during the concert.

The tour continued through America during April and May. In June it reached Australia, where a press conference in Melbourne on 28 June was followed by a concert invaded by

---

* The evidence is on the bootleg *Dupree's Paradise*.

the vice squad. Rock stars often had trouble in Australia.

The vice squad didn't actually *do* anything, they just came backstage after the first of the two Melbourne concerts and pushed people around a bit and were generally offensive – saying, for instance, to a black member of the entourage, 'You're not in America now, boy.' Zappa didn't like it one bit, checked out of his hotel and checked back in again under the name Steven Teech. The second concert went OK, with Zappa auditioning an Australian vocalist called Barry Leef in mid-concert. Afterwards, back in his hotel, one reporter noted the sounds of Zappa practising guitar inside his room, while a roadie named Marty got locked out in the nude with a backfiring fire extinguisher, and a *lot* of groupies found a lot of action. Zappa was back in the rock 'n' roll lifestyle he'd depicted in *200 Motels*. The wheelchair days were properly behind him. He was more than happy with the current Mothers, and altogether more outgoing than he'd been seen to be for a couple of years.

Zappa had told the press conference in Melbourne that already 'in production' were an album with the new line-up in the studios, another *Live In Australia* Mothers album and a new solo album. After Australia, they went back to the States to work on them.

The new studio Mothers album turned out to be *Overnite Sensation*, cut in Los Angeles at three studios – Paramount, Whitney and Boltic Sounds. The line-up for the album was an augmented touring line-up. Those listed as Mothers on the record were the tour band plus Sal Marquez, with Kin Vassy and Ricky Lancelotti getting billing as specific extras.*

In the press kit that emerged with the album, which was in September, there was a statement from Zappa that read: 'The new band doesn't sound anything like you've ever heard before. The instrumental combinations, the sonority of it is so strange . . . The way the tunes are voiced out, the violins will either be on the top or bottom of the chord, the clarinet is in the middle, sometimes alternating with the trombone and the upper edge is usually outlined by a marimba or vibes line. The drums often

---

* 'Lancelotti?' Zappa remarked in a subsequent interview. 'He auditioned, he passed his audition, he rehearsed for two weeks and flunked out. He sang a couple of times on one album.'

play the melody along with everybody else. All of this is accompanied by a harmony line or the duplication of the marimba line on a synthesizer. As you can see, there's lots of complicated lines being doubled all over the place – rhythmically and otherwise.'

As for *Live In Australia*, maybe it was just good PR for Zappa to mention such a thing at a Melbourne press conference. In any event, it never came out, although no doubt his Australian concerts were taped like all Zappa concerts are. God knows where he finds space to store it all back home in the basement, alongside his thousands of old r'n'b 45s and his piles of cuttings, books and equipment. The solo album – the third project mentioned at Melbourne – was to emerge in 1974 as *Apostrophe (')*.

Meanwhile, the tour went on. Zappa spent some time in the first part of August resting in London, preparing for the next lap and, as ever, doing interviews. He told Steve Peacock, then working for *Sounds*, that he was also currently engaged in editing the pre-*200 Motels* film that had been shot in March 1970 – the one of which he'd said at the time 'It's not about The Mothers, it's about something else.'

On 18 August, the tour reached Copenhagen. A day later, Gothenburg. Two days later, Stockholm. Two days after that, his debut concert in Helsinki. Three days later, Oslo. Another three days later, they had zoomed down to warmer weather and did concerts in Rome. Next day, Antibes. Next day, Bologna.

That brought them to the end of August. Without pause, 1 September had The Mothers playing Verona. On the 2nd, Zurich. The 3rd, Linchen. A day's rest. On the 5th, Frankfurt. Next day, Keulen; Brussels two days later; the day after that Amsterdam, and then across to France. The first French date was Lille on the 11th, followed by Paris on the 12th.

Hurrying across the Channel the tour played Birmingham Town Hall on 14 September and the day after that another big London gig, this time at the Empire Pool, Wembley.

Overnite Sensation was released to coincide with this tour. It proved at the time to be The Mothers' most commercially successful album (undeservedly, in my opinion); it was the first done in quadrophonic sound; and the first on the new label Zappa and Herb Cohen had set up, replacing the wound-up

Straight and Bizarre, named DiscReet. This was a combination of a misspelling of one of the quad systems' names – discrete – and the appending of the old Grand Wazoo word 'reet' with the basic word 'disc' to signify that they were going to be good records.

Herb Cohen explained the move to *Sounds* with admirable pith:

'There's no big difference between the new label and Straight/Bizarre except that we decided to combine those two companies into one – partly for economic reasons. Rather than drop one of the names, it seemed much more plausible to drop both and take on a new one. Bizarre fitted a different era, it fitted the sixties; but neither Zappa nor I are ego-involved with the word Bizarre – I don't feel it's something I'd want on my tombstone necessarily.'

In October, the tour moved back to the States and included dates in Austin, Texas and in Chicago, where The Mothers ended the month.

In November the American '73 Tour Lap Two continued through Detroit and Pittsburg and then took a route that jagged curiously up and down between New York State and Canada: 4 November at Brooklyn College, the 6th at Hofstra College in Long Island, the 9th in Syracuse, NY, the 11th at William Petterson College in Wayne, New Jersey; back to New York for a Rochester date on the 17th, in Ontario next day for a gig at Waterloo and another a day later in Hamilton, then back to hit Buffalo, New York on the 21st and the Lincoln Center's Philharmonic Hall on the 22nd; then back to Canada for a Toronto concert and a London, Ontario concert over the following two days; and then back to New York again for another Long Island gig, this time in Stony Brook.

That was on 1 December; on the 2nd they hit North Dartmouth in Massachusetts. Suddenly and quickly, the line-up changed again. Mothers number eight had lost Ian Underwood, though it retained his wife Ruth; it had also lost Jean-Luc Ponty, but had gained Napoleon Brock (tenor sax, flute and vocals), another drummer, Chester Thompson, to supplement Ralph Humphrey's work, and Walt Fowler (trumpet); it had also regained bassist Jeff Simmons.

With this line-up, somehow properly rehearsed within a week, The Mothers returned to LA and on 8 December played the first of several shows in a relatively small venue, the Roxy Club in Hollywood.

The gigs they played there on 10, 11 and 12 December were used as the basis of yet another Mothers album – and yet another live one, of course, at last – the 1974 release *Roxy & Elsewhere*. The elsewheres were to be a Mothers Day 1974 show at the Auditorium Theater in Chicago and a show on 8 May 1974 at Edinboro State College in Pennsylvania – by which time the line-up had shifted again. Mothers number nine, which toured from December 1973 till July 1974, consisted of Zappa plus a ten-piece group. Then it was sleeked down to a five-piece, made up of just Ruth Underwood, Tom Fowler, George Duke, Napoleon Brock and Chester Thompson.

It was an astonishing workload Zappa had ploughed through for the whole of 1973.

In January 1974, Zappa and the now-you-see-them-all-now-you-don't Mothers were still on the road – this time playing larger venues, like the 15,000-seater just down the road from the plush Windsor Arms Hotel, Toronto, where Zappa stayed while he was in town. At an American concert in March, James Euclid Motorhead Sherwood turned up. 'Seemed to be OK,' Zappa told me. And then, remembering something as if from a dream, he added: 'Hey, another guy who came to our concert – you know the song about "Let's Make The Water Turn Black"? Well we played it for an encore at the end of the second show, and standing there right in front of the stage was Ronnie! And I could barely recognize him. I mean, he was *totally* drunk and he had this knitted hat on and he was out there going "DO THE SONG ABOUT THE BOOGERS!", y'know, and I was doing "Who *is* this guy?" – and it was Ronnie!

'So I pulled him up onto the stage – and I had just explained the song to the band a few days before, and they were going; "Yuhk! You know a guy who saves snot on the window??!" and all this sort of thing – squeamish! – and next thing you know, he was up on stage with 'em: it was really funny.'

Early 1974 also saw the debut of his new label, DiscReet –

launched by Kathy Dalton's album *Amazing* (back-up by Little Feat) and by Ted Nugent and The Amboy Dukes' album *Call Of The Wild*. Each released another DiscReet album later in the year.

1974 continued for Zappa himself with the recording of some early bits of what became *Bongo Fury* in January and February, and with the finishing off of the solo album *Apostrophe (')*, which was, apart from that earlier session with Jack Bruce at Electric Ladyland in New York, recorded back at Boltic Sound – a small studio in Inglewood – Pamela Zarubica's home town – and back at Paramount in Hollywood.

The list of musicians credited on that album reads like a scrambled list of different era Mothers:

> DRUMS: Jim Gordon, Johnny Guerin, Aynsley Dunbar and Ralph Humphrey.
> BASS: Jack Bruce, Erroneous, Tom Fowler and Frank Zappa.
> KEYBOARDS: George Duke.
> VIOLIN: Don Sugar Cane Harris, Jean-Luc Ponty.
> PERCUSSION: Ruth Underwood.
> SAXOPHONE: Ian Underwood, Napoleon Murphy Brock.
> TRUMPET: Sal Marquez.
> TROMBONE: Bruce Fowler.
> BACK-UP VOCALS: Ray Collins [!!], Kerry McNabb, Susie Glover, George Duke, Debbie, Lynn, Napoleon Murphy Brock, Ruben Ladron De Guevara and Robert 'Frog' Camarena.
> LEAD VOCALS & ALL GUITARS: Frank Zappa.

The album was released in June of '74, and the same month Zappa's son Ahmet Rodan was born, joining his brother and sister Dweezil and Moon Unit. At the same time, Frank was reportedly looking for a girl 'with a strong voice and acting ability' to play the part of the Queen Of Cosmic Greed in yet another upcoming film project. The girl required, Zappa said, should also be 'adaptable to The Mothers' act'.

The *Apostrophe (')* album was promoted above and beyond

any previous Zappa release. For the first time, TV spots, devised by Frank and his cover art man Cal Shenkel, were used. It paid off, but whether the success of the album was due to TV advertising or to Zappa's intensive schedule of touring, it is hard to say. Either way, for the first time ever, Frank Zappa made the heady reaches of Billboard's album chart. On 29 June, it hit the Number Ten spot. True stardom! It was the tenth anniversary of the birth of The Mothers, and Zappa decided to celebrate. Warner executives looked out of their windows one morning at the beginning of July and found a 50-piece marching band parading up and down outside their building, led by Frank, Herb Cohen, DiscReet vice-president Harold Berkman and MC 'LA's own' Ed Barber.

The concerts kept on coming, including gigs at Constitution Hall in Washington DC, a show in New Orleans where Johnny Winter popped up backstage and stroked Frank Zappa's guitar, and three weekend gigs on 19-21 July at the non-rock venue, the Circle Star Theater in San Carlos.

In August, Zappa's face loomed large on the cover of *Cashbox* – a sign of the unprecedented commercial success of his album – while Frank himself spent a fortnight editing video tapes of concert performances.

In September, Zappa and The Mothers took off again, for another European tour, with which the *Roxy & Elsewhere* album was released to coincide. The tour started in Rome on 6 September and when it ended on 4 October it had passed through Udine, Palermo, Bologna, Milan, Vienna, Frankfurt, Berlin, Hamburg, Oslo, Stockholm, Copenhagen, Helsinki (where Zappa's guitar solo on that night's 'Inca Roads' was taken and used on the recording of that song issued later on the *One Size Fits All* album: extraordinarily, this solo was dropped in on the basic tracks, which were done live in a TV studio three months later – Zappa as editor achieving dazzling technical wizardry here), Gothenberg, Paris, Rotterdam, Brussels, Basle, Lyon, Marseilles and Barcelona.

The Mothers returned to the States after that, and later, in October, Frank was in New York, reportedly working on a new 'rock opera', to be called *Hunchenfoot*. At the end of the month, on Hallowe'en, still in New York, he completed another circle – another editing feat in the movie of his life – when he met Louise Varèse at a special dinner in the city. He wasn't there to socialize (naturally): he was playing two nights at the Felt Forum, having come in from a gig in Boston done on 29 October.

There were more US dates in November, and at some point Zappa also found time to 'read the news' on KOAZ Radio. Then at the end of the year, he and the band recorded a TV Special, called *A Token Of His Extreme*, produced by Mort Libov for KCET-TV in Los Angeles. The music was recorded in two in-concert sessions (later bootlegged as *Indiscreet Picture Show*) and when, the following summer, the *One Size Fits All* album came out, the sleeve notes reported that the basic tracks – which usually means drums and bass and could include rhythm guitar or equivalent – for two of the nine songs on the album had been taken from these TV sessions, December 1974.

For the television show itself, the concert shots were 'overlaid by optical effects and a trick film by Bruce Bickford was integrated.'*

Zappa began 1975 without drawing breath. Having seen the New Year in from the stage of the Long Beach arena, in January he flew to Cannes for MIDEM, the record industry's equivalent of the Film Festival, on unspecified business.

One of the people he met there was Guy Peelaert, the painter who created that distinctive book *Rock Dreams*. A film was to be made, based on this book. Would Zappa like to write the musical scores? Shooting would begin in the spring . . . Nothing further came of this project.

In March, back in America, The Mothers finished recording the *One Size Fits All* album (and the additional material released years later – in late 1978 – by Warner Brothers as the *Studio Tan* LP, issued without Zappa's permission). Zappa got on with mixing the *One Size Fits All* part, which he finished at the beginning of April.

Zappa was also preparing, in March, for the trial, to be held

---

* This TV special forms part of the video 'Dub Room Special'. The TV recording itself was 75 minutes long, though the amount originally transmitted was approximately one hour's worth.

Left: A Warner/Reprise publicity shot of 1976. Right: Paris, October 1974: Zappa at The Mothers' 10th Anniversary party. Below: With long time manager Herb Cohen, outside the Law Courts, Strand, London, April 1975.

Left: The Mothers Group 6. Back row: Jim Pons, Mark Volman and Howard Kaylan. Front row (behind Zappa): Aynsley Dunbar, Ian Underwood and Don Preston. Above: The Mothers Group 7. Back Row: Ralph Humphrey, Tom Fowler, Ian Underwood, George Duke, Jean-Luc Ponty. Front row: Bruce Fowler, Zappa and Ruth Underwood. Right: The Mothers Group 8. Back row: Napoleon Murphy Brock, Chester Thompson, Ruth Underwood, Tom Fowler, Jeff Simmons and George Duke. Front row: Ralph Humphrey, Zappa and Bruce Fowler.

The Mothers Group 9. Left to right: Ruth Underwood, Chester Thompson, Zappa, Jeff Simmons, Napoleon Murphy Brock, Tom Fowler and George Duke. Right: A Warner/Reprise publicity shot of 1976.

Above: On stage in Europe, 1977.
Left: The Zoot Allures band, 1976, soon after the abolition of The Mothers. Left to right: Terry Bozzio, Patrick O'Hearn, Frank Zappa, Eddie Jobson.
Right: Zappa not snorting coke.

EXTRA

WEATHER
Sunny & Warm

Hollywood Evening Bulletin

5 Star Final ★★★★★

PAGE ONE   THURSDAY, FEBRUARY 22, 1979   SECTION ONE

FRANK ZAPPA HAS ARRIVED!

The Artiste demonstrates the 'Sheik Yerbouti' motif

"Sheik Yerbouti" Shocks Nation As Artist Bows Zappa Records

Frank Zappa was the first figure in contemporary music to have created a devoted legion of loyal fanatics all over the world. He has been an innovator and pioneer on most artistic fronts than any pop musician of his generation: recordings, films, television, and live performances.

The concept album was a Zappa innovation, his 1965 double LP, "Freak Out," serving to introduce the Mothers of Invention. The union of modern orchestral forms with rock 'n roll was foreshadowed by Zappa in 1967, when the Mothers were complemented in an Albert Hall concert by ten members of the London Philharmonic. His combining rhythm and blues, rock and jazz with sophisticated compositional elements was years ahead of "fusion music."

Zappa's pioneering efforts in the visual media include a highly original (and highly successful) movie, 200 Motels, and an equally unique television show, A Token Of His Extreme, a Mothers concert overlaid with dazzling optical effects.

Zappa's conceptual and technical mastery of the guitar is a major business phenomenon and, indeed, he is one of the most complete electric guitarists in pop music.

Unlike those groups who view personnel changes as rocking the boat, Frank Zappa has matched changing musical moods with shrewd modification of his group's makeup. His sensitivity to the potential contribution of each musician's personality is admirable, as it his giving each musician an opportunity to expand, musically and theatrically, within the group context.

Each of the Zappa albums has existed in its own time frame while being linked to the previous one, a "conceptual continuity" that can be said to embrace the Frank Zappa film and television ventures as well. The unifying structure gives him conscious control of thematic and structural elements of his work. Long-time Zappa realists are deft at spotting cue turns, catch-words and musical themes that link various phases of Frank's work.

Other celebrated facets of the Zappa legend are a well-developed sense of humor, which includes a refreshing knack of laughing at himself, and an iconoclastic approach to modern conventions and hypocrisies. His integrity and individualism, which he refuses to lend to causes or mass movements, are hallmarks in an industry that thrives on imitation.

Two recent pictoral displays of Frank Zappa. At the top, we find the artiste addressing a New York City concert audience on the highly relevant social issues discussed in the "Sheik Yerbouti" album. Below, the artiste as he appears in his role as the "Broken Hearts Are For Assholes" poster boy.

Two A-Go-Go To Jail

Vice Squad Raids Local Film Studio

CUCAMONGA — Vice Squad investigators stilled the tape recorders of a free-swinging, a-go-go film and recording studio here Friday and arrested a self-styled movie producer and his buxom, red-haired companion.

Booked on suspicion of conspiracy to manufacture pornographic materials and suspicion of sex perversion, both felonies, at county jail were:

Frank Vincent Zappa, 24, and Lorraine Belcher, 19, both of the studio address, 8040 N. Archibald Ave.

The surprise raid came after an undercover officer, following a tip from the Ontario Police Department, entered the rambling, three-room studio on the pretext of wanting to rent a stag movie.

Sgt. Jim Willis, vice investigator of the San Bernardino County Sheriff's Office, said the suspect, Zappa, offered to do even better - he would film the movie for $300, according to Willis.

When Zappa became convinced the detective was "all right," he played a tape recording for him. The recording was for sale and it featured, according to police, Zappa and Miss Belcher in a somewhat "blue" dialogue.

Shortly after the sneak sound preview, the suspect's hopes for a sale were shattered when two more sheriff's detectives and one from the Ontario Police Department entered and placed the couple under arrest.

Zappa, who recently was the subject of a news story on his hopes to produce a low-budget fantasy film and thus bring a share of Hollywood's glamour to Cucamonga, blamed financial woes for his latest venture.

Inside his studio when the raid came was recording and sound equipment valued at more than $22,000, according to Zappa.

Also, a piano, trap drums, vibraphones and several electric guitars were stored among the Dailies litter of the main studio. On the walls, Zappa had such varied memorabilia as divorce papers, a picture of himself on the Steve Allen television show, a threat from the Department of Motor Vehicles to revoke his driver's license, several stag

publishers' rejection letters and works of "pop" art.

Among Zappa's completed musical scores were such titles as "Memories of El Monte" and "Streets of Fontana."

Arraignment for Zappa and Miss Belcher next week will bring them close to home.

Cucamonga Justice Court is right across the street from the studio.

The Artiste in a rare photo showing his knowledge of the French marital rite as he directs the bridal groom to the next phase of marriage.

LATE FLASH

Local resident Gail Zappa, wife of "pop" musician Frank Zappa, has announced that she will give birth to her fourth child on or about August 1, 1979. The expectant arrival will join the other Zappa children: Dweezil, Moon Unit, and Ahmet Rodan. No names for the child have been chosen yet.

Frank Zappa (left) and Steve Allen

'Bicycle Concerto'

Local Artiste, Steve Allen To Play Wacky TV Duet

Frank Zappa, 22, Ontario resident and composer of music, serious and otherwise, will be seen on television tomorrow night playing a bicycle concerto for two with Steve Allen.

The show is at 11 p.m., Channel 4.

"It's very funny," said Zappa. "You play a bicycle by plucking the spokes and blowing through the handle bars."

Other methods of producing "symphophony" are to stroke the spokes with the bow of a bass fiddle, twirl the pedals and let air out of the tires.

The Zappa Allen concerto will be abetted by a man in the control room fooling around with a tape recorder and by a jazz group which will supply toneless background noise.

Zappa studied music and art at Chaffey College. He wrote the score for "The World's Greatest Sinner," a low-budget tale about a sacrilegious impostor who repents. Zap-

ner" had its premiere at Vista Continental Theater, Hollywood, and opened Wednesday at the Ken Theater, San Diego.

Zappa writes musical commercials for TV and radio. They are recorded at Pal Studio, Cucamonga.

ZAPPA RECORDS

Distributed by CBS Records International

MANAGEMENT:
Glotzer Management
824 N. Robertson Blvd.
Los Angeles, CA 90069
213/278-8715

PUBLICISTS:
The Warloke Concern
250 W. 57th St.
New York, NY 10019
212/245-5587

Above: Publicity material (incorporating some very early Frank Zappa press-cuttings) issued by Columbia Records to trailer their deal with Zappa Records, marked by the release of Sheik Yerbouti, *1979.*

Right: Zappa in another silly hat – and communing with the sort of fan he likes best: it's bulbous, it's mechanical and it doesn't answer back.

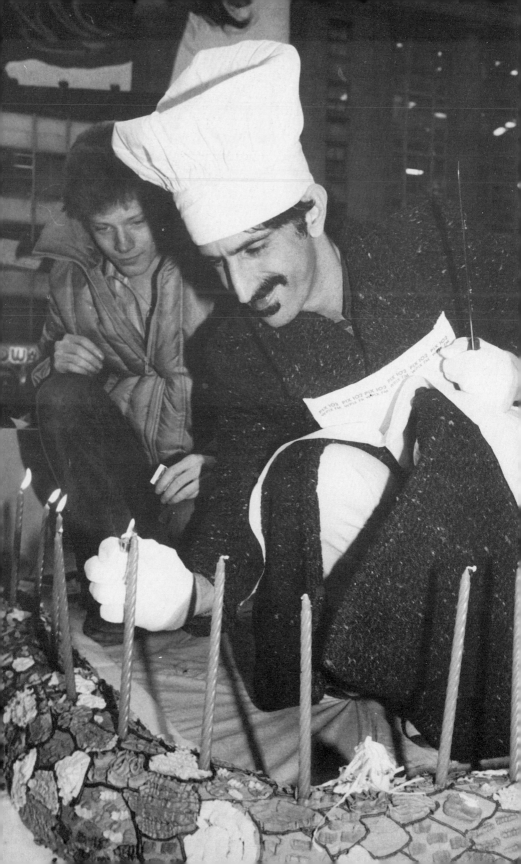

Left: Zappa's birthday snake. Frank publicises the New York City premiere of his film Baby Snakes *by serving slices of the 20-foot long snake-cake to passers-by from a flat-bed truck in Times Square on his 39th birthday, Friday 21st December, 1979.*
Above: Zappa with Dweezil (right) and Moon Unit (left).

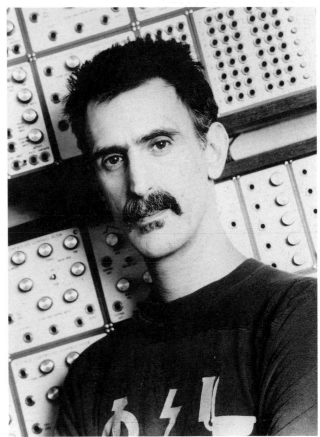

Left: Zappa and equipment truck, France, 1982
Above: During the question and answer session with the audience at 'An Evening With Pierre Boulez and Frank Zappa' at the Schoenberg Hall, UCLA, Los Angeles, 1989.
Right: Zappa at work in the Utility Muffin Research Kitchen, Los Angeles, 1986.

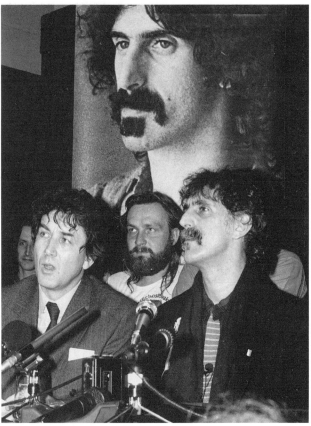

Above: Frank Zappa testifying at the Senate Hearings on 'rating' rock lyrics in 1986.
Left: Press Conference in Prague, November 1989.

Above: Cultural liaison in Prague, November 1989. Zappa somehow looks the most East-European of all of them.
Right: Press conference shared with musician-activist Michael Kocáb, Prague Sports Hall, 24th June 1991, during celebrations marking the departure of the Soviet army from Czechoslovakia. Left to right: Oudrej Hejma (Zappa's translator), Zappa, Michael Kocáb.

On stage at the Alte Oper, Frankfurt, September 1992, with the members of the Ensemble Modern after the premiere performance of 'The Yellow Shark'.

in April, of his case against the Royal Albert Hall. He gave his evidence early, staying at the Dorchester while he hung around, and also holding an evening press reception at a theoretically elegant little club in Mayfair – a club with some tiresomely cute, coy name like Tatters or Dimes or Tramp. Some place where if you *were* in tatters or only had a dime or were a tramp you wouldn't get past the door. This press reception was intended to preview the new then-unreleased album *One Size Fits All* but no-one could hear it above the chatter. Zappa sat quietly on one side of the room being accosted by journalists in twos and threes over a period of around three hours. When someone asked how he could bear to sit through it all trying to play an album that no-one was listening to, he just shrugged and asked what else could he do?

I'd asked him earlier, remarking that he'd shrewdly managed to combine the court case visit with a record company promotional trip, whether that meant that the cost of the trip was being borne by the record company. He said, as if pained: 'No, I pay. I'm paying for the trip and I'm paying for the court case. I'm not walking away from that court case – we waited long enough to get it into court. I'm not supposed to discuss it because it's *sub judice*, but isn't it fabulous? Can you believe those guys? But I have to be back in the States before it finishes because I'm playing Friday in Connecticut . . .'

He and the band did a series of American dates through April and May, opening at Claremont College on 11 April, and including Boston (27 April), St Louis (13 May) and the extravagantly named World Armadillo Headquarters in Austin, Texas, on 20 and 21 May.

The band now consisted of: Zappa, George Duke, Napoleon Murphy Brock, Denny Walley, Bruce and Tom Fowler, Terry Bozzio and – remarkably, after the years of public acrimony – Beefheart.

Beefheart was back to calling himself Don Van Vliet and he was an outstanding Special Mother on these American dates. The excellent results can be enjoyed on the *Bongo Fury* album, which was released later in the year and, briefly, on *One Size Fits All* where he is billed as Bloodshot Rollin' Red. All this was the first collaboration by these ex-schooldays cronies since

161

Beefheart's terrific vocal on 'Willie The Pimp' for Zappa's *Hot Rats* back in '69.

'Just before I came on this tour,' Beefheart told Miles, 'Frank and I had a get-together . . .' Zappa had wanted to know whether, after the intervening abuse, Beefheart still remembered the early days. 'And of course,' Beefheart reported, 'I remembered everything. I even remembered the little mouse that was living in the place he was living. It was a quiet little mouse. We used to feed it cheese.

'I hadn't spoken to him or seen him for five years. I was painting and writing and doing all those things, and I just hadn't come down to Southern California. The minute I came down there we went on a big tour. Ha, that was fun! I'd been with a group for so many years that it was nice to get away and be free again with a very intelligent person. A very old friend . . .

'I just called him up and told him I'd like to see him and he says, "Well, come on down and hear this album I'm working on," and I said, "Well, yeah, I'd like to but I've gotten out of the business!" . . . and he says "Oh no, you can't do that . . . come down and hear some records, you know; we'll go on a tour" . . .'

'When I went down he talked me into it real quick, because he started playing the guitar and I thought "Well, hell, I'm going!" Like the pied piper, I mean, to hear that thing every night? Hoho! . . . I think he's probably the best guitar player on this planet!'

Zappa's account of their reunion was ('of course,' as Miles notes) not the same at all. He said of Beefheart and events: 'He apologized for all the garbagio and asked for a job.' Zappa said Beefheart had 'auditioned' just before Hallowe'en in October of 1974, and that at the audition: 'He flunked. See, he had a problem with rhythm and we were very rhythm-oriented. Things have to happen on the beat. I had him come up on the bandstand at our rehearsal hall and try to sing "Willie The Pimp" and he couldn't get through it. I figured if he couldn't get through that I didn't stand much chance of teaching him the other stuff.'

Zappa said that what happened after that was that he tried

out Beefheart again in the spring of 1975, and found himself feeling: 'Although he still has trouble remembering words and making things happen on the beat, he's better.' So, in Zappa's words, 'he squeaked by' on the second audition and joined the tour.

Beefheart, on having Zappa's account of these events reported to him later, still contradicted them. He told Miles, with some surprise: 'Imagine there being an audition for people who've known one another for that many years. If he did audition me, I didn't notice!'

Whatever, Beefheart's presence on the tour (and subsequent LP) benefited everyone involved, not least Zappa. Its results were what many people felt to be the most creative and fresh period in Zappa's career for years. The combination of Zappa's outfit's tightness and extreme technical proficiency with Beefheart's inspired noises of the soul made for exhilarating, powerful music. Even the lyrics on the resulting *Bongo Fury* album are something fresh, prompted by feelings of dread at the then looming prospect of the USA's bicentenary celebrations, and carving out a theme from this. But it seems to me that the rejuvenated sharpness of Zappa's lyrics was also prompted by his rising to the challenge of Beefheart's writing for the album. The undimmed beacon of Beefheart's poetry, unique in the way it possesses a very fine scalpel, but under the control of an acid-laced brain, shines through *his* songs on *Bongo Fury*, the unarguable 'Sam With The Showing Scalp Flat Top' and 'Man With The Woman Head'.

The evidence that Zappa responded to Beefheart's unique kind of eloquence is there in the album's opening track, Zappa's song 'Debra Kadabra', where the writing is a marvellously resourceful embracing of Beefheart's trademarks and Zappa's ability to 'build things up'. It's a great album, and it would have been special to have been at the Austin, Texas concerts. That town is a hotbed of good music in any case.

It's a pity, but Beefheart dropped out of sight again after these early summer dates. The experience got him back in the rock business, though, and he was to put together a new album of his own, *Bat Chain Puller*, the following year, using, among others, Mother Denny Walley. This album was to become part of a huge contractual tangle that was to do no good for Beefheart *or* Zappa. It involved Virgin Records in England getting court injunctions to prevent Warners marketing *Bongo Fury* there in late '75. By mid-'76 Beefheart's album was in turn embroiled in the legal battles that had by then erupted as a result of Zappa firing his long-time manager Herb Cohen. This meant that lawsuits were flying around, ensnaring the Beefheart tapes, which Zappa held, according to him (though he hadn't produced the album), along with DiscReet Records, Warners and eventually Zappa's own next album, *Zoot Allures*, which had to be released on Warners' label, rather than Frank's DiscReet, because of this imbroglio. But this is a later story.

Back in the summer of 1975, the earlier and larger Mothers' album, *One Size Fits All*, was finally released in July. While Zappa's current projects were looking good, this seemed like a blast from the past and carried with it, somehow, the negative feeling of the era it had come from. It didn't sell well, particularly compared with the *Apostrophe (')* album of the previous year. When, later, he wrote the sleeve notes for the *Zappa In New York* LP, which re-used a song from *One Size Fits All* – 'Sofa' – he noted: 'Since that album was not very popular, this presentation might guide a few curious listeners back in that direction to check it out.'

In August, Zappa's *other* legal battle, the long-running one against MGM Records, finally got settled out of court. In tune with the change in Zappa's mood, he won most of what he'd wanted. He said of it: 'We made a settlement in which we get the masters back plus $100,000. But MGM gets a 3% over-ride on all future use of them.' He won because he was in the right. The basic argument was not about money but about what he saw as their butchery of his work: 'Of the five LPs I recorded for them, they repackaged eleven.'

In September, Zappa decided that though he'd won his fight against MGM, he would not, after all, appeal against the decision in the Royal Albert Hall case. He said, 'It's cost me $50,000 so far and the lawyers want another $15,000 to appeal. It's not worth it.'

Zappa turned his attention instead to a *new* project that demanded a large orchestra, as the Albert Hall concert had been planned to do. This time, though, Zappa was concentrating on his orchestral composing. He brought together 37 musicians, christened them the Abnuceals Emuukha Electric Orchestra and rehearsed them through early September.

Under the batons of Michael Zearot and Zappa, the Orchestra performed on two nights, 17 and 18 September, at the Royce Hall, UCLA, Los Angeles. (Among the musicians were Earl Dumler, Mike Altschul and Terry Bozzio.) The repertoire included: 'Strictly Genteel', 'Pedro's Dowry', 'Naval Aviation In Art', 'Duke Of Prunes', 'Bogus Pomp', 'Black Napkins', 'Dog Breath', 'Dog Breath Variations', 'Revised Music For Guitar & Low Budget Orchestra', 'Kollo', 'Sink Trap', and 'Uncle Meat'.

As one example of Zappa's infinite interweaving of his work, this list is worth thinking through, tracing the strands.

The first five songs on the list were later released, taken from these concerts, on the Warners album *Orchestral Favorites*, issued as late as May 1979, after he'd signed to CBS.* But he'd very possibly have done something similar with them anyway; and of these five, the first is a re-working of a *200 Motels* song; the second, though new then, is itself re-worked on the far more recent orchestral work recorded and performed at the Barbican, London, with the London Symphony Orchestra, in January 1983; the third is new; the fourth retreads *Absolutely Free* LP territory from right back in '66; and the fifth, 'Bogus Pomp' is new – and while *it* is *not* re-worked on the 1983 LSO recordings, Zappa still invoked it as having a perennial yet very specific applicability. He told Karl Dallas:

'I think humour belongs everywhere. You have a pretty dismal world out there and there's no reason why you shouldn't have a laugh when you go to an orchestral concert . . . I think that, for example, the piece "Bogus Pomp" ought to be standard orchestral repertoire because it's a good work-out for the orchestra, not just in terms of the technique that they have to have in order to play it correctly, but it gives them a chance to

---

* Zappa intended to end his Warners contract with a 4-LP set called *Lather*. However, the company hacked this up into *In New York* and three LPs issued without his permission – *Sleep Dirt*, *Studio Tan* and *Orchestral Favourites*. Some material intended for *Lather* remains unreleased.

show off, it puts a little fun into the show, and it's a nice piece of music because there's all these little surprises in it: and it's a virtuoso piece.'

Back at the Royce Hall, in September 1975, the Abnuceals Emuukha Electric Orchestra got its work-out on 'Bogus Pomp' and the others that were to turn up, as noted, on the later *Orchestral Favorites* LP. Tracing through the lines of the rest of the songs from their repertoire – the ones that didn't surface on that album – this is how they lie: 'Black Napkins' had been pre-mièred as a rock number in the Zappa/Beefheart/Mothers tour back in the spring, and a *later* live version, recorded in Japan in February 1976, was to be released on the otherwise *studio*-recorded *Zoot Allures* album later that year; 'Dog Breath' had first appeared as a Mothers single in 1969 and then on the 1972 *Just Another Band From LA* album, done in the Flo and Eddie period; but 'Dog Breath' was also a variation on 'Dog Breath Variations', which itself recurred in this 1975 orchestral reper-toire and was a revisit to material first released back in 1969 on *Uncle Meat* – which was itself actually recorded much earlier still, between October 1967 and February 1968.

Completing the strands, 'Rollo' was new; 'Sink Trap' was a piece first recorded at the *Lumpy Gravy* orchestral sessions done at Capitol Studios in Hollywood in late 1966 and was planned, coupled with the piece 'Gypsy Airs' from the same sessions, as a single on Capitol, before that deal was aborted by MGM; and finally, the Abnuceals Emuukha Electric Orchestra performances/recording of 'Revised Music For Guitar And Low Budget Orchestra' in September 1975 was a revision of the 'Music For Electric Violin And Low Budget Orchestra' on the Jean-Luc Ponty album of 1970, the full title of which makes Zappa's involvement clear: *King Kong: Jean-Luc Ponty Plays The Music Of Frank Zappa/Music For Electric Violin And Low Budget Orchestra*. Later – after the jazz version on the Ponty album and the 1975 orchestral Zappa/Abnuceals version – Warner Brothers released a rock version on *Studio Tan* (1978), this one again entitled 'Revised Music For Guitar & Low Budget Orchestra' and having been recorded by Zappa and The Mothers of the *One Size Fits All* period. Oh, and of course, finally-finally, The Abnuceals Emuukha Electric Orchestra was also the name Frank Zappa had given, all those years earlier, to the musicians he scooped together for that 'original' post-Cucamonga orchestral project, *Lumpy Gravy*.

The autumn of 1975 continued a good year for Zappa and his work. The orchestral concerts went down well, perhaps revealing that his scoring had taken another leap forward. Then in October, the excellent Zappa/Beefheart/Mothers album *Bongo Fury* came out in the States, and by the second half of the month, a newly-pruned line-up was out on the road for Zappa's return to rock concert-work. If it was a shame that Beefheart was not still with them, he was not the only change. The Mothers were now just Zappa, Napoleon Murphy Brock, Terry Bozzio, newcomer session man Andrew Lewis and, back again, our very old friend Roy Estrada.

On 1 November, Zappa did another re-edit job on the past. He did a special broadcast on radio KWST and played tapes which proved to be an aural surprise picnic indeed for Zappa fans. There was: 'Metal Man Has Hornet's Wings' by The Soots (with Beefheart), 1963!; three 1964 Cucamonga instrumentals and versions of something called 'Sandwich Song' and 'Rock Around The Clock'; a pre-*Freak Out!* version of 'How Could I Be Such A Fool'; the very first live recording of The Mothers – 'Whisky Gone Behind The Sun', from the Broadside Bar, Pomona, 1964; 'Mondo Hollywood', recorded live in Hollywood, 1965; and more besides.

From the broadcasting of that material on 1 November 1975, a bootleg album was packaged and released later under the title *Confidential*.

The same week as the broadcast, the London office of Warner Brothers (WEA Records Ltd) issued a statement about the contractual mess that had now emerged in Britain over Beefheart's involvement in the *Bongo Fury* album while Virgin Records Ltd, the independent label of rock's Freddie Laker, Mr Richard Branson, considered Beefheart to be theirs. The Warners statement was clipped: 'Virgin Records Ltd this week obtained in the High Court a renewal of the injunction against WEA Records Ltd and DiscReet Records Ltd, restraining the sale of the new Frank Zappa/Captain Beefheart album *Bongo Fury*. The hearing will take place in due course in the High Court.'

167

Virgin's action stopped Warner Brothers from releasing *Bongo Fury* in Britain. The British music press was given US import copies, and later, imports became generally available in Britain.

So ended 1975.

The following year, The Mothers were to end. So was Zappa's long association with manager Herb Cohen. It was also the end of Zappa's control over DiscReet Records.

Not that 1976 began badly. Zappa, ever the workaholic, started off on another round of his six-months-of-the-year touring, beginning in January with Australia, and still using the small five-piece Mothers from the previous autumn's US gigs. This unit still included Roy Estrada.

In February they played Japan (recordings done in Japan of 'Black Napkins' and 'Ship Ahoy' surfaced later on, respectively, the *Zoot Allures* and *Shut Up 'N Play Yer Guitar* albums).

When Zappa got back to the States he was in good spirits and did some good interviews. One of these was for *Guitar Player* magazine and contained much vivid stuff.

There was technicality galore, and sometimes people can be lured into such stuff by small samplers:

'GP: Are there any devices which you've developed for the guitar?

FZ: There's one thing a guy named Bob Easter constructed for me called the Electro Wagnerian Emancipator. It's a very attractive little device that combines a frequency follower with a device that puts out harmony notes with what you're playing. You can have your choice of any twelve chromatic notes in four parts following your runs . . . Its main drawback is that the tone that comes out of it is somewhat like a Farfisa organ.'

There is informative stuff when Zappa talks of other guitarists and himself. On Eric Clapton's contribution to the *We're Only In It For The Money* album:

'FZ: I invited him over to the studio to do the rap that's on [the album]. People think he's playing on it but he's

not: the only thing he's doing on there is talking.
GP: Did the two of you ever sit down and trade ideas on guitar?
FZ:. . . When I used to live in a log cabin I had some amps set up in my basement and he came over one day and played during one of our rehearsals but he didn't like the amp. We were using Acoustics then and he didn't like them. And remember when he came on stage at the Shrine? Nobody knew who he was. He came out and played the set and nobody paid any attention to him at all, until he walked off and I told the audience that was Eric Clapton.'

And on John McLaughlin, who had recently been superstar of the month:

'FZ: A person would be a moron not to appreciate McLaughlin's technique. The guy has certainly found how to operate a guitar as if it were a machine gun. But I'm not always enthusiastic about the lines I hear or the way in which they're used . . .
GP: How do you see your role as a guitarist different from that of a Beck or a McLaughlin?
FZ: I think that's a matter of advertising more than anything else. Once I get out onstage and turn my guitar on, it's a special thing to me – I love doing it. But I approach it more as a composer who happens to be able to operate an instrument called a guitar, rather than Frank Zappa, Rock'n'Roll Guitar Hero.'

As well as doing interviews, Zappa involved himself in the already-discussed Beefheart album-in-the-making, *Bat Chain Puller*, and by July was producing an album for that much-derided American equivalent of Status Quo, Grand Funk Railroad. (Zappa also plays guitar on the track 'Out To Get You'.) The album was called *Good Singin', Good Playin'*. Zappa maintains to this day that he likes it. On the other hand Grand Funk Railroad disbanded soon after the album's release. Zappa offered the drummer, Don Brewer, a job in *his* band. (In the event, he appeared only on a one-night jam at the end of one concert.)

The band Zappa invited him to join was not the slim five-piece unit of recent months – because Zappa had now disbanded that: and when he did so, he announced that it had been the very last Mothers. He was dropping the name. From now on, instead of doing some albums as Frank Zappa and The Mothers, and some albums as Frank Zappa plus-whatever-musicians, from this point on the single word Zappa would not only serve as his name but as the band's name too. (The following year, kept from control of DiscReet by a characteristic tangle of lawsuits, he founded a new label. This too was named Zappa.)

He explained the band name-change to Miles, less than help-fully: 'Any resemblance between this group and the original Mothers Of Invention is purely conceptual. The kind of things we're doing now are very differnt.'

This different new band consisted at first of Terry Bozzio (one ex-Mother retained) on drums and vocals; Ray White on guitar and lead vocals; Patrick O'Hearn on bass and vocals ('he comes to us from the world of jazz,' Zappa proclaimed suspiciously); Eddie Jobson on multiple keyboards. She did just two gigs and was then 'no longer with us. I let her go.'

He'd let go the other ex-Mothers too.

So. Farewell then, Napoleon Murphy Brock. And farewell Andre Lewis. Au revoir Roy Estrada (for you will be back in a later line-up, whatever its name). Au revoir Roy. Goodnight Mothers.

7. None Of The Above/ The Ocean Is The Ultimate Solution:

The S.S. Zappa Sails Alone

Since the demise of The Mothers in 1976, Frank Zappa's work has more than ever formed the main, almost the only, part of his life. He has more and more come to see musicians as purchasable units, like video-editing suites or new speakers, in among the rest of the big baggage of accoutrements the present-day composer needs to finance, handle and utilize in the course of his working life. Or perhaps even *doesn't* need, in the case of rock musicians. The 1986 release *Jazz From Hell* would be made, with the exception of one track, entirely on the Synclavier, dispensing with musicians altogether yet sounding like a whole bunch of them.

The name The Mothers carried implications of togetherness, indispensability and communal participation which had long ceased to correspond to Zappa's *modus operandi*. It had been years since he'd discussed strategy or musical plans with the group. He'd long since become the straightforward paymaster, with the others the hired hands, as he had many times stressed himself. He'd long since ceased to stay in the same hotels as the other musicians when they were touring. Even with the original Mothers of the mid-to-late-sixties, the consistent tension within the group was between the Mothers' shambling group-consciousness – laid-back, communal, egalitarian, good-time, unambitious, pliable, pop-group-orientated – and Frank's indomitable boss-consciousness – individualistic, hierarchical, ambitious, unmalleable, control-freakish, composer-orientated.

The various assorted line-ups that came to be called Mothers in the 1970s sometimes seemed on a more equal footing with Zappa because he'd chosen them for their technique-based musicianship – so that they were in this respect perceived by Zappa, themselves and the audience as more on an equal footing than the old hoofers from days of yore – yet they were there to be hired and fired. The 'Mothers' tag was a misleading umbrella-title that in reality served only to emphasize the primacy of Zappa's own musical history and career, and jumps such as that from the Kaylan-Volman line-up at the start of the 1970s to the jazz-group centred around the Underwoods three years later underlined that for Zappa a line-up of musicians was an episode in a career that devises and then passes through many episodes. A line-up of musicians is an enabling factor in the making of a Zappa album, or in the staging of a Zappa live-performance, or a handy influence as to the boundaries of, or musical colorations in, a particular composition. 'I respect musicians' idiosyncracies – they add "texture" to a performance,' he notes in his book, soon after defining a composer as 'a guy who goes around forcing his will on unsuspecting air molecules, often with the help of unsuspecting musicians'.

The decision to stop calling them The Mothers and just call everything Zappa as from 1976 was simply a decision to express an already long-established truth. Zappa pointed out that anyone could join his group if they could pass an audition:

'I get cassettes, letters, musical scores, from all over the world because I have the only group which is important and long-lasting, which anybody can join if they're good enough. I audition everybody who comes up, and I'm the only one who offers this opportunity. There's no way that you could join a band like Led Zeppelin, but musicians know that my door is never closed.'

Of course, this also means that the door out the other side again is never closed either. That said, it's also true that once out doesn't have to mean always out. Original Mother Roy Estrada actually rejoined Zappa for the world tour of 1975–6, and for subsequent appearances on *Baby Snakes*, *The Man From Utopia* and *Them Or Us*. Some people keep up their feuds with Zappa, and some manage reconciliation. Some people – Jimmy Carl Black, for one – somehow manage both simultaneously. Re-recruited for one song on 1981's *You Are What You Is*, and by his own admission well-paid for it this time around, ten years later he was to be heard complaining again: because having been paid to be on one song, he ended up on several without extra payment. According to Dominique Chevalier, the only person Zappa truly hates is Jean-Luc Ponty.

Bitterness and dispute were certainly the salient features of the last years of the 1970s. Zappa and Beefheart fell out again after *Bongo Fury*; more injurious to Zappa's ability to get on with his work were a new set of business disputes. After a world tour from October 1975 to March 1976, Zappa terminated his dealings with Herb Cohen – which, according to Dominique Chevalier, meant Zappa couldn't use his film and tape archives any more, and indeed didn't get these back until 1982. DiscReet was effectively removed from Zappa's control.

1976 also saw the release of the *Zoot Allures* album in November (a single-LP originally intended as a double called *Night Of The Iron Sausage*). This was the last Mothers album, and featured the final (twenty-fourth) Mothers line-up – the one that had done the 1975–6 world tour: Napoleon Murphy Brock on tenor-sax and vocals, Andre Lewis (formerly an engineer on Zappa albums) on keyboards and vocals, Roy Estrada on bass and vocals and Terry Bozzio on drums and vocals. Its release coincided with gigs with a new line-up in the States, in which only Terry Bozzio was retained, this time joined by funk-guitarist Ray White, jazz bass-player Patrick O'Hearn and ex-Curved Air and Roxy Music keyboard and violin-player Eddie Jobson (who, Zappa's tour press-kit noted, lent the band 'a sort of damp English charm, smothered in rosy-cheeked appeal'). Rumours were also rife that Zappa had been locked out of his studio by Herb Cohen and that lawsuits were flying. These were true. Two years later he told one of the music papers that he was still suing Cohen and didn't expect it to come to court for another three to five years.

The American leg of the 1976–7 world tour had begun in October, and ran through until December, when some end-of-year gigs had the group augmented by a horn section, Don Pardo and, giving her last Zappa performances, Ruth Underwood. These shows included an appearance on the TV programme 'Saturday Night Live', with John Belushi popping up during 'The Purple Lagoon' dressed as a Be-Bop Samurai Warrior, and culminated in New York City performances that ended with the screening of a slide that read 'Warner Brothers Record Company Sucks'. Zappa constructed the *Zappa In New York* double-album, released in March 1977 on the DiscReet label through Warner Brothers, from these performances.

Warners interfered with the artist's work by removing the track 'Punky's Whips', in case it was libellous. It thereby became something especially sought-after; in 1991, when the CD 're-issue' of *In New York* was released, many who had waited years to hear it were disappointed to find it just another of Frank's lubricious smut-sagas about the sexual proclivities of a musician, and about as engaging to the intellect as 'Billy The Mountain'.

The smaller version of the group then began 1977 with a two-month European tour, starting mid-January. It was unusual in having far fewer set-variations than on your average Zappa tour, but on the other hand many fans welcomed the smallness of the group – 'thus forcing him to actually *play*,' as the UK fanzine *T'Mershi Duween* argued, 'and not just sit around watching the band work out, as he became prone to do'.

That summer, unsurprisingly, Zappa announced that his contract with Warners had expired. He said he'd delivered the albums he owed them in March. As for the Cohen case, was there any bitterness, he was asked?

'Oh yeah, quite a bit.'

He said that his new manager was Bennett Glotzer, who had been manager of Procol Harum, Janis Joplin and Blood Sweat And Tears. He also said he'd acquired a bodyguard: a very large black gentleman called Mr Smothers. Mr Smothers, we were told, sat in on all interviews these days. Later, we learnt that his name was John.

Zappa kept on touring, running through another 'world tour' with a band that comprised a retained Terry Bozzio and Patrick O'Hearn, plus, in place of the others, Adrian Belew, Tommy Mars, Peter Wolf and Ed Mann. Mann was to last through three line-ups, leave after the 1979 Europe tour and then return for 1981-2 and again for the 1987 rehearsals and the 1988 tour;

Mars, with the exception of the 1984 tour, was to last right through till the rehearsals for '88, when he walked out after 'abuse' from Zappa. Wolf was to quit after the early-1979 Euro-dates; Belew, the shortest-surviving member, whom Zappa found playing in a Nashville club and recruited, lasted only for this one tour, though this meant he got onto *Sheik Yerbouti* – where he does the Dylan parody on 'Flakes' – *Baby Snakes* and *You Can't Do That On Stage Anymore Vol. I*.

Zappa did a heavy pitch at Britain in 1978, despite saying how he'd always hated it after being pushed off the stage of the Rainbow ('a miserable little island off the coast of France,' he calls it in *The Real Frank Zappa Book*), selling out four dates at the Hammersmith Odeon. 'Not bad for an old hippie in '78,' he remarked, though he could have noted that another 1960s star who'd never really been a hippie either, Bob Dylan, managed to sell out six dates at Earls Court in the same height-of-punk year. Zappa's new band (out were Bozzio, O'Hearn and Belew; in were Arthur Barrow, Denny Walley, Vinnie Colaiuta and Ike Willis) and the roadies were raided by the police at 5.30 one morning at the band's hotel. The police used wire-cutters to break the hotel-room door-chains. Tommy Mars and Ike Willis were taken barefoot and in handcuffs to the police station. Three others were also arrested. All were later released, four of them on bail 'pending analysis of certain substances'. Zappa slept on unconcernedly in the seclusion of a different hotel and of his own career-long drug-free zone.

Then, just as Dylan went off to Europe after Earl's Court and then came back to Britain to do Blackbushe, so Zappa went off and came back in the summer to play the Knebworth Festival, remarking to the crowd, 'I guess some of you out there were conceived at this sort of thing.' Gail told a timid young reporter not to call her Mrs Zappa: 'You make it sound like I'm his mother.' (Gail sometimes came to major gigs – she was, for instance, around to take the photos for the sleeve of *Zappa In New York* at the end of 1976, and she was to be around in Paris for the concerts there in February 1979, but she never stayed around for a whole tour.)

In Europe Frank and the band made TV appearances in Sweden, Austria, and, in Germany, the hour-long 'We Don't

Mess Around', from Munich. In the autumn, they toured America again, with Ike Willis dropped for the last few dates and Patrick O'Hearn brought back in. In New York, as in Berlin earlier on, there were guest appearances by violinist Lakshmirnarayna Shankar, for whom Zappa would produce an album the following year. The New York Hallowe'en shows also marked the first appearance as a guitarist of long-term teenage Zappa fan and amateur musician Warren Cucurullo, who had already learnt all his mentor's solos. He passed another audition later and joined the band on the European tour of early 1979. His on-stage function was to take some of the guitar-playing and 'comedy' off Zappa's shoulders, leaving Frank free to sit at the side of the stage, drinking coffee, smoking Winston cigarettes and listening to the music, like some dissipated high-school music-teacher overseeing the efforts of his pupils. When Cucurullo left, it was to form the band Missing Persons along with ex-Zappoids Terry Bozzio and Patrick O'Hearn; later Cucurullo joined Duran Duran.

At this stage, Zappa considered himself free of a record contract. There was a period of some months when it seemed he would sign with Virgin in Britain. He talked with Richard Branson but the sticking-point was Branson's lack of enthusiasm for the nine/ten/12-volume set. At the same time Warners followed *In New York* (which had not received good critical notices) with some of the rest of the material Zappa had intended for the 4-LP set *Lather*, assembling and issuing without consultation *Studio Tan* in October 1978 – including some fine guitar and some George Duke keyboards on 'Redunzl', and 'Greggary Peccary' – and a ragbag of recordings from 1974 and 1976 on *Sleep Dirt* at the beginning of 1979. Finally they released the material from Zappa's orchestral foray of 17 and 18 September 1975 with the Abnuceals Emuukha Electric Orchestra as *Orchestral Favorites* in June 1979, conceding that it was 'Frank Zappa's final album for DiscReet Records after a relationship with the company [i.e. Warner Brothers] that stretches back some ten years.'

Plans to have more of his orchestral work recorded – he had been chasing the Vienna Symphony Orchestra – fell through. This revival of concentration on this aspect of his work centred around material he'd been writing since 1975. A modified version would come about with the London Symphony Orchestra at the Barbican in 1983. It was put to Zappa back in the autumn of 1978 that the project was extremely expensive. Usually the first to make that very complaint himself, on this occasion he retorted: 'Well, some rock'n'roll musicians make a bunch of money and stick it up their noses. I stick mine in my ear.'

While he was free of a record-deal, Frank also played guitar for the ex-members of Grand Funk Railroad on their album *Flint* (that was their new group-name), issued on Columbia (1978), and ended 1978 by taking part in the 'Nova Convention' that celebrated the work of William Burroughs at the Intermedia Theater in New York. He was in mixed avant-gardeist company here, with Philip Glass and John Cage. The former is a pioneer of the minimalist movement in 'serious' music that Zappa was later to disparage in *The Real Frank Zappa Book*; the latter shared with Zappa a championing of the work of Conlon Nancarrow, whom Frank first name-checks on 1981's *Tinseltown Rebellion*. Zappa had first come across Cage in person when he came to Pomona College in Zappa's pre-Mothers years and gave a music-demonstration that Frank remembered as mostly Cage gargling with carrot-juice; three decades later Zappa and Cage would both receive invitations to the Frankfurt Music Festival of 1992: but by the time of the Festival, Cage had died (in August 1992) and Zappa himself was admitting he was suffering from cancer. Performance-artists Laurie Anderson, Ed Sanders and Patti Smith, and poets including Allen Ginsberg also took part in the 'Nova Convention'. Zappa contributed a reading from the 'talking asshole' in Burroughs' *Naked Lunch*. Extracts from this performance (2 December 1978) were released on John Giorno's label Giorno Poetry Systems in 1979.

Speculation that Zappa would sign to Virgin was ended when he signed instead another major-label deal. In the USA, Mercury/Phonogram would distribute the Zappa Records label; for the rest of the world, it would be distributed by CBS Records. This would turn out to be his last-but-one major-label deal (so far). To begin with, Zappa relished the encouragement of a new deal and a new and powerful major's enthusiasm, plus his release from a long period of contractual uncertainty and its attendant hindrances to work.

The first project under the new deal was *Sheik Yerbouti*, a double-album, which featured five basic tracks recorded live in the US and Europe during 1978 and overdubbed at Village Recorded studios in New York. There was no American tour in 1979, but *Sheik Yerbouti* was released during an early-1979 European tour, with a band that now included Warren Cucurullo. A pregnant Gail was on the road with Frank on the first part of the tour, flying home after the Paris shows (two evening shows and a matinee in the gruesome 'tent' that is the Hippodrome; sordid details as documented in the subsequent 'in France' on *Them Or Us*). The tour also included London's Hammersmith Odeon, Glasgow in February, and Scandinavia in March, and was notable for visiting smaller towns – Brest and Cambrai in France, for instance – as well as the big cities. The line-up on this tour would be heard later on *Shut Up 'N Play Yer Guitar*, *Guitar*, *You Can't Do That On Stage Anymore Vol. I* and the largely awful *Tinseltown Rebellion*.

If the title for the new album, *Sheik Yerbouti*, a punning allusion to a pop hit single by the forgettable K.C and the Sunshine Band, offended Arabists, one of the songs inside it achieved the balance of offending the Zionists. The Anti-Defamation League of the B'nai B'rith in Pasadena filed a complaint with the Federal Commission following heavy airplay of the song 'Jewish Princess' on the city's KROQ radio-station. The airplay stopped. The League's attorney, David Lehrer, declared in April: 'There's no doubt that the words are anti-semitic and that they promote offensive stereotypes, but the basis for the complaint is obscenity.'

Zappa came out fighting: 'I see it as a question of censorship. The ADL is perpetuating the primitive concept that words can corrupt you. Who are they to decide? If you don't like it, you can turn it off . . . The lyrics [sample: 'I want a nasty little Jewish princess / . . . A horny little Jewish princess / With a garlic aroma that could level Tacoma'] are accurate in terms of Jewish princesses. I'm not the first to make a comment on that phenomenon . . . if it will make them feel better, we're going . . . to record a song called "Catholic Girls". It will be just as true of Catholic girls as "Jewish Princess" is of Jewish princesses.'

Sheik Yerbouti also trod familiar ground with 'Dancin' Fool', which re-stated the theme of the earlier 'Disco Boy' and became a moderately successful single. The album also included 'Baby Snakes' and 'City Of Tiny Lites', and these pointed the way to another Zappa project – a return to the arena of the music *movie*, this time to be called *Baby Snakes*.

Frank hustled it as 'a not normal film about not normal people'. It has interviews with the not normal, interspliced with musical sections taken mainly from *Sheik Yerbouti*, and with the reactions of an audience to the music and to the interviews.

Zappa drew into the film Bruce Bickford, the extraordinary animator he had first come across at the time of the 'A Token Of His Extreme' TV Special in 1975 (which, incidentally, had still only been screened in France, West Germany and Switzerland – you'd think that if the Swiss could take it, so could the USA, but still). Bickford, who works in clay, provides a devastating animation section for *Baby Snakes*, matched up perfectly with the threatening-clouds music of 'City Of Tiny Lites' to produce a truly horror-spiked nightmare, in which as two clay men watch a film, the head of one turns into a hamburger that bites off the other's head, and then every predatory, devouring twitch of clay churns into some other multiplying, frantic thing – all this hamburgerizing of heads and lethal metamorphosis being achieved by convulsions of dissembling clay, giving the viewer something like an alimentary-canalside view of approaching spaghetti and chocolate mousse.

Baby Snakes offers other animation sequences too, plus Zappa interviewing Bickford and skilfully drawing out the genius and lunacy of the man. The completed film was to be premièred at the Victoria Theater on Broadway three nights before Christmas the same year (1979) and in Paris in 1981 was to be awarded the Premier Grand Prix for a musical film at the First International Music Film Festival. (It has now been released on Zappa's video imprint, Honker Home Video.)

Zappa's consistency is quite something. Here he was, at the end of the 1970s, years and years after the Cucamonga porn bust, and eight years after the cancellation on grounds of

179

obscenity of the Royal Albert Hall concert that was intended to promote the music-film *200 Motels*, fighting a censorship battle all over again because of a track on *Sheik Yerbouti* – and still making highly individualistic music-films.

He also spent a month in London rehearsing his band and at the same time producing Lakshmirnarayna Shankar's album *Touch Me There*. Four of the songs were jointly by Shankar and Zappa and, performing under the pseudonym Stucco Homes, Zappa sang on one of these, 'Dead Girls Of London'. (Van Morrison happened to be in the same studios at the time and agreed to do lead vocals on this song, but permissions were never sorted out and this version wasn't released. It remains in the Zappa vaults for possible inclusion in a future mega-set with the working title *The Lost Episodes*.) The album came out on the new Zappa Records label.

In August Gail gave birth to a fourth child, joining Moon Unit, Dweezil and Ahmet Rodan. The *Daily Mail* quoted Zappa as announcing: 'If it's a boy we'll call him Burt Reynolds and if she's a girl she'll be called Clint Eastwood.' The baby was a girl and in the end Frank called her Diva. 'Frank gets to name them: I have them,' Gail told Victoria Balfour in an interview for her book *Rock Wives*.*

In December came the *Baby Snakes* film première, as mentioned above, plus the release of the second Zappa album under his new deal, the 'concept album' that did indeed include the promised 'Catholic Girls', *Joe's Garage Act I*. The title track is a stand-out narrative about the struggles and fortunes over many years of a fashion-following beat combo, in the course of which Zappa and the band provide musical parodies of successive styles that are brilliantly accurate in themselves, and brilliantly produced and mixed into a seamless, elaborate, sustained aural parade that gives you a whole history of pop from doo-wop and garage-bands to heavy metal in a few deft minutes.

Zappa returned to London in January 1980, to promote both his film and his new album. He stayed at the Hyde Park Hotel, had a stomach ailment and sipped herbal tea.

In June he was back again, playing two dates at Wembley as

---

* Beech Tree Books, New York, 1986; Virgin Books, London, 1986.

part of the European leg of a tour that began in North America in March and continued in Europe until August. A two-hour Paris concert in July was telecast 'Live From Palais Des Sports' and nearly an hour's worth of concert in Holland was televised there as 'More Than A Concert'. Zappa used another permutation of musicians: retaining Tommy Mars, Arthur Barrow and Ike Willis but re-introducing Ray White (three years after his previous inclusion) and introducing the short-lived David Logeman on drums.

In August Frank went back into the studio in the States and then played the US autumn tour, which introduced the future heavy-metal star-guitarist Steve Vai in a line-up that, though based around the earlier one of 1980, saw the return of Vinnie Colaiuta, back again in place of David Logeman, and of Bob Harris, back after a *nine-year* absence. This group's dates included Hallowe'en at the New York Palladium, which seemed to be becoming a tradition, and ended up in California in December. Steve Vai was first taken on as a music-transcriber, after introducing himself to Zappa by transcribing 'The Black Page' and sending it to him. He went on to transcribe all of the guitar-solos that ended up in *The Guitar Book* (Munchkin Music, Los Angeles, 1982: 300 pages of guitar-solos from five different albums from *Zoot Allures* to *Shut Up 'N Play Yer Guitar* and *You Are What You Is*). In a 1990 interview, Vai said that to learn the difficult Zappa guitar parts, he taped them and then played them on headphones in his sleep.

Some of this tour's renditions saw the light of day on *Tinseltown Rebellion*, and after the tour's end, Vinnie Colaiuta quit again and later worked for Joni Mitchell, Leonard Cohen and others. Arthur Barrow left the band too, but stayed with Zappa as a sort of coach, supervising the rehearsing of later bands when Zappa himself wasn't around.

1980 also saw the founding of the latest of Zappa's companies, Barking Pumpkin Records: a sign that Zappa was already dissatisfied with the distribution deals he'd struck so recently with Phonogram and CBS. *Joe's Garage Acts II & III*, less of a success than *Act I*, was on Zappa Records in the States, released in 1979, but no albums were released at all in 1980 because Zappa was determined simply to sit out his contract.

Tinseltown Rebellion appeared on Barking Pumpkin, as did *Shut Up 'N Play Yer Guitar* and *You Are What You Is* (all released 1981).* As the music-magazine *The Wire* said of *Tinseltown Rebellion*, with British restraint: 'Too much time on the road documenting his male musicians' foibles can give Zappa's lyrics a relentless sexism that is wearing.' Still heavy on vocals, but better, was the double-album *You Are What You Is* which, though its themes were obvious, delivered a certain patent verve of derision aimed, as on the rather majestic 'Heavenly Bank Account', at the Born-Again Christian industry (one of Zappa's main targets in the 1980s).

The guitar-solos albums (not only *Shut Up 'N Play Yer Guitar* but *Shut Up 'N Play Yer Guitar Some More* and *Return Of The Son Of Shut Up 'N Play Yer Guitar* were at first available by mail-order only, as from May 1981, and were taken mostly from live performances from 1973-1980. Just to make the compiler's job harder, the tracks were given separate names from the names of the pieces they'd first featured in. For example: the item called 'Gee I Like Your Pants' on *Shut Up* is in fact the solo from 'Inca Roads'; and the first thing on the second *Shut Up* album is called 'Variations On The Carlos Santana Secret Chord Progression' but is actually the solo from a live recording of 'City Of Tiny Lites' from the Dallas Civic Arena in October 1980.** To make it yet more complicated, all three *Shut Up* albums were then reissued as a 3-LP box-set under the same umbrella title as the first LP had enjoyed by itself so recently – that is, *Shut Up 'N Play Yer Guitar*. This plethora of releases was an indication of how things would go when, only three years later, Zappa would start releasing it all entirely by himself instead of trying to squeeze it all out through major labels.

* One of the synchronicities repeatedly suggested by the Zappa fanzine *T'Mershi Duween* is between Zappa's work and Kurt Vonnegut's. One of the illustrations of this is that in Vonnegut's 1981 collection *Palm Sunday*, he says he owns a dog called Pumpkin who is always barking.

** On a smaller scale, Zappa has more recently started to do the same thing when 'reissuing' re-edited versions of his albums on CD; on the 1990 CD 'reissue' of *Sheik Yerbouti* the title 'Bobby Brown' has become 'Bobby Brown Goes Down' and, less easy to follow, 'We've Got To Get Into Something Real' has become 'Wait A Minute'. Likewise on the reprocessed CD set of *Joe's Garage Acts I, II & III* (also 1990) there's a minor change to the title of what was 'Wet T-Shirt Nite' and the larger change from what was 'Toad-O-Line' to 'On The Bus'. Anti-train-spotter or what?

Meanwhile in the spring of 1981, Frank contacted a venerable figure in the history of the idol of his youth, Varèse: Nicolas Slonimsky, who had conducted the 1933 world première of Varèse's 'Ionisation' in New York City. Zappa rang him to suggest they got together, and though Slonimsky was aware of FZ only from the 'Zappa the crapper' poster from days of yore, he agreed to meet. Zappa sent a car to pick him up and bring him to the 'Tom Mix cabin' at the top of Laurel Canyon where the Zappas lived (and still live to this day). The two men discussed Varèse, looked through some of Frank's manuscripts and Slonimsky played piano. It was agreed that the pianist/conductor should attend the Zappa concert two days later in Santa Monica. In the event, Slonimsky sat in on the afternoon rehearsal too. Mr Smothers gave him earplugs 'for later' but during the concert, when Zappa introduced Slonimsky as 'our national treasure', he dumped the earplugs and played his own composition 'Minitudes' on electric piano. As Ray Suttle reported in the fanzine *T' Mershi Duween*, the band joined in, adding 'their usual weird dynamics. The audience screamed and whistled and Nicolas Slominsky took a bow at his first rock concert.' Slonimsky was 87 years old.[*]

The autumn of 1981 saw another American tour, including another New York Palladium show on Hallowe'en, with the line-up that would also tour Europe yet again in the late spring/early summer of 1982. This time Steve Vai, Tommy Mars and Ray White were still there, percussionist Ed Mann was back, Bobby Martin was new (on keyboards, sax and vocals), the aptly-named Chad Wackerman was new on drums in place of Vinnie Colaiuta, and new on bass in place of Arthur Barrow was Scott Thunes, whose audition task shows how tough the entrance-examination was for a place at the Frank Vincent Zappa Academy. Thunes was working as a car-park attendant in San Francisco when Zappa (hearing of him from his guitarist brother Derek, who tried to get into the band but failed) installed the would-be bassist in an LA hotel for five days charged with learning 'Mo and Herb's Vacation' from

[*] This episode is recounted, and a photo of Zappa with the 'national treasure' reproduced, in Slonimsky's autobiography *Perfect Pitch*, published by Oxford University Press, Oxford, 1988.

sheet-music. Reputedly this took him 32 hours. He passed, and subsequently survived through the 1982, 1984 and 1988 tours, though it was bad feeling between Thunes and other members of the '88 tour band that led to Zappa's sudden termination of that tour, in disarray and at great expense. The autumn 1981 tour also featured briefly the trained soprano Lisa Popeil: she did two sets on 12 December and is featured on 'Teen-age Prostitute' on 1982's *Ship Arriving Too Late To Save A Drowning Witch*. (The only woman who has ever been a full Zappa band member was the excellent Ruth Underwood, in the 1970s, though Norma Bell was featured on keyboards, sax and vocals on 1975 American dates and on two Jugoslavian dates that December.)

1982 also saw the launch of a new lawsuit – this time against Zappa's accountant for allegedly giving him bad tax advice, which he claimed had cost him an unnecessary quarter of a million dollars. In the summer, he had a hit single on his hands, to help him balance the books.

This was 'Valley Girl', from the 1982 album *Ship Arriving Too Late To Save A Drowning Witch* (which features the 1981-82 tour band, as does *You Can't Do That On Stage Anymore Vol. 1* and *Vol. 3* and the heavy-metaloid *Guitar*. The same band can also be inspected on the videos *Dub Room Special* and *Video From Hell*). In the tradition of early Zappa put-downs of fashionable sub-cultures – such as 'Flower Punk' – but assembled along the lines of his 1970s disco-singles, 'Valley Girl' featured a long monologue by daughter Moon Unit, using the near-impenetrable vogue patois of her school-friends.

This was a hit because it went down well with the people who talked that way. Zappa told Karl Dallas crossly, in an interview the following year:

'Do I feel cut off from young people that talk that way? No, certainly not, because my daughter talks that way and she lives in my house . . . [but] I'm far too old and too ignorant to be able to do that kind of dialect . . . That particular dialect, and the fact that people all over the world have become entranced with it to a certain degree is an indication of really bad mental health, wouldn't you say so? Because the song was originally written as sociological commentary on types of behaviour and values of people who talk like that: air-headed girls who have no values other than what they wear and a party-time atmosphere. Once the thing came out, everybody wanted to be that: an air-headed girl with those kind of values . . .

'Bloomingdales has just opened a Valley Girl boutique where they sell Valley Girl products. We have . . . the rights to make a Valley Girl talking doll. It's true!. . . You pull the string and it will say "Bag your face!" And we've licensed a Valley Girl lunch-box. I mean, this is preposterous!'

Proposals were also put to Zappa for making a TV cartoon series based on the Valley Girl persona, but it never got made. A film 'inspired by' the record was made, however: *Valley Girl*, starring Nicholas Cage, in 1983. It's an interesting example of how ideas only work if they arise at particular times. The Valley Girl – doll, cartoon, whatever – clearly prefigures Bart Simpson, which became a multi-million dollar industry within a very few years of Valley Girl's demise. The two are not unconnected in other ways: Bart Simpson's creator, Matt Groenig, is a friend of Zappa's, and earlier cartoon-work of his, featuring bunches of rabbits, often showed Frank Zappa album-covers lying around in the background.

By the end of the year, Zappa had also completed 'two other 90-minute videos' since *Baby Snakes*, some chamber music that he was trying to organize for Pierre Boulez to conduct, and a new album, *The Man From Utopia* (released in 1983), which featured another reprise of Roy Estrada on vocals, and what Ben Watson in *The Wire* described as 'Steve Vai's transcriptions of Zappa's freeform gibberish. The results, on "The Dangerous Kitchen" and "The Radio Is Broken", are a fantastic collision of discipline and randomness.'

In December, a scruffy-looking figure turned up unannounced at the gate of Zappa's house claiming to be Bob Dylan. Zappa reported to Karl Dallas: 'I get a lot of weird calls here, and someone suddenly called up saying, "This is Bob Dylan. I want to play you my new songs." Now I'd never met him and I don't know his voice but I looked at the video-screen to see who was at the gate, and there, in the freezing cold, was a figure with no coat and an open shirt. I sent someone down to check, to make sure it wasn't a Charles Manson, but it was him.'

Dylan was asking if Zappa would be interested in producing his next album. Zappa recounts: 'He played me his 11 new songs and I thought they were good songs. He seemed like a nice guy. Didn't look like it would be too hard to work with him.'

Apart from all the general ways in which they are poles apart – Zappa's insistence on technical super-proficiency, Dylan's unconcern for it; Zappa's contempt for three-chord songs, Dylan's reliance on them; Zappa's studio perfectionism, Dylan's preference for one-take 'feel' instead – there was, for Zappa, one specific area of difficulty. At this point, the end of 1982, Frank had a fair head of steam going against the TV evangelist movement and the born-again Christian New Right in the States, as his recent work had stressed; Dylan had only made one album since the evangelizing Christian albums *Slow Train Coming* and *Saved* – and even that one subsequent work, 1981's *Shot Of Love*, had certainly not repudiated that evangelizing, and had included songs like 'Property Of Jesus'.

Faced, therefore, with Dylan playing him a new collection of songs ('He basically just hummed 'em and played 'em on the piano'), Zappa confronted him with the question of his Christianity: 'I asked him if it had any Jesus in it. I said: "Do these songs have the Big J in?" and he said no; [but] when I took him upstairs to give him a sandwich, my dog barked at him. I told him to watch out, my dog doesn't like Christians. And he didn't laugh.'

This Zappa-produced Bob Dylan album never happened, unfortunately. Hard as it might have been to envisage, it's possible that the very different strengths of these two major artists might both have flourished within a partnership. Dylan could have done with a perfectionist production, and Zappa could have done with spending some time listening to an artist whose intelligence was so acutely in the service of heartfelt instinct instead of mechanistic boys' toys. As it was, the album Dylan did make from some of the songs he played to Zappa, *Infidels* (1983), was an indifferent and peculiarly anonymous production that made the songs seem an ill-assorted ragbag instead of any kind of cohesive collection. (And it was a collection on which, though he got no explicit name-check, 'the big J' was certainly still around.)

By this time, there is in Zappa's career another shift that was happening all along but which begins to grow more visible: his increased concern to work in the world of 'serious' music composition. As the next chapter seeks to show, it had become apparent by the early 1980s that Zappa's career was straddling two parallel roads. Rather than being a rock musician/composer (frequently using jazz musicians) whose rock work often alluded to the modern-classical world and who made the occasional excursion into that world itself, Zappa was becoming a musician/composer whose work in rock could fund his equally important and time-consuming work as a 'serious' composer.

8. Pedro's Dowry/The March to Dupree's Paradise:

Orchestral Favourites, Porn Wars & The End Of The Road

In April 1981 Zappa had accepted an invitation to be the 'presenter' of a tribute-concert to Edgard Varèse (indeed, he paid for the hiring of the New York Palladium, a larger hall than the musician-organizers had originally booked), and in February 1983, he conducted performances of two of Varèse's works, 'Ionisation' and 'Integrale', by the Contemporary Chamber Musicians of San Francisco. He loved conducting. As he writes in his book, 'One thing the Synclavier can't replace is the experience of conducting an orchestra. The orchestra is the ultimate instrument and conducting one is an unbelievable sensation . . . From the podium (if the orchestra is playing well), the music sounds so good that if you *listen to it*, you'll fuck up. When I'm conducting, I have to force myself *not to listen*, and think about what I'm doing with my hand and where the cues go.' But it was his own work he was keenest to hear performed.

At the beginning of 1983, when he was in London to oversee rehearsals and a performance of some of his orchestral works by the London Symphony Orchestra, under the baton of the young West Coast conductor Kent Nagano (now the Music Director of the Hallé Orchestra in Manchester and of the Orchestre de l'Opéra de Lyons in France), Zappa talked about this side of his work:

'I started writing for an orchestra before I ever wrote a song for a rock 'n' roll band. I've been writing this kind of music since I was 14. I do both at the same time and I have continued to do both at the same time. It's quite possible that in a year I could write two ballets and 20 rock'n'roll songs. It's just part of my workload for that year in the writing department. What you have to do is deal with the musical problems for each form.'

As for the 'classical' side of his work, Zappa said:

'I don't care if I'm known or remembered, respected or get famous. The reason I write music is because I like to listen to it. And if there are other people who like to listen to it, then that's fine . . . I've saved for years in order to make this happen. The process of trying to get this orchestral music played has been going on for years. We've had a deal with the orchestra in Vienna, which was ultimately fucked up by Austrian television . . . We went through the same thing with a Dutch orchestra, from The Hague . . . We went through the same thing with a Polish orchestra, and most recently we went through a problem with the Syracuse Orchestra in the United States . . . We then called London . . . The LSO were not available . . . They were supposed to be taking their vacation, but when the project was presented to the orchestra they said they were interested in doing it and we booked the time and came over and did it.'

It was Zappa who booked Kent Nagano too. As Nagano explained it to fanzine reporter Andy Greenaway in *T'Mershi Duween* no.16, December 1990:

'I was visiting IRCAM* in Paris – some of my friends worked there under the patronage of Pierre Boulez – and I saw the list of various pieces that were to be performed there in the future. Included . . . were some pieces by Frank Zappa . . . I was really surprised and I said "Why are you doing Frank Zappa's music?" and my friend said "Well, it seems he's written a number of serious compositions and he wanted the Ensemble to perform them, and Pierre Boulez has agreed to conduct it."'

'So the next time Frank Zappa toured through the Bay Area . . . I contacted his manager . . . to request that he send me some scores. Then I got a message that Frank Zappa wanted to meet

---

* IRCAM, the Institut de Recherche et de Co-ordination Acoustic-Musical, is a sort of arts-lab organisation set up by Pierre Boulez with backing from the French government. The Ensemble InterContemporain, conducted by Boulez, would perform Zappa's music a year later than the LSO (almost to the day).

189

me during the intermission of one of his [1982] concerts . . . And it was the first time in my life that I'd been to a rock concert. It was a phenomenal experience: it was packed, completely sold out, millions of fans, everyone just incredibly excited and enthusiastic.'

When I spoke to Nagano, in April 1992, I asked if he'd been surprised, at that rock concert, by the level of musicianship. He said: 'Yes. In fact I was *really* surprised. I was also surprised by the decibel level, which was painful.'

Nagano told Andy Greenaway: 'I remember meeting Frank Zappa and his entourage, and meeting his bodyguard . . . [Smothers] scared the hell out of me! Anyway, he showed me the scores, which he allowed me to keep, and they were indeed extraordinary. Extraordinary quality. Very surprising that anybody could write something so original, much less someone who wasn't known in the classical music field. So I asked Frank if I could perform some of the pieces in California . . . [and] for several months I never got a positive or negative answer from him. But what I did receive about four months later was a telephone call asking if I'd be interested in recording a couple of albums of his music with the London Symphony.

'I was delighted. It was much more than "would I be interested?". I considered it a real privilege, a real honour to be able to work with someone like Frank . . . [and] in fact I had never really worked with any what I would call strong world-class orchestras before . . . he gave me my first chance. He made telephone calls, and he did investigations of what my reputation was – but someone has to give a young conductor their first chance, and Frank gave me my first chance, and I'll always be grateful to him for that.

'We did some initial rehearsals together at his home in Los Angeles, and there I realized that it was indeed going to be an extremely exciting project. From my knowledge of his music and his incredible musicianship, I knew that for him it was just as important to have music performed as close to perfection as possible as it was for me. That's one reason why I got my reputation, both negatively and positively – because I rehearse until it's really very, very accurate.'

Someone with a reputation for doing that was exactly what

Zappa wanted. He had already learnt from past experience that orchestral musicians are just as human as rock musos: just as liable to be lazy if you let them, just as distracted from the demands of the music by the demands of everyday life, just as interested in the money, just as inclined to knock it out loaded. (Zappa's book is mercilessly acute and very funny on these matters.)

For Frank, then, Nagano's reputation, and that of the LSO, augured well. As he said, ahead of the concert:

'The London Symphony Orchestra is a fine orchestra and had a good reputation even among the studio musicians of Los Angeles. But: this is hard music. It's going to be hard for anyone to play it – so I'm expecting that the LSO is going to give it a good shot . . . it will be exciting to hear [the seven pieces] for the first time, if they are played right.'

In the event – a concert at the Barbican, 11 January 1983, plus recording-sessions on the days immediately following – Kent was satisfied but Frank wasn't. He was unhappy that many members of the orchestra got tanked up in the interval (he said the backstage bar for the orchestra was bigger and better-stocked than the ones out front for the public), and he was particularly unhappy with the trumpet section – an unhappiness he was not slow to express on his sleevenotes to the albums that resulted from the project. Zappa reported that to repair the trumpet-section faults on the recording of 'Strictly Genteel', 40 edits had to be made in seven minutes' of music. These are undetectable 'because', as Kent Nagano concedes, 'Frank is such a superb editor.'

Six other pieces were recorded: 'Pedro's Dowry' and the splendid 'Bogus Pomp', previously recorded at Royce Hall in 1975 (see *Orchestral Favourites*); 'Envelopes', a rock version of which had appeared on the recent *Ship Arriving Too Late To Save A Drowning Witch*; and three previously unrecorded pieces: 'Sad Jane' (from the ballet *Bob In Dacron*), 'The March' and the lengthy 'Mo & Herb's Vacation'. *London Symphony Orchestra Volume 1* was issued in America, though not in Britain, in June 1983, on vinyl; *London Symphony Orchestra Volume 2* was issued in America and Britain, in September 1987, still on vinyl only, as a double-album. 'Bob In Dacron' and 'Strictly Genteel' are on the vinyl *Volume 2*, but not on the subsequent CD that is meant to replace the vinyl *Volume 1* and *Volume 2*.

Whether an orchestra can rehearse sufficiently to achieve 'correct' performance of music as complicated as Zappa's, aside from factors like alcohol-intake, is essentially a matter of economics. As Nagano observes:

'When he does his rock music, it's no less complicated. But they rehearse until it's perfect and then they go out on the road. Which means if it takes two months of rehearsal, it's two months of rehearsal. In the symphonic world, the financial realities just don't make that possible right now. And it's frustrating for someone who's written music that he knows is totally playable, given enough rehearsal time. I totally understand his point: he's right, in fact.'

Despite Zappa's unhappiness with the LSO performance, he and Nagano remained (and remain) on good terms, with Nagano dropping in on the Zappa family when in Los Angeles. In 1984, Nagano would conduct the Berkeley Symphony Orchestra in an evening of performances of Zappa's work, and in France in 1990, Nagano as Musical Director of the Orchestre de l'Opéra de Lyons would present, at his own behest, another evening of Zappa's music, conducting one of the pieces himself.

In his book, Zappa writes that since the release of the LSO album, he has 'turned down at least fifteen commissions from chamber music groups of varying sizes from all over the world who offered me *cash* to write a piece of music for them. If I were a composer just starting out, I would think that was the greatest thing in the world – but I don't have the time any more, and I shudder to think what would happen to the music if they played it without my being there during rehearsals.

'Complicating matters, these commissions are offered in a way that requires my presence at the *première performance* – during which I would be expected to sit there and pretend it was terrific.'

He adds: 'In the game of new music, everybody has to take a chance. The conductor takes a chance, the performers take a chance, and the audience takes a chance – but the guy who takes the biggest chance is the composer.

'The performers will probably not play his piece correctly (bad attitude; not enough rehearsal time) – and the audience won't like it because it doesn't "sound good" (bad acoustics*; weak performance).

'There's no such thing as a "second chance" in this situation – the audience only gets one chance to hear it because, even though the program says "*World Première*", that usually means "*Last Performance*".'

Zappa was glad to benefit from the eminence of Boulez, in terms of getting this side of his work more 'visibility', but he felt that the Ensemble InterContemporain, too, was under-rehearsed, when it gave its performance of 'The Perfect Stranger', 'Dupree's Paradise' and 'Naval Aviation In Art?', in Paris on 9 January 1984. 'I hated that première,' he wrote later. 'Boulez virtually had to drag me onto the stage to take a bow.'

The studio recordings were done the following day, and the results released, along with several of Zappa's early Synclavier pieces, on the album *Boulez Conducts Zappa, The Perfect Stranger* in August 1984, with a sleeve photo of Boulez and some customarily spiky notes by the composer. It was argued at the time that the Synclavier pieces were 'more successful' than the orchestral work, and the Boulez boys did seem less flexible in their playing than the LSO – but while the French have never been renowned for their understanding of rock 'n' roll rhythms, Zappa himself has always emphasized a mathematical kind of precision rather than 'feel', so it's doubtful whether 'flexible' was what Frank wanted the Ensemble to be. It also strikes me as impossible to compare such different work as the Synclavier pieces and the orchestral ones, and of the latter, even if the composer could envisage better renditions, the Paris recording of 'Dupree's Paradise', at least, yields a wonderful piece.

The same year, Zappa gave the keynote address at the Annual Festival Conference of the American Society of University Composers, held in early April in Columbus, Ohio, and six weeks later was the focus of 'Speaking Of Music With Frank Zappa' at the Palace of Fine Arts in San Francisco, at which he played samples of his work.

* This is certainly true at the Barbican, in the City of London, where nothing is loud enough.

A long excerpt from the Ohio appearance is reprinted in *The Real Frank Zappa Book* – including his excellent analysis of the way in which what popular music gets heard in the USA is determined entirely by a 13-year-old girl called Debbie. *Classical Music* magazine's report of the event (June 1984) noted that Zappa had 'pointed out, in wonderfully graphic terms, the irrelevance of living composers to contemporary society'.

However, Zappa contributed to the greater circulation of 'dead guy' music himself that same year, by recording and releasing an album's worth of baroque trios by his eighteenth-century namesake Francesco Zappa. He performed them on the Synclavier (Zappa calls it the Digital Gratification Consort) with clarinettist David Ocker and Zappoid 'machine rhythms' that 'add a worrying mechanical slant', according to *The Wire* (September 1991). Ocker also wrote what *The Wire* termed 'some excellent demystificatory notes on the function of baroque music ("sawing away while noblemen ate dinner")'. The album is always high in fanzine polls of 'Least Favourite LP'.

By this point, as Zappa observes in his book, he had 'sued the two industry giants, CBS and Warners, and had learned a lot more about "creative accounting practices".'

Yes, the third honeymoon with the major record-companies was over, and Zappa Records and Barking Pumpkin were nearly out on their own, though first there was an interlude of a couple of years in which they came out via a distribution deal with MCA in the USA and with EMI elsewhere (including Britain). The result was the unleashing of an unprecedented amount of 'product' by Zappa, and its appearance via a bewildering sequence of different outlets and on different formats (non-trainspotters can easily afford to skip the next paragraph).

1983 had seen the release in Britain of: the last CBS-distributed LP, *The Man From Utopia*, in March (released on Barking Pumpkin in the USA)*; the 'soundtrack album' to the film *Baby Snakes* the same month in the USA (Barking

---

* For present purposes, 'vinyl' means 'vinyl and cassette'. CDs began to be released in 1986, and from that point onwards retrospective CD issues of most of Zappa's back-catalogue began to be released in addition to new work being issued on the new format, sometimes with a vinyl release alongside it and sometimes not. The first work to be released on CD was in fact a CD-only release from EMI of *Does Humor Belong In Music?*, as early as January 1986. There was no vinyl and no US release in any format.

Pumpkin) but no release in Britain; *London Symphony Orchestra Volume 1* three months later, but again only in the USA; and fourthly a retrospective collection of some of Zappa's pre-Mothers of Invention juvenilia, *Rare Meat*, again issued only in the USA, this time by Del-Fi. 1984 then sees the release of: *Francesco Zappa* through EMI in the UK and Barking Pumpkin in the USA; *Boulez Conducts Zappa, The Perfect Stranger* in August, again through EMI in the UK but on Angel Records in the USA. In October came the rock double-album *Them Or Us*, the UK version coming from EMI and the US from Barking Pumpkin. Only a month after the *Them Or Us* double-album came the appalling *Thing-Fish*, a triple-album box-set 'musical comedy' featuring Terry and Dale Bozzio – the woman who'd been heard relishing her leather-fetish on 'Joe's Garage Act I' and would be heard of again, taking part in *Zappa's Universe* on Broadway in late 1991 – Ike Willis, Ray White, Napoleon Murphy Brock and, on vocals only, Zappa's early r 'n' b guitar hero Johnny Guitar Watson – again on EMI in Europe and Barking Pumpkin in the States. Additionally, the *Shut Up 'N Play Yer Guitar* albums were reissued in the USA . . .

As if this confusion and, more importantly, profusion of 'product' release in 1983 and 1984 wasn't enough, Zappa was at the same time preparing and recording lots more work for release later. He composed a newly commissioned 'classical' piece for string quartet, 'None of the Above', and he studio-recorded what would be the 1986 release *Jazz From Hell*, while the rock-band world-tour of later in 1984 would provide the source-material for several later releases.

This tour, taking in North America, Europe and North America (in that order), began on 18 July and didn't finish till 23 December. It was to be Zappa's penultimate tour. Having more or less toured every year for as long as he could remember, there was no 1983 tour, and after the '84 there would be none again until 1988 – and there's been none since.

The line-up was, naturally, different from that used in autumn 1981 and summer '82. Out, finally, went Tommy Mars, replaced on keyboards by Alan Zavod, who came to Zappa from the Jean-Luc Ponty band; out too were Steve Vai on guitar, by this time on his way to metal-thrash stardom, and Ed Mann on percussion (again); back in after an absence were Ike Willis on guitar and vocals (last around for the summer 1980 tour) and Napoleon Murphy Brock on tenor-sax and vocals, who last appeared with Zappa (before *Thing-Fish*) in the last Mothers line-up, disbanded eight years previously, and was destined not to stay long this time. After the first few American shows, as *T'Mershi Duween* put it, 'Frank gave him the choice of an aisle or window seat back to LA.'

The members of the band still in there from the previous tour were Ray White on guitar and vocals, Bobby Martin on keyboards, sax and vocals, Scott Thunes on bass and Chad Wackerman on drums. Zappa's son Dweezil also played guitar on one or two shows (as he had done at Hammersmith in 1982, and was to do again in 1988), and on one date the middlebrow jazz veteran Archie Shepp played a tenor-sax solo with the band (on 'Let's Move To Cleveland'; this can be heard on the May 1991 release *You Can't Do That On Stage Anymore Volume 4*). Minus these augmenters (and minus Brock), this group is on 1985's video and 1986's CD *Does Humor Belong In Music?* (the video was recorded at one show in New York, the very different audio-CD has tracks taken from many shows), on a small proportion of 1988's *You Can't Do That On Stage Anymore Vol. 1* and on most of 1989's *Volume 3*.

While Zappa and the band were rehearsing for the tour, in June, Kent Nagano was rehearsing the Berkeley Symphony Orchestra for the performance of some of Zappa's 'classical' music on 15 June, as mentioned earlier. Entitled *A Zappa Affair*, the concert contained four 'ballets' featuring giant marionettes, and took place at the Zellerbach Auditorium in Nagano's home town, San Francisco. The composer attended a number of the rehearsals, and took part in getting the theatrical side of it 'looking right'. He also attended the performance. So did the bootlegger who made the subsequent *Serious Music* and *Son Of Serious Music* from what he got on tape: 'Sad Jane/Bob In Dacron', 'Sinister Footwear', 'Pedro's Dowry' and 'Mo & Herb's Vacation'.

The so-called 'giant marionettes' were human-sized. Kent Nagano told me that they were used because the orchestral pieces were ballet-music, and yet 'it wasn't humanly possible for the dancers to do the things Zappa wanted done: not without people hurting themselves anyway. So the logical solution to that was to use marionettes.' (They were made by John Gilkerson, whose work was already well-known around the San Francisco area.) I asked the conductor how he felt about working with them:

'It was really interesting, in that when Frank Zappa wrote the scores they were meant to be theatre pieces. They were written as ballets, so like any such scores, when you just perform them in concert something is missing. The music was made to be heard with its visual counterpart.' He added: 'One day I would like to see the pieces performed by an active theatre company with the technical equipment and the budget to produce, visually speaking, a very high-tech result.'

October saw the release of the double-LP *Them Or Us*. It was an interesting ragbag of material, some live and some studio, and though mostly from 1982 – including the live title track and the Allmans' number 'Whipping Post' – there was also 'The Planet Of My Dreams' from the mid-1970s. Other tracks include the studio-recorded 'In France', with Johnny Guitar Watson on lead vocals, and 'Yahozna', which you're supposed to play backwards in order to spot all the ingredients in its medley of musical allusions. Dweezil guests on a couple of tracks. There was also a book called *Them Or Us* which Zappa issued contemporaneously and which became available through his mail-order supply company Barfko-Swill*. The book, in the form of a story and screenplay, has Zappa 'explaining' his once-famous Conceptual Continuity, and discoursing on his baroque near-namesake Francesco Zappa, Mozart, David Bowie and lots of his own earlier work. According to Dominique Chevalier, it was originally to be called *Christmas In New Jersey*.

Finally for 1984, two more activities: Frank found time to film a small role in an episode of the then-modish TV series

* Barfko-Swill, Box 5418, North Hollywood, California 91616, USA; telephone (818) 786-7546. It also operates a sort of Zappa phone-information service: you just ring up, speak to Jerry Fialca, whose voice sounds disconcertingly like the man himself, and ask him your questions.

Miami Vice, appearing against type as a drug-dealer who gets thrown off his yacht (this was transmitted in 1985 – another busy year, as we're about to see). He also plugged the three-LP 'musical comedy soundtrack' he called *Thing-Fish* by publishing part of its libretto with photographs in the April issue of the American soft-porn magazine *Hustler*. The name of the album was an allusion to the character George 'Kingfish' Stevens in the 1950s TV series 'Amos And Andy', to which the Zappa work made much reference.

The release of *Thing-Fish* proved a struggle, since a woman in the MCA pressing-plant objected to the lyrics and corporate panic ensued, thus abruptly terminating Zappa's final deal with a major. Zappa retaliated by putting his own warning-sticker on the sleeve:

'WARNING/GUARANTEE: This album contains material which a truly free society would neither fear nor suppress.

'In some socially retarded areas, religious fanatics and ultra-conservative political organizations violate your First Amendment Rights by attempting to censor rock'n'roll albums . . .

'The language and concepts contained herein are GUARANTEED NOT TO CAUSE ETERNAL TORMENT IN THE PLACE WHERE THE GUY WITH THE HORNS AND THE POINTED STICK CONDUCTS HIS BUSINESS.

'This guarantee is as real as the threats of the video fundamentalists who use attacks on rock music in their attempt to transform America into a nation of check-mailing nincompoops (in the name of Jesus Christ).

'If there is a hell, its fires wait for them, not us.'

This minor skirmish was a foretaste of imminent battles against the Parents' Music Resource Center, a campaigning organization soon to be founded by Tipper Gore, wife of then Senator and now Vice-President Albert Gore Jr. of Tennessee. Zappa gives a great deal of space to this topic in his book: understandably perhaps, since he also spent a great deal of 1985 fighting this gang of self-appointed moral guardians and their abject appeasers within the record industry itself.

The PMRC wielded power out of all proportion to the size of its membership or the reasonableness of its stance, because its founding posse had close personal links (often undisclosed) to senators and Reagan administration bigwigs; hence it became known as 'the Washington Wives'.

At the end of May 1985, in a national atmosphere of ascendant right-wing triumphalism encouraged by Reaganomics, the billion-dollar clout of the TV evangelist movement and perennial American paranoia – especially about what the developed world's most underinformed youth-population might be up to – the PMRC wrote to the president of the Recording Industry Association of America (the RIAA) demanding, among much else, a rating system for rock records to counteract what they claimed was the industry's dissemination of 'sex, violence and the glorification of drugs and alcohol'. This letter was signed by Senator Gore's wife, the wife of Treasury Secretary James Baker, the wives of nine more US Senators and the wives of two big Washington businessmen.

The RIAA actually rejected most of the PMRC's demands but, almost certainly as an unspoken quid pro quo to secure for the industry the passing of the then-imminent blank tape tax, signalled a possible readiness to give in on the demand for a ratings system. This, of course, necessarily conceded the basic issue as to whether there should be any need even to *consider* any censorship at all, or any kind of recognition given to this self-appointed posse of American moral vigilantes.

This had immediate repercussions. Soon after the PMRC's letter reached the RIAA, the president of the National Association of Broadcasters wrote to 4,500 commercial radio-stations across America suggesting that their licences would be safer if they would avoid playing records with 'explicit' lyrics. This carried not only general echoes of the McCarthy era and the Hollywood blacklist of the 1950s but specific echoes of the secret radio blacklist that had been operated at the end of the 1960s.

Zappa's first public involvement with this issue was in August, when, with a Washington DJ and others, he took part in a CBS *Nightwatch* TV debate taped in front of a live audience, arguing against PMRC spokesperson Kandy Stroud. The DJ said outright that he was reminded of the earlier blacklist. Zappa noted that when the show went out, this comment had been removed. A week later, he did a live radio-interview in

New York, and the DJ there told Frank that he'd seen the black-list early in the 1970s. (Peter, Paul And Mary's pathetic 'Puff The Magic Dragon' really was on the list.)

After that, Zappa took on the PMRC almost full-time through the summer and autumn of 1985, doing a number of interviews on the subject, publishing a savage guest-editorial in the trade paper *Cashbox* – 'Extortion Pure And Simple: An Open Letter To The Music Industry' – writing an open letter to Ronald Reagan (who had of course 'named names' in his pre-vious incarnation during the Hollywood blacklist days), testifying before the Senate Commerce Technology and Transportation Committee in its day of hearings on the matter on 19 September, and subsequently rush-releasing his album *Frank Zappa Meets the Mothers of Prevention*.

The *Cashbox* guest-editorial was of course unlikely to sway the money-men of the industry majors who, as Zappa would point out in his testimony to Congress, wanted their blank tape tax squeezed through the forthcoming Thurmond Committee ('Is it,' Zappa asked in his address, 'a coincidence that Mrs Thurmond is affiliated with the PMRC? I can't say she's a member, because the PMRC *has no members* . . . how many other DC wives are *nonmembers* of an organization that raises money by mail, [and] has a tax-exempt status . . .?'). But what the *Cashbox* piece might have done was a bit of consciousness-raising on the issue among the people at the more creative end of the record-industry spectrum. It was a corrosively articulate piece, castigating 'the elected officials who sit idly by while their wives run rabid with anti-sexual pseudo-Christian legislative fervor' and what he characterized as 'connubial insider-trading and power-brokerage'. He went on to ask:

'If you are an artist reading this . . . did anyone ask you if you wanted to have the stigma of "potential filth" plopped onto your next release via this "appeasement sticker"? If you are a songwriter, did anyone ask you if you wanted to spend the rest of your career modifying your lyric content to suit the spiritual needs of an imaginary 11-year-old?'

Equally, Nancy's husband took no notice of the letter Zappa sent to him on 29 August. 'The President', Zappa reported in his book of four years later, 'did not answer my letter. Instead, he gave a speech . . . wherein he claimed that everybody in the record industry was a pornographer.'

In contrast, Zappa's testimony before the Senate hearing was well-publicized and well-attended by the media and the public. His style of speech was his usual odd mix of brutal directness and parodic American long-winded formality:

'No-one has forced Mrs Baker or Mrs Gore to bring Prince or Sheena Easton into their homes. Thanks to the Constitution, they are free to buy other forms of music for their children. Apparently they insist on purchasing the works of contemporary recording artists in order to support a personal illusion of aerobic sophistication.' This sort of sarcasm got him nowhere – but then neither did arguments that addressed other sides of the issue, as when he said:

'Children in the "vulnerable" age bracket have a natural love for music. If, as a parent, you believe they should be exposed to something more uplifting than "Sugar Walls", support music appreciation programs in schools . . . [which cost] very little compared to sports expenditures. Your children have a right to know that something besides pop music exists.'

Nor was legislative logic any use, as when he said: 'Masturbation is not illegal. If it is not illegal to do it, why should it be illegal to sing about it?' It was pointed out, *à propos* of this kind of argument, that the PMRC wasn't urging new *laws*. Senator James Exon of Nebraska therefore asked:

'I wonder, Mr Chairman, if we're *not* talking about federal regulation, and we're *not* talking about federal legislation, *what is the point of these hearings?*' As Zappa wrote later, this calming intervention 'received great applause, but was not carried by the network news'.

On 30 October, H.R.2911, the blank tape tax bill, got its senate committee hearing (co-sponsored by Senator Albert Gore Jr.) and the very next day the RIAA announced that it had agreed to place 'Explicit Lyrics – Parental Advisory' stickers on rock albums as and when required. Possibly to his own disappointment, Zappa's albums have never been stickered.

The crucial *Meets The Mother Of Prevention* track 'Porn Wars' (later also the title of the relevant chapter in *The Real Frank Zappa Book*) used a crescendo-ing collage of voices taped from the 19 September hearing, vari-speeded, tweaked, re-ordered and manipulated by the Synclavier DMS, in the tradition of the 'found music' of contemporary 'serious' composers like John Adams, and in the tradition of Zappa's own earlier work on albums like *We're Only In It For The Money**. It seems ironic that granted the extreme sophistication and infinite-RAM capacity of the equipment Zappa was by this point able to bring to such projects, the result sounds so very similar to what he had achieved 18 years previously with, at most, a four-track tape-deck. The brief extract of phone-conversation between the girlfriends that comes immediately before the drum-beat intro to 'Bow Tie Daddy' on *Money* manages to show as much about their late-1960s cultural assumptions and lifestyles, in a few seconds, as the lengthy intricacies of 'Porn Wars' ever get to say about the snuffling mendacity of the senators of mid-1980s Washington. (When originally issued, 'Porn Wars' didn't appear on the European release of the album, which suggests that Zappa considers Europeans as insular in their interests as Americans, and that he regards the track as essentially reportage rather than art.)

Zappa didn't stop fighting the PMRC when the stickering went through. He kept tabs on them, building up a dossier of cuttings that he reproduced and issued free as *The Z-Pack* through Barfko-Swill; kept on doing TV and radio-interview campaigning; rush-released the album that November (the same month the stickering decision was announced); and testified before the Maryland State Judiciary Legislature on the same issue on 14 February 1986.

The cause of the latter was that Maryland was considering legislation. A bill was proposed by delegate Judith Toth to extend the existing state pornography laws to include records,

---

* John Adams' *Nixon in China* achieved a certain notoriety. Among others working in these areas is Alastair Riddell, a Melbourne composer of pieces also influenced by Nancarrow and played on a piano 'controlled by a computer'. His work has been issued in the USA on CD on Albion Records (NAO28CD). George Lewis, a Chicago-based musician-composer, has a different use of computers in music: he plays freely-improvised jazz (sax) interacting with a computer that, in response to his noises, throws images onto a screen, and to which he reacts musically in turn. There is now enough computer music to justify a journal devoted to it: *The Computer Music Journal*, published by M.I.T. Press.

tapes and CDs. As Zappa explained in his book: 'The bill had already been passed by the Maryland House of Delegates, and a Senate vote in favor would have placed it into law in Maryland, creating a dangerous national precedent.'

Attending a cocktail-party on the eve of the hearing, organized by the RIAA's lobbyist, Frank went round persuading state delegates who'd voted in favour of the bill to sign a statement retracting their support. Five of them did so, and at the hearing the following day, Frank 'read their names and confessions into the record'. The hearing eventually squashed the bill.

In later years, Frank was to manifest his continued commitment to all this campaigning by using parts of the hearing on his hour-long *Video From Hell*, by making a return appearance on CNN's debate forum *Crossfire* (similar to the CBS *Nightshow*), and by filing papers to set up his own religion – just to fight them on their own turf – as well as by hounding them all through his 1989 book.

Meanwhile, other work had been done in 1985. He spent the early months in the studio restoring fragile old tapes of his early work, and then digitally remastering them, in order to issue them as *The Old Masters Box 1*, a seven-LP box-set (vinyl only, USA only, on Barking Pumpkin) in April. This included a so-called Mystery Disc, originally planned to include an excerpt from Zappa's pre-Mothers Pomona College radio-show and 'all those Ned & Nelda things', and, from the tape of the party held on the opening night of Studio Z in Cucamonga, with Captain Beefheart singing 'Night Owl' and Ray Collins' 'Louie Louie'. In the event it included none of these but did contain a 1 minute 32 second collaged slice of the Studio Z opening-night party.

On 12 April, in San Francisco, the pioneering Kronos String Quartet performed the world première of Zappa's specially commissioned 1984 composition 'None Of The Above'. In this case 'world première' didn't mean 'last performance': the Kronos String Quartet went on to play it again, in Denmark, on 28 April. (It is on the bootleg *Randomonium*.) The following month, the Aspen Wind Quartet performed the world première of another new Zappa piece, 'Time's Beach', at the Alice Tully Hall in the Lincoln Center in New York. This was another piece that had been specially commissioned (by the Walter W. Naumberg Foundation), despite Zappa's assertion, quoted earlier, that after the London Symphony Orchestra sessions, he didn't have the time or inclination to take on such commissions.

January 1986 marked the release of the 1984-tour-based *Does Humor Belong In Music?* (CD only; Europe only) and Zappa's signing of another ill-fated deal: this time for the company Ryko to release 24 CDs over a three-year period! Ryko was the first US record-company to issue their material on CD only; this was a modern and fiercely definite stance to take, which naturally appealed to Zappa. The deal was intended to cover some new work but also to deal with the reissue in the CD format of much of Zappa's big back-catalogue – a process that was happening all across the record-industry as the new format began to be established. Zappa's deal was reported in the trade-paper *Billboard* at the beginning of February (the month in which Frank appeared before the State Judiciary Committee in his 'home state', Maryland).*

Later that year, he produced his son Dweezil's first album, *Havin' A Bad Day*, a somewhat belated follow-up to the 1982 debut single by Dweezil, 'My Mother Is A Space Cadet' (co-written with Moon Unit). The album was issued on Barking Pumpkin/Chrysalis. Frank also devoted some studio-time to *The Old Masters Box 2*, which was, this time around, a nine-LP box-set (again including a Mystery Disc) and as with *Box 1* it was a US vinyl collection only.

This came out in November, as did the album *Jazz From Hell* (recorded in 1984), which featured one guitar-piece, the unusually 'felt' 'St Etienne', and seven pieces 'realized on the Synclavier' computer-to-digital interface. Ben Watson in *The Wire* gushed:

'The bell-like purity of [the Synclavier tracks on] *The Perfect Stranger* has been superseded by more carnal sounds . . . Zappa leaps to the top of the list of worldclass futuro-composers.'

Hm. To some of us, who felt that the Synclavier's function

* See the discography at the back of this book for details of the 25 single-CDs and the eleven double-CDs that Ryko have released. The main part of the deal is finished as of the time of writing, so that the most recent CD-reissues of back-catalogue items are on Zappa's own (and now fully independent) Barking Pumpkin label in the USA, and most future work will be on Barking Pumpkin CDs likewise.

here was to pretend to be a bunch of Zappa's musicians, *Jazz From Hell* sounds unsurprisingly like a bunch of Zappa's musicians having a normal day – actually rather a dreary day – on which we're grateful for the absence of vocals nudge-nudging their way through lyrics to suit the spiritual needs of an imaginary 13-year-old boy. Zappa achieves these synthetic musician-noises by 'sampling' real musicians' noises. Sampling is now widespread and unstoppable, of course, and the musicians' unions hate it, nearly as much as Frank Zappa hates the unions. He has a curt section on the whole musicians-versus-'inventions' question in his book: 'Music comes from composers – not musicians . . . Composers don't have a union – and Musicians' Union actually makes life more difficult for *them* . . . The Musicians' Union helped to create the market for sampling machines, but refuses to admit it.'

'Union people,' he goes on, 'seem to be under the impression that if you "sample" a musician into a Synclavier, you magically (don't laugh) suck the music out of the musician, depriving him of some intangible dignity and/or potential income.'

If *Jazz From Hell* could be cited as a case where the Synclavier *did* elbow musicians out of some work, Zappa was able to cite another case from the mid-1980s where it put music back into musicians. Chamber ensemble the E.A.R. Unit (two keyboards, two percussion, clarinet and cello), founded and led by percussionist Art Jarvinen, asked Zappa to do them an arrangement of his piece 'While You Were Out' (afterwards called 'While You Were Art'), and then, according to Zappa, panicked when presented with something unexpectedly complicated, demanding more rehearsal time than was available. Zappa encouraged them to go ahead and *pretend* to play it, while in fact miming to a tape of the Synclavier playing the piece itself. Zappa told Jarvinen:

'The way to pull this off is to have wires hanging out of your instruments leading into amplifiers and effects boxes on the floor.' They went ahead and Zappa says that neither the man running the concert-series, nor the two reviewers present from major Los Angeles newspapers, nor anyone in the audience, knew that 'the musicians *never played a note*'.

The Synclavier was also employed in 1986 by Miles Davis, on

his album *Tutu*, on which ex-Mother George Duke worked. And in a move that prefigured Frank Zappa's imminent involvement in the shaking loose of the Soviet Bloc, the Estonian rock band Ansambel issued an LP, called *Rock-Hotel*, on which they included a version of Frank's 'Harder Than Your Husband' *in Estonian*, called 'Tüütuks Muutub Hellus'. (This song has also been covered in Czechoslovakia by the band Babeck.)

1987 seemed to reunite Zappa with every area of activity he had ever shown interest in. March saw him knocking on the doors of television, just as he had done 23 years earlier with the world's first non-existent rock-opera *I Was A Teenage Maltshop*. This time it was the ABC network instead of a CBS station, he was able to achieve a meeting ('assisted by Danny Schrier, an aggressive young agent at ICM') instead of just making a written submission, and the project was a proposed TV series called *Night School*. This project, outlined towards the end of *The Real Frank Zappa Book*, was in effect a brilliant analysis of what is wrong with American television, and of the media's role in maintaining the astonishing ignorance of the American public. (By extension, much of this analysis applies just as well to Great Britain.)

As such, it had no hope whatever of getting backed, produced and networked, though it would have been marvellous stuff. *Night School* encapsulated the best side of Zappa's 'practical conservatism' as he dubs it himself – the best side of his indomitable idiosyncratic intelligence, his alertness to issues of government/big-business manipulation, and his bullshit-abolishing articulacy. Among other ideas, it was proposed that the five-nights-a-week, late-night show would get Daniel Schorr, a CBS newscaster who had also worked on national public radio and CNN, (as 'Professor of Recent History') to show 'raw, uncut news footage from the daily satellite feed, point out the material other broadcasters have deleted, speculate on the possible motivations behind the deletions, and refresh people's memories about recent events connected to each day's breaking stories'. You can see at once exactly why that would be terrific and exactly why we'll never see any such thing on our screens. Another idea was to have 'a purposely cheesy sitcom segment', 'The Future Family'. 'Whenever a news item warrants it, "The

Future Family" will "pre-enact" the possible social consequences, twenty years down the road.' Another: 'A summary
will be provided of what our elected officials really did for their
paycheck in Congress each day. Votes on House and Senate
business will be treated like sports scores.' There was also to be
rock music, psychology courses dealing 'almost exclusively with
sexually related topics', and the opportunity to buy *Night
School* 'degrees' for $25. Zappa suggested that the show should
be preceded by a warning: 'This program deals with reality,
using easy to understand colloquial American Language. If you
fear (or have difficulty accepting) either of the above, feel free to
change the channel.'

In the same mood, perhaps, Zappa began 'editing together'
the first of his Honker Home Videos. This was when he
acquired videotape of the Maryland Judiciary Hearing he'd
taken part in to fight Judith Toth's proposed extension of the
state pornography laws early the previous year. Zappa cut up
the tape to make 'a dramatization of the issue' and put this into
the hour-long *Video From Hell*, which would see the light of
cathode in 1989.

Meanwhile June 1987 saw a sudden flurry of release-
activity: the reissue as one collection of *Joe's Garage Acts I, II
& III* (vinyl and CD, the vinyl through EMI in the UK and
Barking Pumpkin in the USA, the CD on Zappa Records in the
UK and on Ryko in the States) *and*, through *Guitar World* magazine, with which Zappa had long enjoyed a special relationship, the cassette-only release inevitably titled *The Guitar World
According To Frank Zappa* (Barking Pumpkin), which at the
time included some otherwise-unreleased material, though it
has since been (re-)issued through normal channels. September
saw the long-delayed release of *London Symphony Orchestra
Volume 2*, and Zappa attended (as a member of the audience) a
concert by the New York Philharmonic Orchestra conducted by
Pierre Boulez at the Lincoln Center, partly of Boulez' own work,
and partly of work by Debussy and Stravinsky.

Continuing his struggle against the TV evangelists, fundamentalists, creationists and nazi idiots, Zappa filed the papers
of application to found his own religion, the Church of
American Secular Humanism (CASH!), in Montgomery,

Alabama. He also made a return-appearance on CNN's debate-show *Crossfire*, this time on the subject 'Does Rock Music Cause Aids?'. Not talking of which, Frank made a videotape interview with groupie Laurel Fishman. She had been at Mother concerts in the 1960s and in 1970 got a backstage pass to a Chicago gig, taking the opportunity to give the group a present of one of her own turds, which 'looked like it had been hand-molded into a perfect sphere, sitting in a mason jar'. She had reappeared on a 1981 tour-date at Notre Dame University, according to Frank, and had starred in the following day's 'breakfast report' to the paymaster by guitarist Steve Vai, which in turn became the basis of the *Them Or Us* track 'Stevie's Spanking' (more appealing for Vai's guitar-work than for the narrative on his sex life). Zappa's video interview with Ms Fishman was on the subject of her sexual proclivities. Here was a woman who really did like vegetables. It must have felt like the old days to Frank.

Likewise, when he put away the video-camera and returned to audio-tape to assemble the mass of material that he would release at the end of the year as *The Old Masters Box 3*, which was *another* nine-LP box-set – vinyl only, US only and this time with no Mystery Disc.

Meanwhile in the autumn, for the first time in a long time, Zappa resumed another activity that had once been recurrent. He assembled musicians and began the rehearsals for another tour. It was to become his last to date. The musicians retained from the previous (1984) tour were Bobby Martin (keyboards, sax, vocals), Ike Willis (guitar and vocals), Scott Thunes (bass) and Chad Wackerman (drums). It was intended to include Ray White again too, but at the first rehearsal he got a phone-call to say that his house had been burgled – some reports suggested it had been burnt down – and he never re-appeared. Old stalwarts Ed Mann (percussion) and Tommy Mars (keyboards and vocals) were intended for re-entry to the ranks, but while Ed Mann did re-join (he'd last been in the 1981-82 line-up), Tommy Mars walked out after a dispute with Zappa in rehearsal. Far older ex-members Flo and Eddie (Howard Kaylan and Mark Volman) were also intended for some form of inclusion, and attended some early rehearsals before dropping out – either because it was discovered that some of the Zappa tour-dates would clash with some of their own, or because they decided that the pre-teen following they had gained in recent years would not be suitable recipients for songs about wanking and spanking.

To this hard-core of personnel were added newcomer Mike Kenneally (guitar, keyboards, vocals) and a horn-section: Albert Wing (tenor sax), Paul Carmen (alto sax) and Kurt McGettrick (baritone sax), plus two of the Fowler Brothers from days of mid-70s yore, Walt on trumpet (and some keyboards) and Bruce on trombone.

Ed Mann says that these rehearsals for what would be the 1988 tour lasted ten hours a day, five days a week for four-and-a-half months. The tour itself started with an American East Coast leg, beginning in Albany New York on 2 February and getting as far into the mid-West as Chicago. At the Washington DC show on 10 February, Zappa introduced his favourite newscaster, Daniel Schorr (putative anchor-man of the impossible *Night School* TV series Zappa had proposed the previous year) and got him to sing 'It Ain't Necessarily So' and 'Summertime'. This first American leg ended back in New York State at Uniondale on 25 March.

The European leg began 15 days later on 9 April at Bourges in France, also played Birmingham NEC, Wembley Arena and Brighton Conference Centre in April, and moved on to dates that included Stockholm, Oslo and Helsinki, Hamburg, Linz and Mannheim, and Bilbao in Spain, ending with some Italian shows. At Stockholm, one of the groups formed in recent years by Zappa fanatics with wholly Zappoid repertoires, the Swedish band Zappsteetoot, was able to join Zappa's band on stage to play on the improvised section of the showpiece number 'Big Swifty' (a piece that originally took up one side of the *Waka Jawaka/Hot Rats* album). In Italy the promoter was a musicologist who gave Frank a cassette, which he played on the tour-bus, that introduced him to Sardinian vocal music: 'five or six old guys singing very low chords with tenor ornamentation'. (In 1990 Zappa would get a field-recording of some of this music, to 'sample' it into the Synclavier.)

The repertoire, which varied a lot from show to show,

209

revealed Zappa's 1980s interest in cover-versions. Not only was there 'Whipping Post', with Dweezil joining his father for the guitar-duels on that number on the US dates, but also covers of Ravel's 'Bolero', Led Zeppelin's 'Stairway To Heaven', with the horn-section playing Jimmy Page's guitar-solo note for note, as transcribed by Zappa, and the Beatles' 'I Am The Walrus'. The new songs were to be gathered together on 1988's *Broadway The Hard Way* album, and the non-new ones on April 1991's *The Best Band You Never Heard In Your Life*; two months later *Make A Jazz Noise Here* was a more classical musically oriented compilation from the same tour.

The tour collapsed in mid-schedule after the last European gig, which was in Genoa on 9 June, and before the scheduled American West Coast leg. They had already played 81 shows on the tour, and now it was costing Zappa lots of money in cancellation fees. It fell apart because on this tour bassist Scott Thunes had the additional duty of being the sort of tour-foreman, and wasn't able to handle this without creating a build-up of resentment and hostility from the other musicians. Eventually they took a vote that they wouldn't tolerate working with Thunes any longer, and asked Frank to drop him. He sacked the rest of them instead, retaining on the pay-roll only Thunes and Mike Kenneally (who hadn't voted against Thunes). It was the end of a long road.

9. You Can't Do That On Stage Anymore?

More Trouble Every Day, Bamboozled By Love

Back to the basement. Well, partly. After the ill-fated final tour (on the American leg of which, 1988 being election year, Zappa had been using the intermissions to urge voter-registration), it was predictable that he would remain busy over the next four years, on a variety of sometimes less than predictable projects. These were to include a TV appearance as a mute humpbacked servant, trying to get financial backing for a Russian horror-film, publishing an autobiography, and deciding whether to run for President of the USA in 1992.

He resumed post-tour '88 busily. April had already seen the release of the double-album *Guitar*, which as the name implies, comprised more guitar-solos, this time from the heavy-metal Steve Vai period 1982–4; and of the *You Can't Do That On Stage Anymore* sampler – another double-album, on vinyl only and not available in the USA – and the CD-only *You Can't Do That On Stage Anymore* (double-CD; all territories). This was the first in a planned series of six double-CDs re-presenting live work taken from 20 years' of performances, and this one went briefly back to 1969 for a cut of 'Louie Louie' recorded in New York with Lowell George on vocals and guitar. In June, while still in Italy at the end of the tour, he presented to officials in Milan a proposal for writing, producing and directing a 'special entertainment event for the conclusion of the World Cup Football Finals' in summer 1990. This was to be financed by the

City of Milan and the Italian Football Committee. His proposed work was to be an opera, to be premièred at La Scala and broadcast worldwide via satellite, with text in English, Italian, German, French, Spanish, Portuguese and Russian, using La Scala's soloists and chorus with the orchestra of Milan's sister-city, the Chicago Symphony. Zappa notes in his book that this proposal was turned down by socialist, communist and anarchist Milanese officials.

Zappa was also writing his book (*The Real Frank Zappa Book*), with Peter Occhiogrosso making a first draft onto computer-disc from tapes of Frank talking and answering questions, and then Frank re-drafting the floppy discs and then sending them to Ann Patty at Poseidon Press. The book records the fact that on 23 August, he wrote the dedication to the book: 'to Gail, the kids, Stephen Hawking and Ko-Ko'. (Stephen Hawking is, of course, a famously intelligent scientist; Ko-Ko was a famously intelligent gorilla who had died just a year or two before Zappa came to write his book. He mentions her again later, in a December 1990 interview.)

Meanwhile one of 'the kids', Dweezil, was releasing his second album, called *My Guitar Wants To Kill Your Mama*. This time Frank did not produce it, but it featured one of his songs as the title-track (Frank's version is on the wonderful *Weasels Ripped My Flesh*), and featured too the ex-Zappa band players Terry Bozzio on drums and Scott Thunes on bass.

In October Frank released more work of his own: two simultaneous issues, in fact. The second volume of *You Can't Do That On Stage Anymore* (with a three-LP vinyl version in the States as well as the double-CD on both sides of the Atlantic) was a complete concert recorded in Helsinki in 1974 with Zappa on sizzling guitar form (as Mike Fish wrote in *The Wire*, 'sample [in the original sense of the term] "RDNZL" for a relentless yet somehow luminous improvisation') and with the band that included Ruth Underwood, George Duke and Napoleon Murphy Brock. At the same time came the single-album *Broadway The Hard Way*, which assembled the new songs that had been performed on the 1988 tour, and which, among other things, added up to yet another Zappa assault on TV fundamentalists.

At 5.30 am on Christmas Day, he finished reading the first set of galleys of his book, as it tells us in the book itself, and promptly began writing the postscript, 'The Last Word', which fulminates about pro-George Bush media bias in the election campaign, AIDS propaganda, God and poison-gas. (Well he would, wouldn't he? How else would Frank Zappa welcome in Christmas Day?)

In an interview with New Zealand media personality Gary Steel, Zappa said that from the end of the 1988 tour until November 1989 he 'was virtually 100 per cent in the studio mixing and editing that tour material. The only time [he] took off was for five trips to Russia and one to Czechoslovakia [in January 1990].' This may have been the case, but nevertheless Zappa did actually find time for many other activities through 1989 as well. He was involved in fighting off the greed-soaked attempt by HARP (the Hollywood Association of Record Producers) to get home-studios closed down because they were 'a threat' to 'proper' studios' business. Zappa's studio, UMRK, was one of those likely to be affected. The issue was resolved with a compromise early in 1990, when it was agreed that home studios could keep functioning so long as their owner-occupiers didn't rent them out to other artists, but not before HARP had used the fine-print in the California zoning laws to close down home studios owned by various musicians, including Steve Vai.

Zappa's trips to the Eastern bloc were in response to the rapidly changing situation there, with the American artist and capitalist entrepreneur inspired to get involved in a number of ways. He went to Moscow to try to get himself a USSR record-deal with Melodiya, the State record-label. He also went back and forth to Moscow in pursuit of (eventually fruitless) discussions aimed at 'facilitating American finance' for a Russian-originated horror film, and (equally fruitless) discussions intended to help an American business acquaintance of his set up a business that would sell deep-frozen muffins to the USSR. Just what the Soviet people needed most.

Frank told Gary Steel: 'After the Czech trip I was side-tracked into some foreign trade stuff that I'm doing with my Why Not? company. It's a Delaware corporation chartered to licensing, consulting and social engineering . . . When I went over there I met all these very interesting people who wanted to do a wide range of business things with people from the West, and there was no way for them to get in touch . . . [I was] kind of like a dating service. Find out what somebody wants over there and try to find 'em a partner over here.'

But frozen muffins? Workers of the Eastern bloc disunite, you have nothing to gain but fast-food outlets.

Zappa was an underground hero behind the Iron Curtain. 'I was really surprised,' he told Gary Steel, 'how they appreciated me in those countries. They have a free glasnost rock'n'roll newspaper, a pathetic thing from Siberia . . . Somebody from a radio station gave me a history of just what they have to go through to get [imported] records . . . I guess some of the stuff I did in the early days was smuggled in there and a whole cult formed around it. On my first trip to Moscow I went to this place called the Stosnomic Centre in Gorky Park. This guy . . . had created facilities where rock'n'roll bands from all over the country could rehearse and he would help them get record-deals and so on . . . in one of these rooms was a Siberian r'n'b band. I walked in and I thought the guy was going to have a heart-attack: he couldn't speak for spluttering. Through an interpreter he says 'Look at this,' and opens his wallet, shows me a photo of his house in Siberia – he's got all of my records on the rack, posters of me on the walls . . . Just so odd. You never know who's listening or why they're listening.'*

Zappa's most significant forays into the Eastern bloc were to take place the following year, 1990, as everything was un-bloc-ing, and as fellow-artist Vaclav Havel had risen from being a blacklisted figure in Czechoslovakia to being its President. However, Zappa has said that although he can't prove it, he knows that the US administration, and specifically James Baker,

* A letter from an East German reader of the British Zappa fanzine *T'Mershi Duween* published in issue no. 10, December 1989, gave this round-up of Frank Zappa releases in Eastern Europe: in East Germany, Bulgaria and Romania, nothing. In Poland, four or five bootlegs on Postcard Records. In Czechoslovakia the sampler *Frank Zappa & The Mothers*, and in Yugoslavia for some reason *Zappa In New York* and *Zoot Allures*. And in the Gary Steel interview in 1990, Zappa said that by then he had clinched a licensing deal for Czechoslovakia 'but there are still other deals that can be done for Hungary, Poland, Romania, Bulgaria and all the rest'.

'applied pressure to stop Havel doing business with me'.*

While Zappa was in the studios and making his trips to Eastern Europe, Hollywood was releasing the Dennis Hopper/Sean Penn film *Colors*, which featured a burst of the original Zappa-penned 'Memories Of El Monte' by the Penguins (though it isn't on the film 'soundtrack' LP); Poseidon Press published *The Real Frank Zappa Book* and was getting it translated into Dutch and Russian; Rhino Records, which had acquired the Bizarre/Straight catalogue (except for Zappa's own work within that catalogue) from Herb Cohen, put out on CD the Lenny Bruce *Berkeley Concert*, first issued in 1968, on which Zappa had been 'Executive Producer', and the GTOs album, on which Zappa had been the real producer. This re-release was timed to take advantage of the fact that ex-GTO Pamela des Barres (Miss Pamela, one-time nanny to Frank and Gail and long since captured for posterity in *200 Motels*) had just published a book of her own, *I'm With The Band*. This came out in Pan Books in the UK a few months after its American publication, apparently after attempts to stop it by one of the stars featured within it, Jimmy Page. Frank and more particularly Gail come out of the book comparatively well, and Pamela ends up a plucky survivor instead of the low-life junkie suicide that might once have seemed inevitable. There was talk of a film based on the book, to be directed by Alan Arkush, possibly with Dweezil as 'Miami Vice' star Don Johnson and Moon Unit as a GTO. Rosanna Arquette was rumoured to have expressed interest in playing Pamela.

Zappa himself put out three Honker Home Videos. One was *Uncle Meat*, the older parts of which had been the always-rumoured-and-never-seen *Uncle Meat: The Movie*, which some fans had been waiting for since 1969, not least the 'infamous' shower scene in which Mother Don Preston and one Phylus Altenhaus rub each other down with hamburgers. The two-hour video release of 20 years later re-incorporates this material, much of it fragmentary 'home movie' footage, into a new whole

---

* From blues-specialist Neil Slaven's interview with Zappa in London in July 1991, on Zappa's way back from another such trip; the interview was published in *Vox* magazine, July 1992.

that also includes Zappa in his basement in 1970 and in 1982. After the credits have rolled, Zappa fills up the tape with disparate extras: a visit to Barfko-Swill and a Bruce Bickford clay-animation for *Night School*. Then there was the video *The True Story Of 200 Motels*, which also includes home-movie footage and Zappadditions to what is basically the Dutch television network VPRO's 1971 documentary on the making of the *200 Motels* film, directed by Roelof Kiers. And then there was the *Video From Hell*, detailed in an earlier chapter.

The 'classical music' side of Zappa's activity was represented in 1989 by a press-conference and debate 'An Evening With Pierre Boulez And Frank Zappa' at the Schoenberg Hall, UCLA, presented by the UCLA Music Department and the Los Angeles Philharmonic Orchestra. This was partly a discussion between the two main guests and MC David Braxton, and partly a question-and-answer session with the people in the audience. Zappa's politeness to Boulez scotched rumours that the two had fallen out over the recording or concert performance of *The Perfect Stranger*.

Somebody asked Zappa: 'What colour is your aura?', to which he replied:

'"What colour is your aura?"! Welcome to California! Welcome to a college in California!'

During this section Zappa recounted the beginnings of another doomed project, saying that he had, 'about four months' previously, 'made a proposal to the World's Fair Organization' for Seville in 1992, to put together a world orchestra and commission composers from all over the world to write five-to-eight minute pieces for this orchestra. He said that in five days' time he was flying out to Madrid for discussions with the Christopher Columbus Committee, 'which is another organization . . . that is putting on a big event in 1992 [and] wants to finance the orchestra. I will believe it when I get a contract for it, but if they decide that they will finance this orchestra, then I will get on a plane and start shopping for musicians all over the world.'

The 'Evening With Pierre Boulez And Frank Zappa' ended with Zappa being asked to identify his 'primary goal', to which Zappa the composer answered: 'That's easy. I'm still waiting for an accurate performance!'

These excursions aside, it was indeed November 1989, as Zappa had reported, when he emerged from his studio-mixing: and he plunged at once into a mass of other activity. He released *You Can't Do That On Stage Anymore Volume 3*, which included the last of the material previously available only on the vinyl sampler issued 19 months earlier. This third double-CD in the series reverted to the ragbag formula, with lots from the 1984 concerts, including a duelling-guitars 'Sharleena' with Dweezil and a couple of cuts of previously-unissued songs – 'Ride My Face To Chicago' and 'Chana in de Bushwop'. There's also some Roxy 1973, some 1981-band *You Are What You Is* material, some Berlin 1968 and more besides. This release features the editing-together of different Zappa line-ups in mid-song – first on 'Drowning Witch', which cuts from the 1984 band to the 1982, then on 'Zoot Allures', which cuts from the earliest extant performance, February 1976, to one from 1982, and finally with some 'King Kong' from three 1982 shows *and* from the ill-fated Rainbow concert of 1971!

On 12 November Zappa gave a (very short) speech at a 'pro-choice' rally at Rancho Park in Los Angeles. (Synchronized rallies were being held all over the USA.) It was not one of his better efforts, and in the course of two short minutes, he managed to denigrate the importance of 'women's issues' and to sound politically naive, nationalistic and thoroughly bombastic. A sample:

'This should not be seen as a matter only affecting women's rights. The matter of choice is something basic to being an American. When someone is antichoice, they are anti-American.' This repulsive, classic argument, used by right-wing populists through the ages, makes Zappa sound more like Senator McCarthy than a libertarian.

November also had Zappa interviewed by Flo and Eddie on their brand-new radio show on WXRK New York, and just before Christmas he spent four hours chatting with the Norwegian branch of his fan-club. And that was the end of the me-decade.

1990 began with the release of the Honker Home Video *The Amazing Mr Bickford*, which included Bickford's extraordinary animation for some of the LSO recordings, and with

217

Frank Zappa's next visit to Czechoslovakia. This time he travelled at the invitation of Czech rock musician Michael Kocáb, a member of a delegation of Czechoslovakians who had just previously met Zappa on a US visit. He flew into Prague from Moscow on 20 January. About 5000 fans and a number of the new government's officials were at the airport to greet him, and he was taken to a meeting with the mayor of Prague at the Troja Chateau. He held a press-conference in the Knights' Hall and then had a question-and-answer session with members of the then three-years-old Czechoslovakian fan-club (total membership: 50).* Then Zappa met underground artists in the Krivan Hotel, where 12 murals painted for the occasion were on display. A month later these were destroyed at the behest of the hotel manager. Zappa sang with the former members of The Plastic People of the Universe.

On 22 January there was a visit to the Loreta Cloister, where Zappa played an historic glockenspiel once played by Liszt, and then he walked to Prague Castle to meet Vaclav Havel. Havel was familiar with some of Zappa's work, and urged him to consider himself as a cultural liaison officer for the new régime in its approaches to the west. Zappa and Havel then watched the changing of the guard and lunched together, with Frank also sightseeing round the castle and signing a deal for the Czechoslovakian release of five LPs. There was also a meeting with Czech cartoon director Jiri Barta, an appearance at a TV studio and a visit to the 'IV Youth Club' where Zappa delivered a monologue with piano accompaniment by the trip's instigator Michael Kocáb. At one of his meetings, Zappa remarked: 'I've come to Czechoslovakia to see communism dying, but it's still kicking. It's necessary to put an end to it.'

That night there was a gathering of Czech pop and rock people at a club called the White Horse, which Zappa attended, and at which he sang two songs over a playback of the *Tinseltown Rebellion* album. The next day he went to a meeting

---

* These included 35-year-old Pravoslav Tomek, who provides much of the information on this visit. He notes that right up until Zappa's visit, 'we all who loved him were under surveillance of the secret police. Some of us were told during interrogations "We'll beat that Zappa out of your heads." ' Tomek's information comes in a letter received from him by Fred Tomsett at the Sheffield HQ of fanzine *T'Mershi Duween*.

with further members of the government at the parliament building, and then back at the Intercontinental Hotel he met aficionado Pravoslav Tomek, who had been making a video of the whole four-day visit, as well as taking photos that are almost comic. They show Zappa walking the streets of Prague with one or two Czechs, and it is always Zappa who looks the most archetypically mittel-European. This solemn-faced, awkward-bodied middle-aged man with a heavy moustache decidedly greying, stands in a dark, heavy overcoat, talking earnestly to other earnest, soberly-dressed men. They all look like site-inspectors from the Czechoslovakian Ministry of Urban Water Supplies.

At their meeting, Zappa at first suggested Tomek send him the video he'd been making but then suggested a personal handing-over instead. Tomek wrote later that all this 'was complicated by the steps the American administration took against Frank's mission to Czechoslovakia before the visit of President Havel to the US and Europe'. As of the autumn of 1991, Tomek still had possession of what was in all a 7½-hour video.

While he was there, Zappa too was filming: fronting some documentary film designed for American television, which he edited in Paris during a stop-over on his way back to the States. He was due to return in May.

Back in the States, he completed his first TV music-score, for *Outrage At Valdez*, a documentary on the oil-spillage scandal, made by the Cousteau Society, to which the composer donated his fee. This was screened in late March in the USA. He also had discussions with ex-Mother Jeff Simmons about a project by the latter to be called 'Queen of the Spy Guitar', though nothing seems to have come of it. Meanwhile The Fall's new album, *Extricate*, included a song about Zappa called 'I'm Frank'; there was a performance of his piece 'Dupree's Paradise' by the Civic Orchestra of Chicago – the training orchestra of the Chicago Symphony Orchestra on 26 April; and the 1988 tour-musician Mike Kenneally started working on writing lead-sheets for a show based in part around *Broadway The Hard Way* that was scheduled to appear as a show *on* Broadway at some future date. It was to be called *Zappa's Universe* and would feature Kenneally, Bobby Martin, Scott Thunes and others.

Penthouse magazine published the 'Porn Wars' chapter of *The Real Frank Zappa Book*, and in Britain the hardback edition of the book sold out its print-run. (A paperback appeared in Europe, including Britain, in August, and a Czech translation was put in hand.) Moon Unit and Dweezil, having finally got a deal for the sitcom they'd long been touting, saw it in production in the spring. Frank commented: 'I won't say it's based on this family but there are certain similarities to the way this household runs.' As originally proposed, the basis of the sitcom was to be that it centred upon a family of weirdos surrounded by deeply normal suburban neighbours. However, CBS changed it round in production, and it ended up wretchedly as yet another deeply normal suburban family with implausibly weird neighbours. The Zappas were unhappy with it, and so were audiences; by the end of the year, after one short season, it had already been pulled. Moon Unit and Dweezil also contributed to a charity album (along with Flo and Eddie, among others) called *Gumby: The Green Album.*

Rumours started circulating in 1989 that Frank Zappa was ill – that he had either contracted cancer of the throat or of the prostate. One or two ex-Mothers dropped hints to this effect 'off the record' in interviews, and gradually the possibility of Frank having cancer, perhaps of his being seriously ill, became widespread in the music industry and around LA. The first indication that there was probably substance to some of this rumour came at the end of May 1990, when he had to cancel a visit to Czechoslovakia and back out of flying to Amsterdam to attend the Music Media Exhibition as a keynote speaker. Cancellation was due to illness. There seemed no doubt any longer that his health was cause for concern among those who admired his work as well as within the personal circles of family and friends. However, he saw no reason to make any kind of public announcement on the subject, so that rumours were all that circulated – which is how it continued to be all through the rest of 1990 and most of 1991, until Zappa's children felt impelled to offer a public explanation for his non-attendance at the Broadway show *Zappa's Universe* that November.

In the interim, though, Zappa was only markedly incapacitated by his illness occasionally. Having cancelled his trips at the end of May, he was giving interviews in June – while in Eastern Europe, 16 June saw the staging of a unique event: an East German Zappa Convention, to which people travelled not only from all over East Germany but from West Germany and the UK too. One person had travelled from Portland Oregon in order to attend. Things were loosening up – such a convention would have been impossible only a couple of years earlier – but not at such a pace that anyone attending could have dreamt that less than two years later there would be no East and West Germany. Similarly, in the case of Czechoslovakia, it was only as from the spring of 1990 that its citizens were free to travel, and no-one looking forward to the removal of Soviet troops the following June could have guessed how soon afterwards there would be no such thing as a Soviet Union to *have* troops. Nor that at the end of 1992 there would be no Czechoslovakia either.

Meanwhile Zappa fell out with Ryko, and cancelled his deal with them, because despite consulting him, they put out the CD of *Sheik Yerbouti* with the wrong cover-art. Ryko ended up retaining the rights to issue some further 'product'; a deal was struck whereby future CD 'reissues' would appear independently on Barking Pumpkin in the States (and on Zappa Records in Britain), and most new work would be handled likewise, but Ryko would go ahead with its planned future releases of *You Can't Do That On Stage Anymore* volumes 4 to 6. Nevertheless, the effect of the dispute was that *Volume 4*, scheduled for release on 4 November, was delayed until May 1991, and Zappa sat out the rest of 1990 without issuing any albums at all.

On 20 September, in Lyons, Kent Nagano supervised performances of Zappa works, choreographed as ballets, played by the Orchestre de l'Opéra de Lyons and performed by the Ballet de l'Opéra de Lyons. Nagano conducted one of the chosen pieces, 'Strictly Genteel', and for the others the conductor was Robert Hughes. Zappa had hoped this performance would include the première of a new piece, 'I'm Stealing The Room', but in the event it didn't. It was rumoured that Zappa's illness had prevented his finishing the piece, but Nagano gave me a

221

different version of events: 'Several pieces were put forward as possibles, but when you make a ballet it's important that you have a choreographer who somehow feels inspired by the music. So the choreographers chose which pieces they wanted, and naturally some pieces got left out. But the music for that piece, so far as I know, was completed.' However, it was certainly the case that Zappa had hoped to attend the evening, and that in the end he couldn't make it.

In October, Zappa asked a friend of his, an ethnomusicologist who worked for an Italian broadcasting organization, if he could go back to Sardinia to make him a field-recording of Sardinian vocal music (to which he'd been introduced by the Italian promoter on the 1988 tour). A few days later, the friend made the trip, and subsequently supplied a tape of what Zappa described as 'five old drunk guys doing an impromptu concert'. Zappa 'sliced it up to make samples for the Synclavier'.

Over a two-day period at the end of the month, the composer sat in his basement studio and recorded a four-hour interview for Dutch radio, destined to be broadcast (by NOS Radio) on his birthday in December. An edited-highlights tape, *The Supplement*, was officially issued by Barfko-Swill at the end of the year. And in late November until early December, Gail, Dweezil, Ahmet and Moon Unit were in Australia, partly for Gail to have discussions with Festival Records and partly because Zappa, fed up with the problems of disseminating his work in the current American cultural climate, wanted Australia checked out as a possible place to set up a sort of colony of artists, as Walter Gropius had done with the Bauhaus group in pre-Nazi Germany. By 5 December, however, Zappa had crossed Australia off his list, and was telling the New Zealand interviewer Gary Steel by phone from his home that he'd been scandalized to hear how powerful the unions were in Australia. Steel told him New Zealand would be better – (well he would, wouldn't he?) Zappa said he'd admired 'the balls' of the decision to refuse to allow the American Navy to bring any nuclear equipment into New Zealand waters; Steel said that actually the government had now reverted to being far more reactionary and it was now business as usual with the USA.

Five days before Christmas, Zappa recorded a telephone-interview (this time from his bedroom, because the phones in his studio were out of order) with Swedish National Radio in Stockholm. The following day, 21 December, he turned 50.

In Britain, on 27 December, Channel 4 Television ran a Shelley Duvall production called 'The Boy Who Left Home To Find Out About The Shivers', in its *Faerie Tale Theatre* slot. This hour-long TV-film featured Frank Zappa in four scenes, as Attila the mute humpbacked servant of the king. Dressed in sackcloth and never speaking, he got pushed around by Christopher Lee and David Warner. What a fulsome tribute to an eminent contemporary composer on the occasion of his fiftieth birthday! That sort of thing (an early 1992 repeat of the Monkees' film *Head* is another instance) seems virtually the only way Zappa gets onto British television. And apparently it is only by the same sort of vehicle or by appearing on talk-shows that he can get onto American television too. In mainland Europe they take contemporary culture more seriously, and are far more inclined to televise Zappa doing his real work – conducting and leading his band in concert-performance, for example. It's the same with radio. In the United Kingdom his music isn't exactly a mainstay of Radios 1 or 3, but he's all right for a guest-spot on *Midweek with Libby Purves* on Radio 4. The contrast with other parts of Europe – even with other small islands on its edges – is highlit by the fact that when, as a Briton, you read in *T'Mershi Duween* that 'Icelandic State Radio are [*sic*] planning a five hour Zappa broadcast soonish. Why can't we do that here?' the question merely prompts aguffaw.

The Zappa offspring started 1991 by appearing in the 40-minute *Give Peace A Chance* video and then Dweezil's band, which now included younger brother Ahmet on lead vocals, went on tour. They were support to the newly re-formed Spinal Tap, and, playing at the Anaheim Disney Hotel, Dweezil included in his set a revised version of his father's song 'Broken Hearts Are For Assholes', the lyrics amended to address the issue of the Gulf War.

In February there was a 25th Anniversary reissue of *Freak Out!* on vinyl (a CD would follow in mid-July), and this happened to coincide with Frank reaching a provisional out-of-court settlement with the six ex-Mothers Of Invention who

223

were suing him for 'unpaid royalties' in Los Angeles, arguing that he'd profited from the release of old tapes (the *Old Masters* box-sets) without paying them. They had also been suing him for 'defamation', because when they'd tried to launch their legal action on the royalties matter in 1985, Zappa had been quoted at the time as responding that their action was 'the product of chemically-altered imaginations'. Under the terms of the out-of-court agreement (which was destined not to last out the year) – or *because* of its terms, rather – Zappa cancelled his plans to issue a CD of the whole of the now-legendary 1968 Royal Festival Hall concert.

Meanwhile on 4 March a single taken from concert performances of 20 years later, comprising Zappa band covers of Led Zeppelin's 'Stairway To Heaven' and Ravel's 'Bolero', were issued in 12-inch vinyl and CD formats. The following month, Zappa released a new double-CD, *The Best Band You Never Heard In Your Life* (a title chosen to express its author's continued resentment at the way the third leg of that tour had never come to pass), which included the two tracks from the single as well as covers of the old Cream 'classic' 'Sunshine Of Your Love', 'Purple Haze' (from a soundcheck) and 'When Irish Eyes Are Smiling'. It was also distinguished by what one review described as 'sumptuous new textures' and 'a horn section of huge panache' on revisits to Zappa repertoire items from 'Eric Dolphy Memorial Barbecue' (fused from three different shows) to 'Zoot Allures' (from Brighton), and from 'Zomby Woof' to 'Let's Move To Cleveland' and 'The Torture Never Stops'.

On May Day Dweezil's band, by this time touring Europe, reached the Marquee, where their insanely loud set included a Dweezil guitar-piece built around a medley of something between 20 and 50 songs. Barking Pumpkin released his third album, a double called *Confessions*, again featuring Moon Unit, Ahmet, Mike Kenneally and Scott Thunes. Frank Zappa's *You Can't Do That On Stage Anymore Volume 4*, delayed from 1990 by wrangles with Ryko, also came out in May, and on the 11th, some of his music was performed at the Brighton Festival, the Composers' Ensemble playing 'Igor's Boogie', 'Little House I Used To Live In', 'Uncle Meat', 'The Be-Bop Tango' and 'The Black Page No.2'.

In June, not content with having issued a double-CD's worth of 'new' material in each of the preceding two months, Zappa now released another CD: *Make a Jazz Noise Here*, which also drew its material from the 1988 tour, though this time with more of an emphasis on modern-classical music. In 1992 the CD of *Make A Jazz Noise Here* would be withdrawn because of permission problems with the copyright-holders of the Stravinsky and Bartok ingredients on the record.

Later in June 1991 Zappa flew back to Eastern Europe, this time to attend concerts in Czechoslovakia and Hungary to celebrate the departure of Soviet troops from these countries. In fact, for the Prague concert, on 24 June, Frank not only attended but performed – his first guitar performance since the collapse of the 1988 tour – though only for a few minutes. The concert was essentially by his old Czech mate Michael Kocáb and his band, and Frank told the crowd, through an interpreter, that he was happy the Soviet troops were leaving and that he hoped the Czechoslovak people could keep their country unique. Then he played a reggae improvisation with Kocáb's band, including a guitar-solo several minutes long. This has since appeared on a Czech CD of the concert, *Prazsky Vyber – Live – Adieu CA*.* There was a comparable event in Budapest, at which Zappa again guested with a local band.

On his way home, he stopped off in London to see his UK record distributor, the world-music indy Music For Nations, and to do some interviews. He appeared on Libby Purves' 'Midweek' show on Radio 4 on 3 July and did a Radio 1 interview that was broadcast on the 12th, and the Neil Slaven interview for *Vox* magazine (eventually published almost a year later in the July 1992 issue). His interviews included his announcing that he was still doing 'a feasibility study' on whether to stand for the US Presidency in the 1992 elections. This involved getting US radio-stations to invite listener-response, which Zappa reported later was extremely favourable. By the autumn, no decision on whether to go ahead and stand had been announced, and then Zappa's illness was announced instead,

---

* On AP Records of Prague, catalogue no. 0001-2311. 'CA' was the Czechs' abbreviated name for the Soviet army.

leaving it implied that, like Edward Kennedy, he would be dropping the election idea at least for the time being.

Later that July the CD reissues of *Freak Out!* and *Ship Arriving Too Late To Save A Drowning Witch* were issued, the latter offering, unusually, nothing new beyond the back-cover design. Meanwhile the Ensemble Modern, a 25-piece chamber orchestra, commissioned Zappa to write a piece for them to première at the following year's Frankfurt Festival (for the week beginning 14 September 1992), and they were in Los Angeles for two weeks in the second half of July (1991) to do some preliminary, pre-composition work directly with Frank.

In August, Zappa issued a ten-LP box-set . . . but with a difference. This time he got hold of some bootleg records that were in circulation among collectors and on sale at record fairs, and reissued pressings of them himself as a set called *Beat The Boots*. They were offered in three formats: as a ten-LP set with a T-shirt and badge; or as a set of eight cassettes likewise; or as eight separate CDs. He didn't spend money cleaning them up: he just put them out himself, saying that if people were going to buy this crap they might as well buy it from him. The concerts were from Stockholm 1967 (*'Tis The Season To Be Jelly*); Boston 1968 (*The Ark*); New York City 1971 (*Freaks & Motherfuckers*); Stockholm and Sydney 1973 (*Piquantique*); South Bend, Indiana 1974 (*Unmitigated Audacity*); Saarbrucken 1978 (a double-LP); Paris, 1979 (*Anyway The Wind Blows*, another double-LP); and New York City's Palladium Hallowe'en Concert from 1981 (*As An Am*). When these were issued, without any further payment being made to any of the musicians who had played the music on them, one of them, Arthur Barrow, phoned his old friend Frank on behalf of several others as well as himself, to ask if such payments were to be forthcoming. Gail told him there were to be no payments, because the recordings were still sort of 'unofficial'. When he pointed out that they were now being released officially (and commercially), Gail told Barrow never to ring the house again, and hung up. A case of going on how you meanly started. The Zappas and the Mothers: still squabbling about money after all these years. But things were about to change, and with unexpected speed.

In November 1991, *Zappa's Universe* was staged for four performances at New York's Ritz Theater, organized by Joel Thome but with Zappa himself involved in its coming into being. It was billed as 'A crossover music theater event' and 'a tribute to Frank Zappa in his 50th Birthday Year'. The first (short) section of the show consisted of Thome conducting his Orchestra Of Our Time playing Satie's 'Socrate', linking this tenuously to Zappa by a programme-note to the effect that both were concerned about censorship issues. The second (main) section of the show was a rock band Mike Kenneally had put together with himself on guitar, Mats Oberg and Marc Ziegenhagen on keyboards, Scott Thunes on bass, Morgan Agren on drums and Jonathan Haas on percussion: a mix of old Zappa musos and members of Zappsteetoot. Kenneally took Zappa's vocal and guitar parts. On some numbers the group had the orchestra playing behind it, and on some numbers there were guests, including the *a capella* groups Rockapella and The Persuasions, opera-style singer Maureen McNally, Steve Vai and Dweezil taking solos and guitar-duetting on 'Dirty Love', and Dale Bozzio, who helped act out 'Wet T-Shirt Nite'. At the first performance, *T'Mershi Duween* correspondent Geoff Wills reported, someone in the audience was 'so overcome' by this audio-visual spectacle that he was moved to exclaim, 'Dale! I'd eat the peanuts out of your shit!'

Polygram recorded the first show for a home video release and taped the first two nights' shows for release of highlights as a 'soundtrack album'.

On the day of the first performance, CNN ran a TV news item about Frank Zappa having cancer, which 'outed' his family into issuing a statement, read out by Moon Unit and given out as a newsflash an hour before the concert, at which Zappa had intended to act as 'host', was due to begin. The statement ran:

'As many of you know, [Zappa]'s been diagnosed by journalists as having cancer. We'd like you to know his doctors have diagnosed prostate cancer which he's been fighting successfully. He's been feeling well and working hard and planned to attend. Up until the last minute we were hoping he would feel well enough to get on the plane and come here. There are occasionally periods when he's not feeling as well and it's really unfortunate that it happened during this event.'

Soon after eight o'clock and at the start of the first show, Moon Unit and Dweezil appeared on stage and announced their father's non-appearance. This time they didn't mention cancer at all, referring instead to 'a dose of flu'. At this point, significant numbers of the first-night audience left. Subsequently, the media picked up on the story and in some cases (the *Daily Mail*, for instance) ran a version in which Zappa had only months to live. This was a doom-mongering guess, though as it turned out, not so very inaccurate. In truth, Frank Zappa had two years left to him.

All through 1992 and 1993, the real state of his health remained only privately known; outsiders could only make guesstimates based on what we know about the work projects and appearances Zappa cancelled in 1992, and on what's known about prostate cancer itself.

Because this form of cancer is so common, it follows that it is a common cause of death. In Britain, where breast cancer is the commonest cause of cancer death in women, pushing lung cancer into second place, male cancer death is most commonly from lung cancer (77 men a day) and prostate cancer comes next. It kills 8,400 men a year in Britain.*

Yet, prostate cancer is not necessarily a serious illness, and almost comes with the territory for middle-aged men in the West (especially, in the USA, among black ones). Within a month of the *Daily Mail* declaring that prostate cancer had Zappa at death's door, the *Independent on Sunday* ran a piece headed 'Common Complaints: Cancer of the Prostate Gland' which began by claiming that it 'seems to be an inevitable part of growing old'. Having said that, however, 'Dr Tony Smith' goes on to say that its cause is a mystery, that it often spreads to the bones and that in a third of cases by the time it is discovered it has spread too far for surgical cure. 'The prostate is the gland, a little smaller than a golf ball, that makes the fluid in which the sperm are carried . . . and it can be felt and assessed by a doctor during an examination of the rectum . . . If the cancer is

---

* Figures are from a World Cancer Research Fund leaflet using 1990 statistics, published 1992 by WCRF.

deprived of male sex hormones its growth slows down and often stops.' They used to counter it with female sex hormone injections; today, while suppressor and blocking drugs are used instead, drastic measures are still on offer. 'Removal of the testes achieves the same results and is often preferred.'

In May 1992, one of the musicians who kept in personal touch with the Zappa household reported privately that he was looking fine, had a healthy appetite and was working hard. This suggested that he was doing well enough to be described as 'in remission', which means that his cancer was being contained. If that were true, then the cancer may well not have spread, or if it had, then this too might have been contained and not be progressing. In which case, with medical treatment improving all the time – with it being possible, for instance, to induce 'boney spreads' to 'melt away' – Zappa's might still have been considered a relatively unserious condition at that point.

It was impossible to convert any of this into a prognosis. Just as it's possible to look ill and thin after a bout of depression or flu or overwork or dieting, it's also perfectly possible to have prostate cancer and look glowing with health. While the truth known to Zappa and his family was that in fact he had been misdiagnosed until it was too late to halt the cancer's progress, the outside world had no way to tell whether things were truly serious until Zappa himself chose to say so. In the meantime, all was speculation, fuelled by Zappa's inactivity.

If Zappa was largely out of action as from November 1991, others still worked on his music. Two days after the last performance of 'Zappa's Universe', the Birmingham Contemporary Music Group (that's Birmingham, England) gave the first of three performances of several works by Zappa and other current composers. The first performance was in Edinburgh on the 11th; they played Birmingham on the 22nd and made a recording of the material for BBC Radio 3 on the 29th. The works performed included Colin Matthews' 'Hidden Variables' and Mark Anthony Turnage's 'Kai', followed by Zappa pieces arranged by Philip Cashian and conducted by Stefan Asbury: 'Uncle Meat', 'Black Page No.2' and a stately whole-orchestra arrangement of 'Little House I Used to Live In (Piano Intro)'. Early in 1992 the Composers Ensemble performed a very short version of 'Revised Music for Low-Budget Orchestra' in London, and that April the Royal Northern College of Music put two of Zappa's pieces alongside work by Weill and Stravinsky in a concert at its home base in Manchester, combining its Wind Orchestra and its Jazz Band for the British premieres of 'Envelopes' and 'The Dog Breath Variations', conducted by Clark Rundell.

The Zappa tribute-bands continued to ply their wares too. As fanzine *T'Mershi Duween* commented: 'Over the last five years, there seems to have been a plague of them, from the Muffin Men in Liverpool to bands in Holland, Germany, Italy, Sweden and even Brazil . . .' By 1993 there was also a Japanese Zappa tribute-band.

The Muffin Men headlined at the Zappa Party Part II Freak Out in Münster, Germany, on 24th May 1992 and played a Zappa 52nd birthday celebration in Liverpool that December. In July 1993 they toured Europe, sharing some bills with the band of ex-Mothers long known as the Grandmothers. The month before, while Grandmothers' founding member Jimmy Carl Black was touring Britain with Eugene Chadbourne, he reported that Captain Beefheart too was a victim of illness, in his case multiple sclerosis. Black said bluntly that Beefheart was 'sick, but not as sick as Zappa'.

Meanwhile 1992 had seen the inexplicably tardy back-catalogue CD release of the *Roxy & Elsewhere* album, though with none of the extras that fans had long looked forward to hearing. Various Zappa videos were queueing up for British Board of Film Censors certificates prior to official British release. Rhino Records put out a 19-track sampler of the old Bizarre/Straight material, excluding both Zappa and Wild Man Fischer. *You Can't Do That On Stage Anymore Volume 5* and *Volume 6* – a double-CD in each case – were released in the summer, and in October came the further double-CD *Playground Psychotics*, reprocessing yet more material from the Flo & Eddie era. In the spring of 1993, having arrived at a new settlement with the old Mothers of Invention, Zappa finally released the long-mooted *Ahead of Our Time*: an official CD, at last, of the 25-year-old Royal Festival Hall concert of 1968. In September 1993 came the equally belated release of the *Uncle*

Meat video. In contrast, both audio and video recordings of *Zappa's Universe* were released by Polygram a mere two years after the event. A full circle of sorts was completed by the CD being issued on none other than Verve Records in the USA. Concurrently (November 1993) Zappa issued what was to be the final record-release in his lifetime: *The Yellow Shark*.

It was when this music was recorded, in the autumn of 1992, that speculation that Zappa's illness was truly serious was much intensified, by what people saw of him in Germany when he appeared, and failed to appear, at the Frankfurt Music Festival to conduct the première of his work 'The Yellow Shark'. This had been commissioned by the Ensemble Modern in 1991 and worked on jointly by Zappa and the Ensemble through 1992: the one new project Zappa had not cancelled due to illness in recent times.

In the event – which took place three times, at the Alte Oper (Old Opera House), on 17, 18 and 19 September – 'The Yellow Shark' proved not to be a wholly new work but an umbrella-title for a collection of short pieces, some of which were new. In advance the programme was said to be constructed as follows. The new pieces were to comprise compositions for the Synclavier – 'Living In The Drum' and 'Beat The Reaper', this last accompanied by Canadian dance group Lalala Human Steps, as was to be the case also for a Synclavier performance of the older composition 'G-Spot Tornado', a work for two pianos, 'Ruth Is Sleeping', and four new works for the whole Ensemble, conducted by Peter Rundel: 'Amnerika', 'Get Whitey', 'The Yellow Shark' and 'Channel Mr. Boggins'. These were to be intermixed with a brass arrangement of 'Pound For A Brown On The Bus', a Synclavier arrangement by the Ensemble of 'Girl In The Magnesium Dress', a string quartet version of 'More Of The Above' (presumably a revisit to 'None Of The Above') and an Ensemble performance of 'The Be-Bop Tango', with 'The Dog-Breath Variations' planned as an encore. As a further part of each evening's event, Zappa himself was to conduct the Ensemble for three 'Improvisations' (the third to incorporate the text of 'Bobby Brown').

The reality was different. *T'Mershi Duween* correspondent Non Bohman reported it as follows: 'The first piece, "Overture", began with sinister Synclavier sounds as the Ensemble walked onto the dimly-lit stage. . . . Then FZ appeared and took the EM through strange musical cues using his specialised sign language. There was a manic percussion solo by Rumi Ogawa-Helferich behaving like Keith Moon's Japanese sister. This piece was just a warm-up, said Zappa, but it sounded phenomenal.

'Zappa off and EM conductor Peter Rundel on for "Dog/ Meat", a sparkling rendition of "The Dog-Breath Variations" followed by "Uncle Meat". Next was "Outrage At Valdez" for the Ensemble. This is the 1992 Zappa sound: compositional devices conceived on the Synclavier and translated to orchestral forces. . . . The virtuosity of "Time's Beach II" was brought to an end by the string players activating "cow moo" boxes. I think "III Revised 1992" for string quartet was [also] a version of "Time's Beach", although this material is so complex that . . . I couldn't be sure. This segued into "The Girl With The Magnesium Dress" for small ensemble (piano, three percussion, celeste, guitar, mandolin) . . . Back to full ensemble [twelve wind, two keyboards, three percussion and eight string; exotic instruments used for "The Yellow Shark" included alphorn, cimbalon, didgeridoo and banjo] for "The Be-Bop Tango" . . . Zappa came back on to conduct the EM while viola player Hilary Stuart told us about 'Food Gathering In Post-Industrial America' . . . This piece was replaced on the 18th and 19th by "Beat The Reaper" . . .

'After the intermission came "Ruth Is Sleeping" . . . The full ensemble played "Amnerika" (amnesia/America) . . . This segued into "None Of The Above" for string quintet . . . The Ensemble joined in for "Pentagon Afternoon" . . . Suddenly the Ensemble struck up a corny military march and Peter Rundel stormed off in disgust. Enter FZ in ridiculous party hat, followed by Hermann Kretzschmar in a huge blue top hat. "Welcome To The United States" consisted of Hermann reading selected texts [questions] from the US immigration form . . . Zappa coaxed appropriate musical themes and moods for each question [including] . . . two full ensemble assaults on "Louie Louie". FZ and HK marched off as the Ensemble played a loop of the first few bars of "A Pound For a Brown On The Bus". Peter Rundel regained the conductorship and "Pound"

was played through (wind and percussion only) . . . The full
Ensemble played "Get Whitey" . . . A suitable showstopper
ended the concert – 'G-Spot Tornado' [with the dance troupe
La La La Human Steps: three males and three females].' The
encore was a faster-still repeat of 'G-Spot Tornado' without the
dancers.

This first night, telecast live on the German pay-TV channel
Première, was greeted with great enthusiasm by the press and
critics, who also presented Zappa with a Lifetime Achievement
Award at a post-performance party.

But Zappa had had to be carried to the edge of the stage by
his bodyguard, and on-stage had shuffled rather than walked.
At the party afterwards, he stayed only twenty minutes. Next
day it was announced that he was feeling ill; he received medical
treatment and cancelled his appearance at the second evening's
performance. He managed to appear again for the final night –
but then flew back to Los Angeles, thus bowing out of the
performances he had planned to be a part of later the same
month in Berlin (22nd and 23rd) and Vienna (26th and 27th).*

At the press conference Zappa had given in advance in
Frankfurt on 21 July, the question of his health had been raised.
Asked if he was still thinking of pursuing a political career, he
replied straightforwardly: 'No, my health is not good enough
for that.' Another journalist then commented: 'What about
your health? I read you have cancer.' Zappa responded 'Yep,
you read right.' And back home in L.A., he added one more
public statement on the subject, telling the press: 'I was in bad
shape but I'm better now. I'm not in hospital, I'm in my kitchen.
I'm not dead. I have no intention of checking out any time this
week or within the forseeable future.'

So even at the end of 1992, while Frank Zappa's illness had
clearly become a very dark shadow hanging over him, it was
still possible for the observer to feel hopeful, as, still pursuing
the conceptual continuity of his life and work, Zappa continued
to insist, à la Varèse, that 'the present-day composer refuses to
die!'

* These went ahead without him, including an extra date in Vienna (though this
also excluded the dance troupe). Recordings were made of these performances – there
was also a radio broadcast from Berlin.

In a very short time, however, the rediscovered Motorhead said in an interview that Zappa's cancer had reached his back, and in response to persistent questioning and media-rumour, Frank himself issued a clarifying statement that left little room for hope:

'I'd been feeling sick for a number of years, but nobody diagnosed it. Then I got really ill and had to go to the hospital in an emergency. They did some tests and found out it had been growing undetected for anywhere from eight to ten years. By the time they found it, it was inoperable.'

Zappa also said: 'Time is the thing. Time is everything. How to spend time.' In March 1993, the composer was still able to receive, as visitors, whole troupes of musicians, among whom were the Meridian Arts Ensemble, who were proposing to record some of Zappa's work. He was, they reported, sufficiently alert to be able to make an array of suggestions about how they might handle their recording project. When they called on him again seven months later, Gail told them they could see him but he was in bed these days. They went in and saw him but found him barely able to speak.

By this time, as was revealed when *The Yellow Shark* CD was released in November 1993, steps had been taken to put Zappa's trademarks and copyrights into the ownership of 'the Zappa Family Trust'.

On Saturday 4 December, 1993, two and a half weeks before his 53rd birthday, Frank Zappa died at home, with his family around him. He was buried in a private, non-Christian ceremony the next day. Only after this was his death made public, with the family issuing this brief statement:

'Composer Frank Zappa left for his final tour just before 6pm Saturday.'

The composer had had mixed expectations of this final tour. He was not one who had looked forward confidently to a certain after-life. Yet, true to his character, he had clung to a sceptical form of hope which he could not sustain yet had no wish to discount:

'I believe,' he had speculated, 'there's an electro-chemical process that animates this bag of shit that everybody has to drag around. So it's not impossible that at the point where the electro-chemical process ceases to be strong enough to make the bag of shit move around, that energy may be exchanged, and may dissipate and have an existence of its own. I believe those energies and processes exist. I just don't think they've been adequately described or named yet. If you start defining these things in nuts and bolts scientific terms, people reject it because it's not fun – it takes some of the romance out of being dead. But basically, I think when you're dead – you're dead. It comes with the territory!'

Zappa's death left many work-projects unfinished and many plans unrealised. He had remained at work as late as was physically possible. As late as June 1993, he was at work on a new Synclavier album, to be titled *Dance Me This*, described as being 'designed to be used by modern dance groups'. In August, Zappa was quoted in Tower Records' American magazine *Pulse* as saying that the business manager of the Ensemble Modern, Andreas Molich-Zebhauser, had told him 'about an interview Edgard Varèse gave once where he said he envisioned a film to accompany his piece "Deserts". I had never heard of that before. Varèse said that the images didn't need to relate to the music. Well, the Ensemble is booked for a concert in Cologne on 27 May, 1994. Andreas thought of the extensive data bank of video images I've collected and got the idea to commission me to do a 22-minute film.

'The other project we discussed was for May 1995 when the Ensemble would perform an evening dedicated to my theatrical works like "Billy The Mountain" and "Brown Shoes Don't Make It", arranged for classical ensemble. I think it will make an entertaining evening and an entertaining CD.'

A more concrete project on which Zappa and the Ensemble had been working was a recording of music by Varèse, performed by the Ensemble and produced by Zappa. This is due for release on Barking Pumpkin under the title *The Rage and the Fury*.

Other items more or less completed and awaiting release at the time of writing – they had once been expected to arrive in 1992 – include *Civilisation Phase III* (its original title was going to be *Lumpy Gravy Phase III*) and a two or three CD set of previously unreleased studio recordings to be called *The Lost Episodes*.

235

All Frank Zappa's work was created out of a set of dramatic contradictions within the remarkable man. For a workaholic cigarette-addict who despised the use of alcohol and drugs, he hung out with – in some ways even modelled himself upon – an awful lot of no-hoper junkie wastrels. For an artist with a passionately demanding musical sensibility, he showed a monumentally crass (and undiminished) taste for smut-songs, their lyrics as carelessly crafted as their music is clever. From someone so sharp, it opened a telling further abyss of misjudgement always to miss the critical point by defending these songs with rallying-cries of 'humour' and 'sexual honesty' when those two qualities are exactly what are absent. All around him grown-ups of widely variegated senses of humour unite in finding this side of Zappa's work wretchedly, *uninterestingly* unfunny, and grown-ups who have spent the last two decades and more seeking the potential truths suggested by successive waves of honourable sexual politicking, find Zappa's writing about as sexually 'honest' as Benny Hill.

For a man who earned such an unusual level of loyalty from his family, and who prided himself on his libertarian, no-bullshit child-raising philosophy, he was remarkably authoritarian in his running of the household. Not content with naming the children unilaterally, he even had to be the only one who got to choose names for the *dog*. As for the others, they could do what they liked as long as he thought it was OK too. For eldest son Dweezil, being his own person has meant growing up to be just like dad. Not only a rock-musician/composer: that would be no more nor less understandable than if he'd become a sociology professor. But Dweezil Zappa is a rock-musician/composer who plays lead guitar, who records with his dad's musos, who got his father to produce the debut album that should have been saying, 'This is *me*!', and who gives his own songs titles that sound like no-one else in the world but his father. If you're Frank Zappa Junior, there's not much independent spirit about calling your songs 'You Can't Judge A Girl By The Panties She Wears' and (the admittedly canny) 'I Can't Fuck Without Falling In Love'.

As for Gail, she had long-since given up what most people would call a career of her own. In the mid-1980s she talked to

the compiler of the sobering book *Rock Wives*, the intrepid
Victoria Balfour, the only person known to have prised an interview out of Bob Dylan's bigtime early lover Suze Rotolo *or* out
of this particular rock wife. Gail told Balfour that she didn't
want a job because 'Frank would have seriously questioned it';
she thinks that wives with careers are 'competing with their
husbands'. She knew Frank wouldn't have stood for that, even
though it 'is not a philosophy that Frank and I have discussed.
Frank and I try to talk to each other as little as possible. We
make an effort not to speak . . . because there's really nothing to
talk about unless something isn't OK.'

This meant unless something was not OK for Frank. When
something was not OK for Gail, that was shut-up time too. 'I
think that there are some women who should figure out right
away, as soon as possible, that there are some things that you do
not talk to your husband about – things that have to do with
yourself and how you feel about the relationship that you're
not sure about. It's not the job of your husband to answer
your questions.' Balfour asked her about groupies, and seeing
Frank with other women, for instance; and Gail said: 'I hate it a
lot . . . I have psychic pictures of what happens. There's no
escaping it – I don't have to go there. There are a number of
ways you can deal with it. You can scream, which will get you
nowhere . . . What you ultimately have to face is being honest
with yourself . . . to figure out what your priorities are, and if
you know what they are, you'll be less likely to do anything to
trip yourself up. You'll be less hysterical if it's going to push
somebody in the wrong direction.'

So for Gail to keep her 'job', she had to make sure she didn't
'trip herself up' on any of her own needs; meanwhile what was
her 'job'? 'Mostly you just block for Frank so that all he has to
do is do what he does with not too many distractions.'

You could hear through the plucky-little-woman-talk the
voice of the male authority-figure who had laid down the rules.
No talking. No distractions. Your job is to service me. Shield me
not only from the outside world but from the emotional life
inside here too!

Zappa confirmed that this was how he liked it. He said in his
book: 'At home, a normal day for me is spent working by myself

237

and not talking to anybody . . .' And 'I'm lucky; I don't have to do the mundane stuff because Gail seems to find it *fascinating* . . . She grumbles about it sometimes, but I think that *deep down* she *likes* it . . . This division of labor works best when we see each other the least. Don't get the wrong idea from that – Gail is also my best friend.' Yes Frank, but were you Gail's? 'We talk about business when we have to, but the rest of the time we don't talk at all . . . I have to work the night shift and she has to work the day shift. We see each other on the edges when the shifts change . . . Every three or four weeks I'm back on daylight – and I dread it . . . All those questions Gail was dealing with when I was sleeping on the day shift, now *I have to answer – live, in person.* I can't edit . . .' Exactly.

This is, in cruelly exaggerated form, what almost all men are like. I can hear a voice behind my shoulder right now saying, 'But that's how you are too!' Most men's work is to some extent a way of avoiding the emotional demands of themselves and their families, and without question getting into the power-cocoon of the company car, going to the office and having important executive meetings beats staying at home, mopping up the smeared boiled egg and doing the ironing. You see this sexual divide very early on. Small girls want to know why someone is crying, and how to put a bandage on somebody who's hurt, and they like to hang around when visitors come, adult or not, clocking all the dynamics, all the subtle multi-layered exchange of human feeling and interaction. Small boys avoid all this: they want to commune with machines – simple, noisy things they can *control.*

Frank Zappa seemed to cling to this version of the world exceptionally hard, avoiding real life at all costs. He put it succinctly back in 1982: 'I'm not interested in sharing other people's emotional freight.' There was a time when that sounded cool; but the climate of the times is warmer than that now. He thought of himself as this open, receptive person who bestrode a world stage – the campaigner, the man of political ideas, the internationalist, the engaged artist, the no-bullshit truth-detector – but actually he was a man who spent most of his life locked away in a basement, inside a semi-fortified house, on the edge of the world's most impersonal city; a man with no interest in the riches of the world – not food, wine, trees, literature, cinema, theatre, architecture, travel, nor even much music besides his own.

He was a man who said he didn't have friends (he had to wrap these difficult concepts in reductive, distancing inverted commas: 'I don't have "friends"!') and who avoided social life and all the awfulness of ordinary people ('I don't have time for "social activities"'); a man who, nearly thirty years ago, was so unnerved by the prospect of a small joint of marijuana luring him into letting go that he grew the hard shell of a lifelong loud antipathy towards anyone else's enjoyment of it. He had to be in charge. So he worked alone as much of the time as he could manage, and, when he had to work with other people, at home or outside it, he kept things safe by always being the boss, the one who defined and allocated the others' 'jobs'. The only kind of freak Frank Zappa ever was was a control-freak.

Yet the patriarch who ruled his household as firmly as any of his Sicilian ancestors could have done, nonetheless inspired in his family a rare level of love and loyalty. What other successful rock business careerist stayed married to one person all through the last twenty-five years? How many other California households can claim to have lived together in unity and self-respect as did the Zappas, in a time and place where disaffection and inter-generational contempt have become such strong cultural norms?

And the man who said he had no friends in truth had many, and attracted the loyalty of people from many walks of life, including, as individuals, many of the rock musicians Zappa had so derided as a breed, as well as other, different talents: people like Kent Nagano, whose first-hand contact with Frank led to unreserved admiration. Nagano told me: 'I respect him very, very much, as an artist, as a musician and as a really *fidel* friend.' Even Ringo Starr, Zappalganger of the film *200 Motels* almost as far back in time as were The Beatles, told *Q* magazine that Zappa was 'probably the nicest man I ever met in this business'. And the admiration felt by the members of the Ensemble Modern, a personal as well as a professional one, was written on their faces at the end of the Frankfurt performances.

Towards the end of Zappa's fiery life there were even times when he unbent a little, and sounded ready to drop his olympean disparagement of almost everyone else on the planet: times when he sounded almost reconciled to being ordinarily human. In a National Swedish Radio interview, broadcast on Zappa's 50th birthday, it was put to him:

'You've been pretty sharp in your criticism of American society through the years. But Americans I've talked to say you're just considered a weird guy and no-one pays any attention to you.'

'It's true!' replied Zappa good-naturedly.

Not so. On it goes. The cultural influence of the Zappoid Universe, in its old and its recent forms, rolls on in cumulative co-existence. This year some people will be listening to orchestral Zappa music from *The Perfect Stranger* to *The Yellow Shark*; others will be ordering his son-of-Duchamp Mona Lisa promo poster, or the one with him sat on the toilet; in Eastern Europe someone will be listening to the Synclavier playing music composed by Francesco Zappa a couple of hundred years ago; and some Wayne's World figure down in Alabama will be purchasing the almost as venerable *Hot Rats*.

Offering thirty years' worth of his own music across what was an unprecedented, and remains an unrivalled, breadth of musical terrain, Zappa, like any great artist, changed the contours of that terrain for others. It's part of life's complexity that this wasn't his intent. He made his music not for the world but, as he often said, in order to hear it himself.

'Let me sum it up for you. Information is not knowledge. Knowledge is not wisdom. Wisdom is not truth. Truth is not beauty. Beauty is not love. Love is not music. Music is the best.'

Dizcography

This discography does not list singles or EPs, nor any releases in territories other than the USA and the UK, even where there *is* no US or UK equivalent. (For example: 13 sampler-LPs were issued in Europe only, and one in Europe and Brazil; in [West] Germany, two sets of single-LPs were coupled together when re-issued: *Burnt Weeny Sandwich* with *Weasels Ripped My Flesh*, and *Hot Rats* with *Chunga's Revenge*; there is also a recent Japanese issue of very early material.)

Nor are those UK albums listed which, having been originally issued through CBS and later withdrawn, were re-issued through EMI. Therefore the original CBS issues are listed but not the EMI re-issues. The EMI records listed here are thus only those whose original release was on EMI. (However, because it is not a mere replication but a re-formatting, the discography *does* list the EMI repackaging of *Joe's Garage Acts I, II & III* into a three LP box, replacing the originally issued CBS single-LP *Joe's Garage Act I* and the originally issued CBS double-LP *Joe's Garage Acts II & III*.)

Cassette-releases are not listed, except for *The Guitar World According To Frank Zappa*, which was a cassette-only release. For all practical purposes, however, if an item is listed as available on vinyl or on CD, a cassette equivalent will also be available.

Finally, there have been various limited-edition, and in other ways obscure, interview-discs and -cassettes and an interview-CD released in one territory or another. These are not listed.

These caveats aside, the discography covers both the *history* of Zappa's album-releases and the *currently available* forms of all his album work.

The first aim of the discography is to list the original release-date of each album and its original American and British label and catalogue number. Reading across the first four columns will yield this information, and takes the chronology right through from the July 1966 release of the double-LP *Freak Out!* to the November 1985 release of the LP *Frank Zappa Meets The Mothers of Prevention.* Note, however, that while *Freak Out!* always should have been a double-LP, its initial release in the UK, on Verve Records, was in truncated, single-LP form; its 're-release' restored it to its intended double-LP form. Note also that 'S' in the UK Verve catalogue numbers, and '6' in the US Verve catalogue numbers, were to indicate at the time that a stereo version was available; mono versions were issued at the same time without the 'S' and '6' codes. Later the mono options drop away. The brackets around both the 'S' and '6' indicate that these codes are only present on the stereo versions. The brackets themselves are not part of any of these catalogue numbers. Where these works are still available on vinyl in the UK (now on Zappa records), a single asterisk (*) is appended to the catalogue number given. Where the UK vinyl release has been deleted (or never existed) but an American vinyl release is still available on import on the Barking Pumpkin label, a double-asterisk (**) has been appended to the album title. One extra oddity: the American MCA re-issue of *200 Motels* is still available too. All other original vinyl releases have been deleted. The fifth and sixth columns across the page list the labels and catalogue numbers of the subsequent, retrospective CD releases of all this work. As suggested in the text of the book, in many cases Zappa has re-structured, re-mixed, added to and/or subtracted from the original vinyl versions. In some cases separately issued single LPs have been combined onto one CD 'reissue': hence the CD catalogue number for *We're Only In It For The Money* is as for *Lumpy Gravy*, and *Over-Nite Sensation* is as *Apostrophe (').*

From 1986 onwards, the original release chronology is maintained but the position is different, because from then on, new 'albums' of work begin to get CD release either concurrently with, or even in place of, a vinyl release. Usually. For example, January 1986's *Does Humor Belong In Music?* was a new work that was issued only on CD (and only in the UK). On the other hand November 1986's *The Old Masters Box II* was only issued on vinyl (and only in the USA). On the other hand again (no doubt, as a Zapparachik, you have three hands) no new work since October 1988 has been issued on vinyl at all except the *Beat The Boots* box-sets.

In summary, from 1986 onwards in the listing, the CD releases are not retrospective 'reissues' but original issues.

Note, finally, that double-LPs, triple-LPs and vinyl box-sets are indicated by '2-LP', '3-LP box' etc. Double CDs are indicated as such by codings within their catalogue numbers: in the case of UK Zappa Records numbers, this is indicated by CDD (instead of CD) at the beginning; in the case of American Ryko numbers, it is indicated by an extra oblique stroke (/) and digit at the end (eg. Ryko RCD 10064/5).

These explanatory notes are by the author. The listing itself, though it includes some additional research by the author, is essentially by Fred Tomsett, editor of the British Zappa fanzine *T'Mershi Duween*, which can be written to and subscribed to (at £8 a year UK, £9 Europe, $26 airmail US and elsewhere, cheques payable to T'Mershi Duween) at: *T'Mershi Duween*, PO Box 86, Sheffield S11 8XN. Fred says: 'Thanks to the Torture Team, Andy Greenaway and Black Page.'

Picture creditz

The publishers would like to thank the following for supplying pictures: DiscReet Records; Michael Gray; Philip Lloyd Smee; Pictorial Press; Anthony Russell; Associated Press; Joel Axelrad; Barrie Wentzell; United Artists; Claude Gassian; Warner/Reprise; Michael Putland; Robert Ellis; CBS Records; EMI; Pravoslav Tomek; Lutz Kleinhans; Alan Johnson.

Date	title	UK vinyl	US vinyl	UK CD	US CD
07/66	Freak Out! (2-LP)	Verve (S) VLP9154 (single LP) *263004 (2-LP reissue)	Verve V (6)5005	Zappa CDZAP1	Ryko RCD40062
05/67	Absolutely Free	Verve (S)VLP9174 2317035 (reissue)	Verve V(6)5013	Zappa CDZAP12	Ryko RCD10093
01/68	We're Only In It For The Money	Verve (S)VLP9199 2317034 (reissue)	Verve V(6)5045	Zappa CDZAP13	Ryko RCD40024
05/68	Lumpy Gravy	Verve SVLP9223 2317046 (reissue)	Verve V(6)8741	Zappa CDZAP13	Ryko RCD40024
11/68	Cruisin' With Ruben & The Jets	Verve SVLP9237 2317069 (reissue)	Verve V65055	Zappa CDZAP4	Ryko RCD10063
04/69	Uncle Meat (2-LP)	Trans- atlantic TRA197	Bizarre MS2024	Zappa CDDZAP3	Ryko RCD10064/5
04/69	Mothermania	Verve SVLP9239 2317047 (reissue)	Verve V65068	–	–
??/??	The Worst Of The Mothers	–	MGM SE4754	–	–
??/69	The **** Of The Mothers	–	Verve V65074	–	–
??/??	The Mothers Of Invention	–	MGM GAS112	–	–
??/??	Pregnant (2-LP)	–	Verve 2356049	–	–
10/69	Hot Rats	Reprise K44078	Bizarre RS6356	Zappa CDZAP2	Ryko RCD10066
02/70	Burnt Weeny Sandwich	Reprise K44083	Bizarre RS6370	Zappa CDZAP35	Barking Pumpkin D2 74239
08/70	Weasels Ripped My Flesh	Reprise K44019	Bizarre RSLP2028	Zappa CDZAP24	Ryko RCD10163
10/70	Chunga's Revenge	Reprise K44020	Bizarre MS2030	Zappa CDZAP23	Ryko RCD10124

244

Date	title	UK vinyl	US vinyl	UK CD	US CD
08/71	Fillmore East, June '71	Reprise K44150	Bizarre MS2042	Zappa CDZAP29	Ryko RCD10167
10/71	200 Motels	United Artists UDF50003	United Artists UAS9956 MCA 24183 (reissue)	–	–
05/72	Just Another Band From L.A.	Reprise K44179	Bizarre MS2075	Zappa CDZAP25	Ryko RCD10161
07/72	Waka/Jawaka	Reprise K44203	Bizarre MS2094	Zappa CDZAP10	Ryko RCD10094
12/72	The Grand Wazoo	Reprise K44209	Bizarre MS2093	Zappa CDZAP31	Ryko RCD10026
06/73	Over-Nite Sensation	DiscReet 41000	DiscReet MS2149	Zappa CDZAP18	Ryko RCD40025
04/74	Apostrophe (')	DiscReet 59201	DiscReet DS2175	Zappa CDZAP18	Ryko RCD40025
09/74	Roxy & Elsewhere (2-LP)	DiscReet 69201	DiscReet DS2202	Zappa CDZAP39	B. Pumpkin D2 74241
??/75	Frank Zappa & The Mothers Of Invention (Transparency)	Verve 2352027	Verve 2352027	–	–
06/75	One Size Fits All	DiscReet 59207	DiscReet DS2216	Zappa CDZAP11	Ryko RCD10095
10/75	Bongo Fury	–	DiscReet DS2234	Zappa CDZAP15	Ryko RCD10097
10/76	Zoot Allures	Warner Bros K56298	Warner Bros DS2970	Zappa CDZAP22	Ryko RCD10160
03/78	Zappa In New York (2-LP)	DiscReet *69204	DiscReet DS2290	Zappa CDDZAP37	B. Pumpkin D2 74240
09/78	Studio Tan	DiscReet K59210	DiscReet DSK2291	Zappa CDZAP44	B. Pumpkin D2 74237
01/79	Sleep Dirt	DiscReet K59211	DiscReet DSK2292	Zappa CDZAP43	B. Pumpkin D2 74238
03/79	Sheik Yerbouti (2-LP)	CBS *88339	Zappa SRZ21501	Zappa CDZAP28	Ryko RCD40162
05/79	Orchestral Favorites	DiscReet K59212	DiscReet DSK2294	Zappa CDZAP45	B. Pumpkin D2 74236
09/79	Joe's Garage Act I	CBS 86101	Zappa SRZ11603	–	–
11/79	Joe's Garage Acts II & III (2-LP)	CBS 88475	Zappa SRZ21502	–	–

245

Date	title	UK vinyl	US vinyl	UK CD	US CD
05/81	Tinseltown Rebellion (2-LP)	CBS 88516	B. Pumpkin PW237336	Zappa CDZAP26	Ryko RCD10166
05/81	Shut Up 'N Play Yer Guitar	–	B. Pumpkin BPR1111	–	–
05/81	Shut Up 'N Play Yer Guitar Some More	–	B. Pumpkin BPR1112	–	–
05/81	Return Of The Son Of Shut Up 'N Play Yer Guitar	–	B. Pumpkin BPR1113	–	–
09/81	You Are What You Is (2-LP)	CBS 88560	B. Pumpkin PW237537	Zappa CDZAP27	Ryko RCD40165
??/82	Shut Up 'N Play Yer Guitar (3-LP box)	CBS 66368	B. Pumpkin W3X38289	Zappa CDDZAP19	Ryko RCD10028/9
05/82	Ship Arriving Too Late To Save A Drowning Witch	CBS 85804	B. Pumpkin FW38066	Zappa CDZAP42	B. Pumpkin D2 74235
03/83	The Man From Utopia	CBS 25251	B. Pumpkin FW38404	Zappa CDZAP53	
03/83	Baby Snakes	–	B. Pumpkin BPR1115	Zappa CDZAP16	B. Pumpkin D2 74219
06/83	LSO Volume 1	–	B. Pumpkin FW38820	Zappa CDZAP34	–
??/83	Rare Meat	–	Del-Fi RNEP604	–	–
08/84	Boulez Conducts Zappa, The Perfect Stranger	EMI DS38170	Angel 38170	EMI CDC-7471252 (original) Zappa CDZAP49 (reissue)	B. Pumpkin D2 74242
??/84	**Francesco Zappa	EMI EJ2702561	B. Pumpkin ST74202	Zappa CDZAP48	B. Pumpkin D2 74202
10/84	Them Or Us (2-LP)	EMI *2402439	B. Pumpkin SVB074200	Zappa CDZAP30	Ryko RCD40027
11/84	**Thing-Fish (3-LP box)	EMI 2402943	B. Pumpkin SKC074201	Zappa CDDZAP21	Ryko RCD10020/1
04/85	The Old Masters Box I (7-LP box)	–	B. Pumpkin BPR7777	–	–
04/85	The Old Masters Box I Sampler	–	B. Pumpkin BPR7X41	–	–
11/85	**Frank Zappa Meets The Mothers Of Prevention	EMI 2404921	B. Pumpkin ST74205	Zappa CDZAP33	Ryko RCD10023

Date	title	UK vinyl	US vinyl	UK CD	US CD
01/86	Does Humor Belong In Music?	–	–	EMI CDP-7461882 (original) Zappa CDZAP54 (reissue)	–
11/86	The Old Masters Box II (9-LP box)	–	B. Pumpkin BPR8888	–	–
11/86	The Old Masters Box II Sampler	–	B. Pumpkin BPR8888X	–	–
11/86	Jazz From Hell	EMI EMC3521	B. Pumpkin ST74205	Zappa CDZAP32	Ryko RCD10030
??/86	London Symphony Orchestra	–	–	–	Ryko RCD10022
06/87	Joe's Garage Acts I, II & III (3-LP box)	EMI FZAP1	B. Pumpkin SWCL74206	Zappa CDDZAP20	Ryko RCD10060/1
06/87	The Guitar World According To Frank Zappa (cassette only)	–	B. Pumpkin GW002		
09/87	London Symphony Orchestra Volume 2	*Zappa 5	B. Pumpkin SJ74207		
12/87	The Old Masters Box III (9-LP box)	–	B. Pumpkin BPR9999	–	–
04/88	Guitar (2-LP)	*Zappa 6	B. Pumpkin BPR74212	Zappa CDDZAP6	Ryko RCD10079 /80
04/88	You Can't Do That On Stage Anymore Sampler (2-LP)	*Zappa 7	B. Pumpkin BPRD174213	–	–
04/88	You Can't Do That On Stage Anymore Vol. 1	–	–	Zappa CDDZAP8	Ryko RCD10081/2
10/88	You Can't Do That On Stage Anymore Vol. 2 (3-LP)	–	B. Pumpkin BPR74217	Zappa CDDZAP9	Ryko RCD10083/4
10/88	Broadway The Hard Way	*Zappa 14	B. Pumpkin D174218	Zappa CDZAP14	Ryko RCD40096
11/89	You Can't Do That On Stage Anymore Vol. 3	–	–	Zappa CDDZAP17	Ryko RCD10085/6
04/91	The Best Band You Never Heard In Your Life	–	–	Zappa CDDZAP38	B. Pumpkin D2 74233

Date	title	UK vinyl	US vinyl	UK CD	US CD
05/91	You Can't Do That On Stage Anymore Vol. 4	–	–	Zappa CDDZAP40	Ryko RCD10087/8
06/91	Make A Jazz Noise Here	–	–	Zappa CDDZAP41	B. Pumpkin D2 74234
08/91	Beat The Boots (10-LP box) alternatively sold as individual constituent CDs as follows:	–	Foo-ee RI–70907	–	–
	As An Am	–	–	ESMCD956	Foo-eee70537
	The Ark	–	–	ESMCD957	Foo-eee70538
	Freaks & Motherfuckers	–	–	ESMCD958	Foo-eee70539
	Unmitigated Audacity	–	–	ESMCD959	Foo-eee70540
	Anyway The Wind Blows	–	–	ESMCD960	Foo-eee70541
	'Tis The Season To Be Jelly	–	–	ESMCD961	Foo-eee70542
	Saarbrucken '78	–	–	ESMCD962	Foo-eee70543
	Piquantique	–	–	ESMCD963	Foo-eee70544
06/92	You Can't Do That On Stage Anymore Vol. 5	–	–	Zappa CDDZAP46	Ryko RCD 10089/90
07/92	You Can't Do That On Stage Anymore Vol. 6	–	–	Zappa CDDZAP47	Ryko RCD 10091/92
07/92	Beat The Boots II (available only as a box-set: of 11 LPs, 8 CDs or 7 cassettes)	–	Foo-eee RI–70372	–	Foo-eee R2–70372
10/92	Playground Psychotics	–	–	Zappa CDDZAP55	B. Pumpkin D2 74244
03/93	Ahead Of Their Time	–	–	Zappa CDZAP51	B. Pumpkin
11/93	The Yellow Shark	–	–	Zappa CDZAP57	B. Pumpkin

249